3000 800024 24591
St. Louis Community College

W9-CZU-411

FV

WITHDRAWN

 St. Louis Community College

Forest Park
Florissant Valley
Meramec

Instructional Resources
St. Louis, Missouri

GAYLORD

The Electronic Eye

The Electronic Eye

The Rise of Surveillance Society

DAVID LYON

1994

University of Minnesota Press
Minneapolis

Copyright © David Lyon 1994

The right of David Lyon to be identified as author of this work has been asserted in accordance with the Copyright, Designs and Patents Act 1988.

First published in 1994 by Polity Press
in association with Blackwell Publishers

First published in 1994 in the United States by
University of Minnesota Press
2037 University Avenue Southeast
Minneapolis, MN 55455-3092

All rights reserved. No part of this publication may be reproduced, stored in a retrieval system, or transmitted, in any form or by any means, electronic, mechanical, photocopying, recording, or otherwise, without the prior written permission of the publisher.

Library of Congress Cataloging-in-Publication Data

Lyon, David, 1948–
    The electronic eye : the rise of surveillance society / David
Lyon.
        p.   cm.
    Includes bibliographical references and index.
    ISBN 0–8166–2513–1 (hc)   0–8166–2515–8 (pb)
    1. Electronic surveillance—Social aspects.   2. Computers and
civilization.   3. Information technology—Social aspects.
I. Title.
TK7882.E2L96   1994
303.48'33—dc20   93–35598
                                                  CIP

The University of Minnesota is an
equal-opportunity educator and employer.

Contents

Preface and Acknowledgements

Great excitement was generated during the 1970s and early 1980s about the arrival of new social conditions. Computer and communications technologies had made possible the 'Information Society'. All manner of benefits awaited us; new prosperity, new democratic and educational opportunities, a 'global village' thanks to new telecommunications, and a realignment of workplaces and class relations. There is no denying that advantages do indeed accrue from such technological development, but a little historical reflection and sociological imagination makes warning bells ring.

A number of writers – including me, in *The Information Society: Issues and Illusions* – took it upon themselves to assess just what was going in the so-called information revolution. I argued that each situation should be analysed in its own right, that new technologies may well be implicated in some radical social changes that we don't yet understand fully, but that utopian dreams of wholesale societal megashifts were at best misleading hyperbole and at worst dangerous delusions.

Since then, the debates surrounding new technology have tended to become much more sober, if not sombre. The failure of computer-based service economies to lift the world out of recession, the advent of electronic war, and the dismayed realization that computers have a huge capacity to track the tiny details of our personal lives, have all helped foster more forbidding social forecasts. Even fearing the spectre of 'Big Brother' scarcely seems to do justice to the new mood. The term 'surveillance society' was first coined in 1985; the warning note is growing in volume.

Of all the questions raised by new technologies, the one that strikes me as being most socially pervasive is the garnering of personal information to be stored, matched, retrieved, processed, marketed and circulated using powerful computer databases. The result of my investigation is this book, in which I examine the major dimensions of what we now speak of as 'surveillance'. Whereas once this had a fairly narrow meaning, to do with policing or espionage, surveillance is used here as a shorthand term to cover the many, and expanding, range of contexts within which personal data is collected by employment, commercial and administrative agencies, as well as in policing and security.

But I do not conclude that surveillance is solely sinister. Having tried earlier to puncture inflated optimism about the information society, I now try to soften the scaremongering alarms about surveillance society. Rather than view contemporary societies in which surveillance capacities are constantly augmented by computers merely as the sites of tighter social control, I suggest that surveillance often shows two faces. The processes that may seem to constrain us stimultaneously enable us to participate in society. We may be tracked by our Social Insurance Number, for instance, but the same computerized system ensures we receive unemployment benefits. The electronic eye may blink benignly.

The question then becomes more subtle. At what points, under what circumstances, and by what criteria is the current computer-aided surveillance undemocratic, coercive, impersonal or even inhuman? And when is it innocuous or a channel of positive blessing? Such questions must be addressed historically, sociologically, and politically. They involve normative judgements at every level. And they entail engagement with present day debates about post-modernity, partly because new technologies are already implicated in those discussions and partly because conventional views of 'self' or 'citizen' are disputed within them. My own route through these troubled waters, let it be said from the outset, is guided by converging traditions of Christian social thought. I may not see the Morning Star very clearly, but readers should at least know how I tried to set my course.

A number of people have been extremely inspiring, helpful and supportive as I have been involved in writing this book and they deserve sincere thanks. From the early 1980s, conversations with Mike Harrison, Mike Parsons, Harold Thimbleby and others in the REGIS group convinced me that electronicially mediated communication has some special features, such as malleability. Mike LeRoy and David Pullinger persuaded me that electronic surveillance was the theme I ought to pursue. Along the way, strong encouragement came at the right time from Anne Goldthorpe and Zygmunt Bauman in Yorkshire, and Rebecca Sutherns, who was a valued research assistant and friend in my early days at Queen's. Howard Davies, Bob Fortner, Rob James, Gary Marx and Jim Rule kindly read a draft of the whole book and made detailed and insightful comment.

Zygmunt Bauman, Yolande Chan, Kathy Carter, Roberta Hamilton, Bob Pike and Elia Zureik read the whole or part of the book and drew my attention to its more glaring problems while also spurring me to continue. Several cohorts of students at Bradford and Ilkley College and the Open University in the UK and especially in SOCY 426 at Queen's, have provided just the sort of ongoing sympathetically critical feedback that one needs on tackling a project like this. Polity Press people should also be saluted for their care and enthusiasm. Having said all that, I alone am still responsible for the final result.

Financially I have benefited by support from the Advisory Research Committee of the School of Graduate Studies at Queen's. My greatest debt, however, is emotional and practical. I am deeply grateful for the love and fun enjoyed with Sue, Tim, Abi, Josh and Min. Sue's pottery studio, helping with homework, making music, cycling country roads and canoeing the wilderness lakes is as much my life as the book in your hand.

Parts of Chapter Three appeared in an earlier incarnation as 'A New Surveillance? New Technologies and the Maximum Security Society, in *Crime, Law and Social Change*, 17 (3) 1992, and similarly select parts of Chapter Four appeared as 'An Electronic Panopticon? 'A Sociological Critique of Surveillance Theory', *The Sociological Review*, November 1993. Both are reprinted by permission of Marvel Comics Inc., who have also granted permission to reprint the cartoon on page 43. The *Penitentiary Panopticon* on p. 64 is from *The Works of Jeremy Bentham* by John Bowring, 1843 (2nd ed.), pp. 38–9, and is reproduced by permission of The Bodleian Library, Oxford, shelfmark 265.i.228, vol. 4.

David Lyon, Kingston, Ontario

Part I

Situating Surveillance

1

Introduction: Body, Soul and Credit Card

'An individual in Russia was composed of three parts; a body, a soul and a passport.'

Vladimir Medem[1]

Surveillance in Everyday Life

This book, while it certainly doesn't ignore 'bodies and souls' is primarily about the 'passport' aspect of human existence. That is to say, I focus on that dimension of social life which today is vital to most relationships and transactions, apart from those of the most intimate or familial kind. Passports get us across borders, who drivers' licences are taken more seriously than our own word for proving who we are. In much of modern life we deal with relative strangers, and to demonstrate our identity or reliability we must produce documentary evidence. Indeed, the Russian proverb above should really be updated to indicate that human beings would now be defined more accurately as 'body, soul and credit card'.

The other side of the coin, however, is that organizations of many kinds know us only as coded sequences of numbers and letters. This was once worked out on pieces of paper collated in folders and kept in filling cabinets, but now the same tasks – and many others, unimaginable to a Victorian clerk – are performed by computer. Precise details of our personal lives are collected, stored, retrieved and processed every day within huge computer databases belonging to big corporations and government departments. This is the 'surveillance society'.[2]

No one is spying on us, exactly, although for many people that is what it feels like if and when they find out just how detailed a picture of us is available. 'They' know things about us, but we often don't know what they know, why they know, or with whom else they might share their knowledge. What does this mean for our sense of identity, our life-chances, our human rights, our privacy? What are the implications for political power, social control, freedom and democracy? This book addresses just such questions.

In one, limited, sense the electronic component of surveillance is nothing new. Wiretapping and other forms of message interception have been the common currency of espionage and intelligence services for many decades. But what this book explores is how, to an unprecedented extent, ordinary people now find themselves 'under surveillance' in the routines of everyday life. In numerous ways what was once thought of as the exception has become the rule, as highly specialized agencies use increasingly sophisticated means of routinely collecting personal data, making us all targets of monitoring, and possibly objects of suspicion.

Surveillance, as described here, concerns the mundane, ordinary, taken-for-granted world of getting money from a bank machine, making a phone call, applying for sickness benefits, driving a car, using a credit card, receiving junk mail, picking up books from the library, or crossing a border on trips abroad. In each case mentioned, computers record our transactions, check against other known details, ensure that we and not others are billed or paid, store bits of our biographies, or assess our financial, legal or national standing. Each time we do one of these things we actually or potentially leave a trace of our doings. Computers and their associated communications systems now mediate all these kinds of relationships; to participate in modern society is to be under electronic surveillance.

All this did not develop overnight, and indeed part of what we must examine is the relatively long history of the 'surveillance society.' Today's situation cannot be understood without reference to the long-term historical context. Ever since modern governments started to register births, marriages and deaths, and ever since modern businesses began to monitor work and keep accurate records of employees' pay and progress, surveillance has been expanding. Surveillance denotes what is happening as today's bureaucratic organizations try to keep track of increasingly complex information on a variety of populations and groups. Yet it is more than just 'bureaucracy.' Surveillance is strongly bound up with our compliance with the current social order, and it can be a means of social control.

At the same time, surveillance systems are meant to ensure that we are paid correctly or receive appropriate welfare benefits, that terrorism and drug-trafficking are contained, that we are made aware of the latest consumer products available, that we can be warned about risks to our health, that we can vote in elections, that we can pay for goods and sevices with plastic cards rather than with the more cumbersome cash, and so on. Most people in modern societies regard these accomplishments as contributing positively to the quality of life. So surveillance is not unambiguously good or bad; and hence the dilemmas surrounding the use of computer databases for storing and processing personal data.

Surveillance expands in subtle ways, often as the result of decisions and processes intended to pursue goals such as efficiency or productivity. Moreover, its subtlety is increased by its present-day electronic character. Most surveillance occurs literally out of sight, in the realm of digital signals. And it happens, as we have already seen, not in clandestine, conspiratorial fashion, but in the commonplace transactions of shopping, voting, phoning, driving and working. This means that people seldom know that they are subjects of surveillance, or, if they do know, they are unaware how comprehensive others' knowledge of them actually is.

Though modern surveillance originated in specific institutions such as the army, the corporation, and the govenment department, it has grown to touch all areas of life. This was brought home to me personally during a recent move from Britain to Canada. My family and I could not fully participate in Canadian society until our details had been transferred into a number of electronic databases. This began on arrival at Toronto International Airport, as the travel-tired family lined up at Employment and Immigration Control. Details had to keyed into the computer before we could continue to our destination in Kingston, Ontario.

No sooner were we installed in Kingston than we had to obtain health care cards, Social Insurance Numbers, bank cards and a university staff card, each of which relates to personal details stored in a compouter database. We could not be employed, acquire medical or accident coverage, or obtain money without these. However much we like cycling, it is hard to get around without a car, so we had to get drivers' licences, which again link our records by computer. Surprisingly soon after arriving, we started receiving 'personal' advertising mail which indicated once more that yet other computers contained data about us, gleaned from the telephone company, which also lists – and sells – essential facts about us. Other agencies than the phone company do just the same.

As soon as we began the process of buying a house, the quest for electronic verification intensified. Mortgage companies demanded details of the crucial Social Insurance Number (which would reveal immediately whether we were *bona fide* citizens, permanent residents or temporary workers) because such financial transactions are of interest to the tax authorities. Equipping ourselves with a cooking stove, washing machine and fridge involved similar proof of (credit-) worthiness in terms of bankcard and credit-card numbers. As a university professor, I find myself in the relatively privileged position of either possessing the right number sequences to unlock these electronic doors or of being able to explain that things will soon be in place. But the same processes are clearly experienced in quite different ways by those lacking access to the appropriate plastic cards or numbers.

In other words, participating in just about every aspect of modern life depends upon our relationship with computer databases; and to process our personal details we rely not only upon professional experts and bureau-cratic systems, which have increasingly become a feature of modern life in the twentieth century, but upon electronic storage and communication devices. What difference, if any, does this make to social, political and cultural life? The answer to this crucial question draws us into a number of important debates, sometimes in disciplinary areas that are convention-ally separate. I shall list these below, but thoughout the book I shall show how they must be considered together if we are properly to grasp the dimensions and implications of the 'surveillance society.'

The genius, and the usefulness, of sociology lies in locating particular events and trends in their broader structural and historical context. In this way we can begin to distinguish between the short-term aberration from some norm and the long-term break with existing conditions, between the socially significant and the trivial or the transient. This book aspires to place elctronic surveillance – in a broad sense, rather than the narrower 'security-and-intelligence' sense – in just such a social and historical context, and to show where it came from, what – if anything – is new about it, what are its future prospects and wider implications, and what might seem to be appropriate responses to its development. This should become clear as we consider the various debates within which electronic surveil-lance is properly situated.

Surveillance in Modern Society

Until a decade ago, surveillance occupied no distinct place in the sociological lexicon. Despite the fact that James Rule's groundbreaking study of *Private Lives and Public Surveillance* had appeared in the early 1970s, quickly establishing itself as the standard text,[3] it was not until Michel Foucault's celebrated, and contentious, historical studies of sur-veillance and discipline had appeared that mainstream social theorists began to take surveillance seriously in its own right. Surveillance, insisted Anthony Giddens[4] and others, should be viewed not merely as a sort of reflex of capitalism (monitoring workers in the factory), or of the nation–state (keeping administrative tabs on citizens), but as a power-generator in itself.

Of course, we can now look back at many other sociological studies and see how they concerned processes very closely related to what today we call surveillance. Prominent here is work carried out in two major traditions, the Marxian and the Weberian. Karl Marx focuses special attention on surveillance as an aspect of the struggle between labour and capital. Overseeing and monitoring workers is viewed here as a means of maintaining managerial control on behalf of capital. Max Weber, on the other hand, concentrates on the ways that all modern organizations develop means of storing and retrieving data in the form of files as part of the quest of efficient practice within bureaucracy. Such files frequently contain personal information so that organizations, especially government administrators, can 'keep tabs' on populations.

Foucault's more recent contribution to surveillance theory, though sophisticated, may be simply stated. Modern societies have developed rational means of ordering society that effectively dispense with traditional methods like brutal public punishment. Rather than relying on external controls and constraints, modern social institutions employ a range of disciplinary practices which ensure that life continues in a regularized, patterned way. From army drill to school uniforms, and from social welfare casework to the closely-scrutinized factory worker's task, the processes of modern social discipline are depicted in sharp relief. Others have taken his analysis beyond the spheres he considered, for instance into the ways women are disciplined to dress and present themselves as 'feminine' in male-dominated society.[5] Furthermore, as these examples imply, people co-operate and collude with the means of control.

Specialized knowledge strengthens the power of each modern agency, and taken together they seem to colonize ever-increasing tracts of so-called private life. The categories and classifications imposed, whether they be the time for performing a work–task or raising a rifle or the calculation of health or crime risk, induce, according to Foucault, progressively sharper distinctions between acceptable and unacceptable behaviour. This in turn defines the 'normal' human individual, thus creating what we think of as social order. In this way people are produced as subjects – or, more accurately, objects.

Foucault's role in surveillance studies is curious and paradoxical. With careful empirical studies of surveillance, such as Rule's, available, it yet

took someone who was notorious for his disdain of data to set the debate
fully in motion. One of the oddest things about Foucault is his silence
about that acme of rational classification, the computer. Surely, if anything
accelerates the process of monitoring the routines of everyday and
producing people as objects it is the computer! But the task of applying
Foucault's analysis to the social role of information technology – and quite
an array of plausible interpretations is available! – has been left to others.
The apparent relevance of Foucault's analysis may be obvious, but the way
that some of the connections have been made actually arouse further
controversy.

For one thing, many commentators have lighted eagerly upon
Foucault's image of the Panopticon prison plan[6] as an examplar of
electronic surveillance. Some apply it only to specific social milieux, such
as industrial organizations, while others glimpse here the contours of a
completely new social formation, comparable to Marx's depiction of the
'mode of production'. At one extreme this can be taken to mean that
wherever computer databases process human data we are caught up in
some system of total, prison-like domination, which seems to me to be
nonsense. However, even milder versions of this idea rightly raise the
question of resistance; what can be done in the face of such all-
encompassing power? This is what this book tries to explore.

The idea of the 'surveillance society' is used to capture this particular
dimension of modern social life.[7] The perspective outlined in this book
takes account of what Marx, Weber and Foucault have to say, but is not
exclusively aligned with any one of them. In any case, the sociological
debate has been joined by others, notably Anthony Giddens, who locate the
processes of surveillance within modern society as one of its major
isntitutional dimensions. His work is a useful springboard[8] for surveillance
studies, but, as we shall see, it too invites modification, particularly in the
light of the electronic character of surveillance.

In the sections that follow I indicate the kinds of debates within which
surveillance features. These debates overlap, and greater integration
between them could only be beneficial. The order in which they are listed
implies no priority.

The Social Impact of Technology

Electronic surveillance has to do with the ways that computer databases are
used to store and process personal information on different kinds of
populations. Examining the 'surveillance society' may be seen as a case
study in the interaction between technology and society. I say 'interaction'

advisedly, because there are several stances on the society/technology relationship.

Some writers place the emphasis on the ways that new technologies determine the direction of social development. This impression could be given, for instance, by titles such as Alvin Toffler's *The Third Wave,*[9] which seem to imply that social change is technology–driven. Both extreme optimists and extreme pessimists on the question of the social role of technology are prone to this error, which is known as technological determinism. It underestimates both the role of social factors in shaping the technology in the first place, and also the variety of social contexts that mediate its use.

Other commentators put such stress on the social relations expressed in the technologies that they seem to have little time for considering how specific technologies might have intrinsic constraining or enabling consequent for social relations. Some Marxists succumb to this temptation, following Marx's gloss that machinery is 'a power inimical [to the worker] and as such capital proclaims it from the rooftops and as such makes use of it'.[10] In the laudable attempt to uncover the social relations obscured by apprently asocial machines like computers, they sometimes seem to deny that the artifact itself could have some consequences that are intrinsic to it.[11]

Electronic surveillance, I argue, is both socially shaped and has social impacts, but the nature of the shaping does not necessarily render the impacts predictable in any straightforward sense. Certain capacities of the technological systems themselves make them attractive for use in ways hitherto unimagined. This kind of approach comports well with Gary T. Marx's studies of what he calls the 'new surveillance'. In the course of a major analysis of undercover police work in the USA, he found that the use of computer technologies does indeed make a difference, for a number of important reasons.[12]

Computer matching provides a good example of this relatively independent characteristic of new technology. The power of computer systems to relate data from various sources and gathered with different purposes has inspired numerous experiments with personal information. Two or more unrelated computerized files of individuals are matched to identify groups of people in a similar category, such as suspected law-breakers.

Computer matching is a technique used first by government departments in the late 1970s, and it was widespread by the early 1990s. Quite *how* widespread is not always known exactly. During 1991, for instance, the Ontario Information and Privacy Commission proposed that a task force be established to discover just how extensive computer matching is within and between different departments of the provincial government.[13]

In Australia, especially since 1987, computer matching has grown apace, so that by October 1990 there were thirty-one active and proposed major data–matching programmes involving government departments.[14]

In the USA, the technique began in 1977, when the then Department of Health, Education and Welfare matched welfare files of federal government departments in what turned out to be a somewhat abortive attempt to expose fraud.[15] To illustrate its potential in other areas, a bizarre case concerns an America business, Farrell's Ice Cream Parlour, which sold the name-list of those claiming free sundaes on their birthdays to a marketing firm. Soon after, the ice-cream eaters were surprised to find draft registration warnings in their mail! The marketing company had sold their details to Selective Service System, who had in turn sold them to the Department of Defence.

More routinely, employee records of the American Civil Service Commission have been matched with those of family welfare recipients in order to root out fraud, and, at the other end of the social spectrum, the Department of Heath and Human Services matches relevant files to check that no doctors are double-billing the health insurance schemes of Medicare and Medicaid.[16] Comparing files on such a huge scale is clearly only possible using computers so, such investigations are technologically facilitated. But once begun, computer matching has huge implications. Anyone can be caught in the computer dragnet, and may be presumed guilty until proven innocent. Existing privacy laws have been powerless in this respect.

It is this kind of realization that lends weight to the view that such computer systems grow 'out of control'. David Burnham's fascinating – and frightening – book, *The Rise of the Computer State*,[17] for instance, implies that new computer technologies augment themselves beyond the direct control of anyone, let alone elected decision-makers. At odds with this 'autonomous technology' position, however, are observers who see new technology almost as a tool of capitalism or of repressive states. Kevin Wilson's *Technologies of Control*,[18] for example, portrays the home networking of computers as 'data-based social control'. Here, computer-power appears to be used deliberately as a means of obtaining compliance.

The stance taken in the following pages is that while new technologies do indeed have a kind of self-augmenting capacity (the phrase, by the way, is Jacques Ellul's)[19] this does not make them immune from sociological scrutiny. The process by which they are augmented is all-too-often a 'black box'. We should open the box and analyse the contents; we may well discover some deeply social factors shaping the technologies. At the same time, I do not wish to underestimate the extent to which new technologies may contribute to the processes of social control. But the story is a subtle one, and cannot be reduced to any crude categories that assume that surveillance is born of a malign collusion of economic and political power.

One interesting challenge to surveillance studies presented by processes such as computer-matching is that an essentially technical procedure may contribute to the blurring of conventionally conceived boundaries. Anthony Giddens, for instance, distinguishes between surveillance as 'gathering data on' and 'supervising' people.[20] But this may be less salient as forms of 'supervision' by various agencies – including employers, who might once have monitored their workers in a more direct manner – are actually achieved by 'data gathering'.

These then are the general contours of the technology-and-society debate within which electronic surveillance may be situated. The niceties of debate must not, however, be allowed to obscure the significance of the particular case considered here. Our topic represents the single most controversial and potentially alarming social issue prompted by the massive expansion of computer power in human affairs. Modern society makes us all radically dependent upon the realm of expert knowledge, on people 'in the know'. The key question addressed here is, what difference for good or ill does it make to mediate that knowledge through powerful computer systems?

Technology and Totalitarianism

The vexed question of computers, power and domination conjures up a variety of sinister images. The best know of these is Orwell's dystopia, *Nineteen Eighty-Four*, where telescreens constantly monitor all activities. The nation-state now comes into the foreground, and with it the commonplace post-war contrast between totalitarianism and democracy. If Giddens is right to say that 'Totalitarianism is, first of all, an extreme focusing of surveillance'[21] then the enhanced role of new technology within government administration and policing should give us pause.

It is important to note that the influence of Orwell's *Nineteen-Eighty-Four* has been felt far beyond the merely literary. The metaphor of 'Big Brother', in particular, now expresses a profound cultural fear in areas quite remote from what Orwell originally had in mind. The impact of Orwell's dystopia has also been sociologically significant. James Rule explicitly refers to *Nineteen Eighty-Four* as the situation of 'total surveillance' from which he derives the concept of 'surveillance capacities'.[22] Others, such as Christopher Dandeker in *Surveillance, Power and Modernity*,[23] carry the same concepts into sociological analysis of the 1990s.

The fact that the advanced societies are falling over themselves to adapt and upgrade their computing capacities does not on itself mean that they are sliding down a slope into tyranny, However, if intensifying surveillance is a crucial component of totalitarianism, democratically-minded citizens would be justified in at least asking questions about the role of new technologies in government. After all, was it not in a highly civilized, rational, bureaucratic society that the techniques of the Holocaust were conceived and executed? As Zygmunt Bauman reminds us, moral standards are easily rendered 'irrelevant' to the technical success of bureaucratic operations. The objects of bureaucratic operation – people – are easily dehumanized.[24]

Over the past decade Social Insurance Numbers have been used for more and more purposes in Cananda, machine-readable passports have been introduced in Germany, electronic identity card systems have been proposed in Britain and Australia, and the driver's licence has become a *de facto* personal identifier in the USA. Yet such developments occur all too often without extensive public discussion and policy debate. Sir Norman Lindop, chairman of the British Data Protection Committee, reporting as early as 1978, commented that

> We did not fear that Orwell's *1984* was just around the corner, but we did feel that some pretty frightening developments could come about quite quickly and without most people being aware of what was happening.[25]

As we shall see, just what Lindop feared has occurred, and not only Britain.

Other problems also exist besides bureaucratic momentum and public ignorance. One is that personal databases proliferate in areas which are not directly within the ambit of administration and policing but which, given the increasing ease of communications between computers, may interact with them. This happens by all manner of routes, including the leakage of public sector data to the private sector *via*, for example, insurance companies, private policing (whose findings are used by statutory police forces), and the monitoring of exmployees; this last has generated data used extensively within and outside government administration in vetting applicants for posts or promotion. In addition, being accepted as a fully participating member of society today depends more and more on one's ability to consume, and much contemporary surveillance is in fact commercial. How far are ordinary people's life-chances circumscribed or enhanced by such processes? Surveillance, which was once thought of as touching only the realm of political citizenship, now affects our involvement in society at a more basic level.

A further issue of note is the relative lack of countervailing organizations committed to investigating, and if necessary resisting, the spread of electronic surveillance. Other modern institutions seem to have provoked the forming of social movements that call them in question; capitalistic organization has been accompanied by the rise of labour movements, industrial expansion by Green movements, and so on. But to which groups or coalitions could one realistically turn for a critique of or reasoned opposition to electronic surveillance? Granted, civil liberties associations, consumer councils and some labour unions do play an active part in trying to contain or democratically channel its growth. But one doesn't have to be a pessimist to note the relative lack of such resistance.

On the positive side, we should note that there are some strong hints of a growing realization of the importance of surveillance issues. A casual review of popular media shows more frequent treatment of 'computer and privacy' issues, and during 1992 an important step was taken with the founding of Privacy International. This new organization exists to draw together data on surveillance data protection from widely scattered countries across the world.[26] From the point of view of those concerned about surveillance this is a welcome move, especially as surveillance is an increasingly global phenomenon. The long-term impact of such attention and activity remains, however, to be seen.

I have already alluded to one reason for the relative lack of public resistance to contemporary surveillance. That is, many of its achievements are viewed – rightly – as positive social benefits. Why resist systems whose advantages simply carry with them a number of acceptable risks?

Another reason is no doubt the feeling that statutory agencies already take care of such matters. Data protection agencies, such as the Canadian Information Commission or the French Commission Nationale de l'Informatique et des Libertés (CNIL) have for some time acted as watchdogs or whistleblowers in their respective countries. Data protection and privacy legislation certainly offers some established limits to the unhindered growth of electronic surveillance, but, given the rate of technological change facilitating the processes mentioned above, such legal measures tend to lag behind to a significant and perhaps dangerous degree.

Added to this is another serious difficulty; lack of agreement on exactly what is the perceived problem. All too often the stock response to issues of surveillance is couched in the language of 'privacy'. Indeed, in North America the relevant legislation is normally termed 'The Privacy Acts'. The chief difficulty here is that the concept of privacy is stretched beyond its (socio)logical limits. Anxiety about totalitarian tendencies is inappropriately addressed under the 'privacy' rubric, though that may be one concern among others; 'Liberty' might make a preferable candidate.

Equally, the possible limits on autonomy within the marketplace, imposed by commercial surveillance, are hardly confronted head–on when 'privacy' is brandished in resistance.

At the same time, simply abandoning privacy is as misguided a response as adopting it in an omnibus fashion. Neglecting the issue of privacy is to ignore some of the most profound challenges of the growth of electronic surveillance, even though that issue cannot properly cover some of the most significant issues raised by it.

The Problem of Privacy

Privacy was first mooted as a serious question for legal consideration during the last century. Expressed classically in the USA by Samuel Warren and Louis Brandeis, privacy is 'the individual's right to be left alone'. Although in 1928 Brandeis warned, ominously, that 'The progress of science in furnishing the Government with the means of espionage is not likely to stop with wiretapping', little did he guess just how far even 'the most intimate occurences of the home'[27] would become potentially transparent to a range of agencies courtesy of computer-power.

By 1948 – the year the transistor was invented – the United Nations declared as a human right that 'no one shall be subject to arbitrary interference in his privacy, home or correspondence'. The word 'arbitrary' was clearly intended to contrast with, say, 'lawful', but who is to say what should be thus exempted? Or, for the matter, what exactly constitutes 'interference'? Thirty years later, when the microchip made its first appearance, such questions seemed even further from resolution. By then, governments and other large organizations were already making extensive use of computer power to store and process personal data, and the more precise term 'information privacy' was proposed as a means of coping with the consequent broadening of perceived threats to privacy.

But what exactly is threatened by the rapid rise of computerized record-keeping, either by state or economic institutions? In Victorian times, the fear was that members of the public might obtain unseemly access to the private lives of élite people, such as politicians or the rich. British Royalty, among others, continue to struggle with this. With electronic surveillance, however, the equation is reversed. It is the lives of ordinary citizens that are thought to be at risk from large and powerful agencies. Indeed, the practice of computer-matching, mentioned earlier, tends to place the poor, the vulnerable, the minority at a particular disadvantage relative to big bureaucratic forces.

Unfortunately, and with a few important exceptions. sociologists have not given extensive attention to the debate over privacy and data protection. Until recently, many sociologists seem to have so preoccupied with opposing privat*ism* and familial*ism* that matters of human dignity, self-identity and personal space have fallen into neglect or left by default to other disciplines. Over recent decades the discourse on privacy has been dominated by legal opinion. Consequently, while some useful work has been done in an attempt to define privacy for the so-called information age, legal writers and philosophers have had to fall back upon what one of them, Geoffrey Brown, calls 'crude and homespun sociology'.[28]

The danger of such a relative lack of sociological analysis and discussion is that legal conceptions of privacy lose touch with technological and social realities.[29] Sociological and historical investigation highlight the cultural variations in privacy, and can show both what people actually fear and how well-grounded those fear are. Considerable headway has been made in this regard in the comparative studies produced by Canadian historian David Flaherty.[30] His work also addresses the key question of what social, political and economic difference is made by the advent of electronic surveillance. Beyond this, sociology may well play a part in uncovering and evaluating perceived threats to human liberty or privacy produced by apparently innocuous practices such as the management of consumer demand.

North American data protection laws, for example, tend to cover only government databanks, leaving huge swathes of commercial surveillance almost untouched. Thus when in 1991 Lotus advertized new business software on CD–ROM disks that reveal at the push of a button the names, addresses, marital status and estimated income of eighty million American householders, no law stood in its way. Indeed, the software had been approved for distribution by an experienced American privacy advocate, Alan Westin. Even before it was formally launched, however, Lotus received so many complaints that they withdrew the product. The incident indicates not only the weakness of legislation but also the paucity of privacy as an organizing concept. In an information technology environment such concepts requir overhauling.

Ironically, one of sociology's central themes since it began to define the parameters of modernity is precisely the relation of the so-called 'private' to the 'public' sphere. This debate – particularly as precipitated by feminist critique – is of immense importance to matters considered here under the rubric of electronic surveillance. The public/private dichotomy originates in classic liberalism. The former refers to the realm of politics and the state, which acts as an umpire, enforcing public laws. The latter includes the domestic realm, but can also refer to private interests, private enterprise and private individuals. Sociologically, this is connected with the way that industrial production increasingly sent men 'out' to work and relegated women to the 'home'.

From the feminist critique it is plain that notions of public and private have been used to throw a veil over conflicts, struggles and abuse that occur all-too-often within the so-called private sphere. Thus the distinction carries heavy ideological freight. Dilemmas abound here too. Historical research shows that many women welcomed intervention in abusive situations.[31] Today, telephones with 'caller ID' facilities that display the caller's number to the called household are similarly welcomed by women in danger. The problem is that the same system, used in reverse, is a gold mine of consumer data for companies wishing to target specific buying groups. Our 'phones may reveal more than we wish to disclose!

During the 1990s, new telephone services promise to offer a major challenge to conventional concepts of privacy, particularly as far as this term applies to the domestic sphere, the 'home'. Caller ID is just one of them, but this has already generated considerable controversy in the countries where it is available.[32] While the telephone companies sell the services as a means of gaining control over what communications *enter* the home, marketers rub their hands with delight at their new corner on data *leaving* the home by the selfsame channel. It is indeed a Janus-faced technology, but one prominent critic, Marc Rotenberg, warns of a coming showdown as members of the public become aware that caller ID is a means of obtaining personal information without consent. 'From Ma Bell to Big Brother' is his slogan for it.[33] The once 'private' home is made 'public' means of convenient communications systems purchased by its residents.[34]

If it was ever appropriate analytically to separate 'public' and 'private' spheres, it certainly is not in then late twentieth century, when the boundaries between them have been thoroughly obscured. Indeed, to return to our central theme, information technology now enables further blurring of the boundaries, on a massive scale. The home, once a sacrosanct liberal haven from 'public' life, increasingly finds itself to be the site of surveillance. Government administration gains easy access to details of who lives with whom, and this affects voting capacity or welfare entitlements, while commercial agencies encounter few obstacles to analysing the financial standing and consumer preferences of each household in a given street.

All this throws into radical doubt the usefulness of 'privacy' as a concept that can cope sociologically (let alone legislatively!) with the challenge of electronic surveillance. At the same time, it would be premature to jettison any and all appeals to privacy, or to a 'personal' realm. The personal is indeed political and power relations are evident in the public/private distinction. But one can still argue for a personal dimension to social life.[35] The nature of that 'personal' sphere constitutes another area of debate into which questions of electronic surveillance propel us.

Clearly, new dialogue is urgently needed between social scientists, legal thinkers and policy-makers if today's challenges to taken-for-granted assumptions about privacy and its security are to be contained or neutralized. Needless to say, such a dialogue would in part be contingent upon the willingness of sociologists to have an 'applied' role; and this in turn requires some redefinition.[36]

Personhood and Postmodernity

Lastly but by no means least, electronic surveillance must be situated within a cluster of problems that, for want of a better term, I have labelled 'personhood and postmodernity'. Personhood has to do with human identity, dignity, liberty and responsibility, which in different ways are assumed to be challenged by the rise of electronic surveillance, and in terms of which rules regulating its spread are framed. 'Postmodernity' refers to a debate about a social transformation supposedly taking place towards the end of this century, in which we move beyond the modern condition. I have placed personhood and postmodernity together to indicate that the study of electronic surveillance raises some fundamental philosophical questions that sociology *per se* cannot resolve but without attention to which sociology cannot proceed.[37]

A paradox lurks here. The impact of information technology in human affairs is sometimes taken to be one indicator that we are entering a qualitatively different phase of social development from that known as 'modernity'. Among other things, in the condtion of postmodernity it is sometimes said that we can no longer be as sure as we were of the status of human presonhood – apart from its being culturally and historically relatives. At the same time, the growth of electronic surveillance has thrown up questions about 'privacy' that ultimately can only be addressed in terms of some conception of personhood and human identity. Can those involved in the critique of electronic surveillance, the framing of law, and the establishment of policy, agree enough on what is important to construct appropriate measures relating to it? A couple of examples will give a flavour of the problem.

In *The Postmodern Condition*[38] Jean-François Lyotard paints a picture of society that is heavily dependent upon new information technologies. He follows Daniel Bell's[39] assertion that 'knowledge' has emerged as a new axial principle of contemporary societies, and that new means of information processing are deeply implicated in this development. At the same time, this 'postmodern condition' is characterized by the 'collapse of metanarratives'. That is to say, modern verities such as the redemptive belief in science, technology or democracy, having fallen into some disrepute during the twentieth century, have now lost whatever universal power they might once have been thought to posssess. Lyotard asserts not only that they have collapsed, but that in a quest for some kind of certainty people clutch at the apparently certain methods of computer science as a substitute.

Information technology, in this account, stands in an ambiguous relation to postmodernity, part problem, part remedy. People trust themselves to complex technologies because they seem to promise convenience, efficiency, security and reduced uncertainty. Simultaneously, we worry that in so doing we may be denying something important to a worthwhile human life. But what that 'something' is becomes increasingly hard to define. We end, Lyotard might conclude, by depending on the very systems about whose efficacy we entertain nagging doubts. We collude with surveillance systems, whether willingly or reluctantly, wittingly or unwittingly. But if we object, we are unsure of our grounds for so doing.

Similar themes are taken up by Mark Poster, who argues persuasively that the postmodern could be classified as a 'mode of information'.[40] He too places the development of information technology – and particularly what we shall refer to as its surveillance capacity – at the centre of contemporary social transformation. He asks, for instance, where the human self is located if fragments of personal data constantly circulate withing computer systems, beyond any agent's personal control?

For Poster, the language of 'privacy invasion' is irrelevant, a throwback to modernity. In today's databases we see 'the constitution of an additional self, one that may be acted upon to the detriment of the 'real' self without that 'real' self ever being aware of what is happening'.[41] So what exactly is the status of our 'electronic image'?[42] And how does it affect or even connect with our other, more familar relationships in everyday life? And if we query the desirability of this 'virtual world', is it enough to counter it with a 'freedom of information' strategy, as Poster seems to advocate?

Both of these accounts present us with an intriguing and important challenge. Should current trends in the processing of personal data be interpreted as simply more of the same, and thus amenable to the kinds of analysis that began with Max Weber's studies of rationalization and bureaucracy? Or should they be considered as significant aspects of a deeper social transformation that requires the entire recalibration of sociological concepts? Is the kind of surveillance that characterized the growth of modernity being supplanted by a new, postmodern surveillance, or is it merely the old surveillance writ large? Either way, the issues of what constitutes human personhood and of how that fits with conceptions of social order cannot be evaded.

Although these issues are addressed later in the book, a word on my own stance may be appropriate here. While I regard some from of surveillance as an inherent – and not necessarily evil – feature of all human societies, it seems to me that the chronic quest for personal data-collection that typifies modern life demands specific and urgent critical attention. Questions of justice and fairness must be raised when people's everyday activities are monitored and their habits, commitments and preferences classified by the would-be omniscient organization. Such classification is both an outcome not only of social differences but of advantage and disadvantage, and often serves to reinforce inequalities of life-chances. And while it undoubtedly enables us to participate in society in numerous important ways, it also constrains us and encourages us to comply with the social order. The more marginal or nonconforming we are, the stronger the web of constraint-by-surveillance becomes.

Surveillance is thus a morally and politically loaded activity, amenable to critique and to challenge; and not only from the macro-level political point of view. Issues of social inequality and social control are also connected with issues of trust and personal integrity. Particular forms of communication are a vital aspect of what it means to be human. What we disclose to whom, and under what conditions, is highly significant. What once we might have revealed, consciously, about ourselves to someone we trust – friend, doctor, priest, therapist – may now be involuntarily disclosed by electronic means to organizations or machines that we cannot know, let alone trust, in the same way. Our identity is understood by others – and by inanimate machines – more from our data-image than from our personal communication.

In other words, living in 'surveillance societies' may throw up challenges of a fundamental – ontological – kind. Not surveillance as such, but the specific surveillance trends of the late twentieth century seem to raise questions for which as yet we have far from adequate answers. While it would be foolish to imagine that this book would provide such 'answers; I hope that at least the questions will be made clearer. My own stance, which guides my choice between both theoretical and practical alternatives, is nurtured by traditions of Christian social thought. These call for care about all situations in which human dignity and justice are threatened. At present, the large, 'metaphysical' questions are all too frequently ignored,[43] rather than engaged by a critical analysis based on specific views of justice and human personhood.[44]

Understanding Surveillance Society

The chapters of this book are organized under three connected headings. In the first, *Situating Surveillance*, the growth of electronics surveillance is placed against the backdrop of modernity – its historical, social and cultural context. Given the huge scope of this task and that which follows it in the rest of the book, I draw upon illustrative material from a variety of sources rather than attempting to paint an exhaustive empirical picture. Two major issues are addressed in the remainder of the first part. First, do new technologies spell a qualitatively new surveillance? and secondly, if so does this add up to the emergence of a more authoritarian, prison-like society?

Part Two, *Surveillance Trends*, documents the specific ways in which surveillance is currently being augmented using new technologies, both in and between administrative and commercial contexts. Surveillance related to state functions takes up two chapters, as does surveillance in relation to capitalism, But wheras in other treatments the accent is on the productive sphere, in this book I lay great emphasis on the implications for surveillance of *consumption*. The role of computer matching, smart cards and universal personal identifiers is especially significant in this part of the book. Additionally, we shall see how surveillance has become very much a global, not just a national phenomenon, which also has implications for responses to it.[45]

In Part Three, *Counter-Surveillance*, the actual challenge of electronic surveillance is reappraised in the light of the analysis contained the first two parts of the book and the various responses to that challenge are examined and evaluated. Privacy is seen as one strand among others in an appropriate strategy of limiting electronic surveillance. Without for a moment minimising or dismissing the personal and social challenges of surveillance, however, I recommend the abandonment of merely negative, dystopian perspectives. They act as a hindrance to both adequate social analysis and appropriate ethical practice.

In order to understand the 'surveillance society', then, we must engage with several kinds of debate, and communicate across several different disciplinary areas. The sociologies of technology, politics and law are three such, but these in turn have to be seen in relation to debates over social control and surveillance on the one hand, and over modernity and post-modernity on the other. And none of these is satisfactorily discussed without reference to some concept of personhood, or some outline of what constitutes the good society.

Beyond mere 'understanding', however, sociology exists in close relation to its object of analysis , society. Sociology has become a crucial component of the social self-understanding, and thus also of the ongoing reproduction, of modern societies.[46] It is my hope that the analysis offered in these pages will make some small contribution to defining the social, political and cultural meanings of electronic surveillance so that, in dialogue with it, more room will be made for just, fair, loving and responsible social practice.

2

Surveillance in Modern Society

A Prehistory of Surveillance

Surveillance is not new. Since time immemorial, people have 'watched over' others to check what they are up to, to monitor their progress, to organize them or to care for them. The rulers of ancient civilizations, such as Egypt, kept population records for purposes such as taxation, military service and immigration. And the Book of Numbers records how even the nomadic people of Israel undertook more than one census to record population details as far back as the fifteenth century BC.

The Israelite Censuses seem to have been a means of regrouping after the flight from slavery in Egypt and of ensuring some semblance of military order among people who had shortly before been a ruthlessly exploited ethnic minority underclass. Later on, the census, though still maintaining military overtones, also served as a way of apportioning land as the wanderers settled in Palestine. The division of a people into tribes and clans, and the recording of names and ages in each, permitted oversight and order. Once the numbering was complete, leaders could calculate how many were suitable for fighting and what land would be required where.

Less long ago, Domesday Book, a record of English land-holding begun in 1086, contained a massive collection of facts about people and property. This so-called *descriptio* enabled the Norman administration, having established itself militarily, to consolidate its power. William I inaugurated a massive scheme of land transfers, redistributing property and imposing new systems of taxation. The effect, as Vivian Galbraith notes, was to 'harness the wealth of England to a new system of feudal baronies'. It was a 'written record of the new order, as seen through Norman eyes'.[1]

The *descriptio* contained in the Domesday Book attempted a comprehensive survey of all tenancies and inheritances, in contrast with the piecemeal approach taken earlier. Disputes were bound to arise, with the land transfers especially, and Norman administration had to counter them. It was essential to know, and to establish by the written word, who was liable for what. Domesday Book, as a 'logical outcome of Conquest',[2] sought complete knowledge, as a means to complete control.

The survey for the *descriptio* was highly detailed, and clearly not popular with those required to give account. The *Anglo-Saxon Chronicle* records with some chagrin how the survey was 'made so narrowly that there was not a single hide or yardland, nor – shameful to relate . . . – was there an ox or a cow or a swine left out, that was not set down in his writing'.[3] Because some land-holders deliberately concealed 'hides', a special *inquisitio geldi* was initiated to catch them out, so that the new government could extort the last penny in dues.[4]

Why the *descriptio* was called Domesday Book is unclear. Although the book was first kept in the *Domus Dei* – House of God – at Winchester, the English Treasurer, writing in 1179, explained that it refers metaphorically to the Day of Judgement, when, according to Revelation, the dead will be judged by what is written in the book.[5] This seems both appropriate and likely.

What exactly is going on in these historical examples? We may observe how power is maintained through such surveillance activities, and how the survey or 'inquest' was experienced negatively by those called to account in Norman England. But it is also noteworthy that administration of this kind depends upon the development of writing. Changing technique, one might say, facilitated alterations in the surveillance capacity of rulers. This important insight, though expressed a little differently, is central to the work of Harold Adams Innis.[6]

As Innis put it, *all* forms of communication technology have a 'bias'.[7] He suggests that in ancient states citizens were bound together over time by the use of writing, whether on stone, parchment, or clay. Recorded details of past transactions and rules were more secure than human memory. Only when papyrus became widely available to the Romans, through their conquest of Egypt, could they hold together administratively the vast spaces that would be known as the Roman Empire. But papyrus fell into disuse after the decline of Rome, and it took the growth of printing – the 'Gutenberg revolution' – before a further major change could occur in administrative power. Now the political sphere could expand enormously, given the novel availability of written texts. This is of course highly pertinent to the development of surveillance as a dimension of modernity; printing facilitated the development of modern democratic governance.

And it also raises the question of whether the late twentieth-century use of information technology portends further alterations in organizational power.

If surveillance itself is not a novel phenomenon, has its character changed? In the Egyptian, Hebrew, Roman and English examples given here, certain features appear. To take the Norman English example, in the fior place surveillance connects with the power to help organize and control populations; King William wished to consolidate his rule through the Domesday survey. Then, surveillance may be experienced negatively as well as positively. The post-conquest English landholders resisted the prying *inquisitio*. Finally, improved recording techniques – writing or printing – facilitate new levels of surveillance. As we examine surveillance in the modern era, it is worth bearing these issues in mind: what kind of power is involved? how is surveillance experienced, and with what effects? in what ways do better techniques contribute to greater surveillance capacities?[8]

Surveillance and Modernity

Surveillance as we know it today – that is, as an institutionally central and pervasive feature of social life – did not emerge until modern times. While its primitive forms may be seen for instance in the eleventh century with Domesday Book, its expansion from the nineteenth century was dramatic. Systematic surveillance, on a broad scale as we shall understand it here, came with the growth of military organization, industrial towns and cities, government administration, and the capitalistic business enterprise within European nation-states. It was, and is, a means of power; but not merely in the sense that surveillance enhances the position of those 'in power'.

Paradoxically, as we shall see, surveillance expanded with democracy. Indeed, it is associated with the post-Enlightenment political 'demand for equality',[9] and with populations previously denied access to full political involvement. At the same time, older local, familial, and religious kinds of surveillance declined or were diluted. Historically, then, the development of surveillance is complex. The question of who watches whom and with what effect cannot be answered without reference to specific social situations at specific times.

Before proceeding any further, we should note that although until fairly recently sociologists have not written a lot about surveillance *per se*, the theme is extensively explored under other rubrics from the time of the nineteenth-century sociologists onwards. Of course they themselves were children of modernity, and as such held ambivalent attitudes to it. On the one hand, being so close to the transformations they attempted to describe, they were in an especially good position to evoke the sense of a sea-change in society. On the other hand, the very magnitude of change sometimes blinded them to continuity and persistence. A glance at these commentaries will serve as a rough guide to what follows, and I shall pick up these more analytical threads once again towards the end of the chapter.

One abiding feature of societies we call modern is the economic system of capitalism, which brought with it a strong surveillance dimension. For Karl Marx, surveillance was located within struggles between labour and capital in the business enterprise and the capitalist system. Previous means of co-ordinating workers on a large scale had involved coercion; under capitalism, labour was no longer coerced. According to the new doctrine, the worker was, in a formal sense, free. But the capitalist manager still had to maintain control of workers so that they would keep the business competitive by producing as much as possible within a given time at the lowest cost.

Hence what we now know as 'management' was developed to monitor workers and to ensure their compliance as a disciplined force. The idea of bringing workers together under one roof, in factories and workshops, has often been seen as a way of maximizing technical efficiency, making full use of machinery, and so on. But it can equally well be argued that the use of factories to ensure labour discipline through the oversight of workers' activities was at least as important, if not more so.[10] Marx's recognition of this makes his work vital to an understanding of modern surveillance.

Probably the best-known figure in the early analysis of surveillance is Max Weber. While he acknowledged the role of surveillance in capitalist enterprises, he resisted the restriction of surveillance to the context of class relations. For him, surveillance is bound up with bureaucracy, of which capitalist businesses are but one type. Modern organizations are characterized above all by their *rationality*, a feature that both gives them coherence and distinguishes them from previous forms of organization.

In the capitalist workplace, for instance, this rationality entails accounting by means of double entry book-keeping. Everything is geared towards making possible carefully calculated decisions. All administration is based on written documents, processed by a hierarchy of salaried officials, and impersonal rules based on up-to-date technical knowledge. Efficiency is allegedly maximized through this system, but so is social control. Members come to accept the rules as rational, fair and impartial. The director of a bureaucracy can predict with certainty that orders will be implemented in a rational manner. As Christopher Dandeker says, for Weber, 'rational administration is a fusion of knowledge and discipline'.[11]

Jumping to the later twentieth century, the work of Michel Foucault points beyond bureaucracy. He places surveillance in the broader context of discipline in society-at-large, not just organizations. Indeed, only since Foucault has surveillance been accorded a central position in social analysis. For Foucault, modern society is itself a 'disciplinary socieaty', in which techniques and strategies of power are always present. Though these may originally develop within specific institutions such as armies, prisons, and factories, their influence seeps into the very texture of social life.

Power, in this view, is not a possession but a strategy. Power makes for constant tension and struggle as those subjected to it resist it with their own tactics. In modern societies people are increasingly watched, and their activities documented and classified with a view to creating populations that conform to social norms. The knowledge of what happens is thus intrinsically bound up with power.

This perspective, as I hinted earlier, has advantages and drawbacks. In the modern world, access to information does seem to be increasingly connected with power — especially today, with the availability of cheap and efficient modes of data processing. On the other hand, Foucault's perspective seems to revolve around the concept of power in a way that almost excludes other proper sociological considerations; Power, expressed as domination or violence, is all there is. Little space remains for examining how people actually interact with each other in surveillance situations, still less for approaching these questions from a different standpoint.[12] When it comes to electronic mediation of communication, however, there is more scope for considering approaches derived from Foucault, and we shall return to this theme in later chapters.

Whether it is an aspect of class relations, or rationality, or a pervasive dimension of society itself, surveillance must be seen, sociologically, as a central feature of modernity. Never before have social organizations developed that could so comprehensively touch the routines of ordinary people in everyday life.

But surveillance may also be viewed as the other side of the coin of democracy. As Alexis de Tocqueville astutely observed, modern mass democracies depend upon bureaucratic documentation and intervention. Ironically, suggests de Tocqueville, democracy produces privatized citizens whose paramount concern is personal welfare. This renders such individuals particularly vulnerable to the crushing strength of central state institutions.[13] As surveillance develops, so an individual anxiety about 'privacy' emerges, stimulated by what are felt as the encroachments of government administration.

From the earliest days of modernity, then, administrators collected and recorded personal details of given populations, and capitalist business organizations monitored and supervised employees in order to enhance their efficiency. Increasingly, heavy dependence was placed on the role of knowledge in generating and maintaining power. While the term 'information society' only came into vogue during the 1980s following the widespread adoption of so-called 'information technologies',[14] in an important sense modern societies have been 'information societies' since their inception.[15]

In what follows I shall begin by looking a little more closely at the different contexts within which modern surveillance has been established: the military, the nation-state and the capitalist business organization. We can now say a little more about the three questions posed on page 24, and I shall pursue these in what follows: One, is surveillance power synonymous with bureaucracy? In short, who is correct; Marx, Weber, Foucault, or none, or all of them? Two, if we examine this power, it does not seem to be experienced in an overwhelmingly negative way. At least some surveillance seems to occur in settings that allow its subjects to 'answer back'. Does this reciprocity always obtain? Three, as in the modern world we become dependent upon experts, on those 'in the know', how far does control of information become the key political question?

The Military, War and Modern Surveillance

From 1585 to his death in 1625 Maurice of Nassau was Captain-General of Holland and Zeeland. Confronted by the challenge of the Spaniards in the Low Countries, he turned to Roman writers for a model he might adopt. Systematic drill was the idea that struck him most forcibly, and to make drill even more effective, he divided his army into small tactical units.[16] Soldiers were taught to regularize their matching, as to load and fire their matchlock guns in the forty-two moves analysed by Maurice, thus permitting constant volleys of fire. Drill, more closely supervised than ever before by a new cadre of officers, made armed action semi-automatic.

Thus the modern army made its appearance, complete with an embryonic bureaucracy, a separate class of officials or officers, uniforms, and disciplined drill, all in the quest for efficiency and the need to reduce unit costs. Careful analytical thought went into each aspect of Maurice's new regime. It was a product of rational calculation. All these features would reappear to some degree in other modern organizations, the factory, the office, the prison, the school.

It would be nice to think that one could isolate a symbolic starting point for modern surveillance in this way, but before continuing a note of caution should be sounded. A good case can indeed be made for saying that modern surveillance practices originated in military drill. But this should not be taken as confirmation of Leon Trotsky's aphorism that 'war is the locomotive of history'.[17] The military background to modern surveillance is but one – though a singularly important one – of several key influences that are interrelated in complex ways.

It makes much sense to think of modern societies as having several major institutional dimensions, none of which may be reduced to another. Anthony Giddens proposes four such dimensions; capitalism, industrialism, military power, and surveillance.[18] He rightly suggests that surveillance is fundamental to all the kinds of organization associated with modernity. It is visible, for instance, in capitalist workplace supervision, government administration, and the monopoly by the nation-state of the means of violence. Having said that, military development certainly offers a convenient and salient starting point for surveillance studies.

Christopher Dandeker[19] argues persuasively that the armed forces represented the most significant component of the early modern state. They were organizationally complex, attracted the greatest expenditure, and involved the largest number of people. Warfare with other societies helped create the modern state as an entity separate from civil society and with the organizational means of supervising the population of a given territory. The military led the way, at least in Europe, in providing a bureaucratic model of organization for others – such as the business enterprise – to follow. Beyond this, warfare encourage the extension of state supervision of society for military objectives.

One aspect of this extension has already been mentioned, namely the formation of professional military organizations separate from the rest of society. Though these grew into the bureaucratized mass armed forces of the mid-twentieth century, for various reasons they are now shrinking in size as the military enterprise becomes more capital intensive.[20] Another facet of state supervision, however, is the way that whole societies gradually became involved in the process of warfare. Though this occured in different ways and at a varying pace in different societies, such mass mobilization found its most dramatic expression in the world wars of the twentieth century. Allegiance to the nation state for the 'war effort' was secured in part at least by accompanying extension of citizenship rights, and promises such as 'homes fit for heroes'. The connections between the warfare state and the welfare state are strong and significant.[21]

In Britain, for instance, large scale bureaucratic surveillance was required for conscription from 1916, both in a register of fit men and modes of dealing with groups such as conscientious objectors. But public opinion had to be monitored in new ways, and production and distribution regulated as never before, to ensure that in conditions of total war victory was achievable. Security services stepped up their surveillance activities, reporting on suspicious persons, intercepting letters and cable messages, and collecting data on several categories of potentially risky people.

Once established for the Great War, the whole system was relatively easily re-established in 1939, and soon augmented by new features such as a national identity card scheme. Thus the protection of citizens from external threats involved the erosion of some long-cherished civil liberties, particularly assembly, movement and provision of information. And innovations such as British identify cards did not simply disappear after the war. Not until a motorist challenged in the court the apparently arbitrary right of the police to demand the card was that system dismantled.[22]

Following the war, certain other measures continued; for instance, the more centralized management of industrial disputes. But war measures were also transposed into novel attempts to manage the economy in such a way as to minimize socially damaging fluctuations, and also into rationalized systems providing social security and welfare for those who one way or another had failed to keep up within the market.

Several facets of surveillance can thus be found embedded in the history of modern military and war-related activities. These range from the observation and calculation of soldiers' movements for efficient battle-readiness to the bureaucratic organization of armies and their officers, and from the mobilization of whole civilian populations for total war to the growth of security and intelligence services as departments of state. Each of these involves either direct supervision of subordinate groups by others or the garnering of documented details of personal life with the purpose of co-ordination or control. Moreover, such surveillance is often placed in a positive light because the over-arching goal of such endeavours is to procure national security, military supremacy or the defeat of an aggressor.

The Nation-State and Modern Surveillance

One essential element of surveillance is the generation and collation of files or dossiers on individuals. These exist in military settings, especially in the field of intelligence. But keeping files on individuals is more broadly characteristic of the civilian state, and indeed of all bureaucratic organizations. As Weber correctly observed, the written file is the documentary foundation of all modern management within such organizations. The files are intended to ensure technical efficiency and predictability.

Besides the realization of organization ends, however, is the way that files serve a surveillance function. People's activities can be supervised and thus co-ordinated or controlled by an organization that has a record of an individual's past conduct. Weber agonized over this. He was worried that impersonal calculations that drew together organizational rules and personal files would end by 'pigeonholing the spirit' as the bureaucratic ideal gained dominance.[23] But Foucault's insight is that 'disciplinary power' resides in the file which, as Giddens says, 'allows the individual to be kept under minute and scrupulous observation'.[24] This goes beyond Weber's concerns, and also takes us directly into issues central to the so-called 'dossier society'[25] of advanced computer databases used in modern government.

For the present, however, it would help to look back and examine the historical backdrop to the dossier society. Why do we inhabit such extensively administered societies in the late twentieth century? What happened between Domesday Book in the eleventh century and the interlocking networks of government and administrative databanks of the twentieth? The brief answer lies in the birth of modern society, with its constitutive components of industrial capitalism, the nation-state and the new military.

The development of a money economy, as opposed to one based on local transactions, barter, and exchange, provided the means of paying salaried officials. Both the qualitative and quantitative growth of administrative tasks within these societies – or, more accurately, nation-states – called for some adequate system for holding everything together. For Weber, that system is bureaucracy which, as it evolved, commended itself as the superior means of achieving organization goals.

And what were the administrative tasks that mushroomed in nineteenth-century nation-states? These were the continuation of the kinds of activity already alluded to in post-Conquest England: the collection of taxes and other dues, the registration of property and, later, those vital statistical details of births, marriages and deaths, gathered in a uniform and consistent manner. As the franchise was extended, so eligible voters has to be listed; when war was declared, conscripts or volunteers had to be called up, and so on. Indeed, the development of one task often leads to another in order to complete the jigsaw of bureaucratic advantage. Bureaucracy sometimes appears to have a life of its own.

Consider this local example of life in Kingston, Ontario in the 1840s. For a brief period of three years Kingston was the capital of East and West Canada, but this was a decisive time for the establishment of the modern nation-state. Alexander Galt, Canadian Minister of Finance, pointed out that

Our population, annually increased by immigration, compels more extended arrangements for the administration of justice and the wants of civil government. Our infant enterprises need to be fostered by the aid of public funds and our great public resources nurtured and expanded by the erection of public buildings . . . [26]

Among the administrative tasks facing this young country – not yet a full nation-state – were recording property transactions, caring for the native population, regulating fishing, licencing and collecting dues for lumbering, and passing immigrants up the waterways to the interior, as well as providing government services for transport and communication, roads, bridges, canals, and ports, taxation and customs and excise.

From 1841, under the supervision of Lord Sydenham, the various administrative services were rationalized into distinct departments, each with its own head. Administration, finance, defence, education and welfare, natural resources and development; each found its place within the overall scheme. In short, the seeds of modern bureaucracy in Canada were sown at this time. The main outlines of modern administration, still largely recognisable today, took shape.

These then are the kinds of administrative tasks undertaken by the burgeoning nation-state during the nineteenth century. While they were all increasingly organized on a bureaucratic basis, most of them involved personal documentation, and can thus also be seen as contributions to the rise of 'surveillance society'.

It is important to note that this nascent 'surveillance society' has more than one face. It may be viewed either from the perspective of social control or from that of social participation. The administrative machinery constructed during the nineteenth century can be understood both as a negative phenomenon – Weber's 'iron cage' of bureaucratic rationality or Foucault's 'disciplinary society' – or, more positively, as a means of ensuring that equal treatment is meted out to all citizens. It is a mistake to focus exclusively on one face of surveillance.

The European-style nation-state differed from earlier, more traditional ones in at least one crucial respect; other means than direct violence were increasingly sought to contain disorder. As agricultural land was enclosed for larger scale use, and newly landless labourers sought employment in the cities and relief in the parish, constant fears were expressed about the potential for unrest. But the means used to ensure order involved progressively more use of the separation – or 'sequestering' as Foucault has it – of populations who deviated from the desired norms of 'society'. In Britain and elsewhere the workhouse, the hospital and the prison served as places where the disobedient or the deviant could be 'put away' or be 'reformed' into constructive citizens. In this way institutions like prisons could become not only places of punishment, but places where ideals were upheld and realized. The vision of order over against potential chaos could be maintained and even exemplified in prisons.

Something similar may be said for the city, although some doubt exists as to how far the apparently rational schemes of the urban planner really did contribute to the public good. Stanley Cohen's account of Lewis Mumford on the city is instructive here:

> The dark shadow of the good city is the collective human machine: the dehumanized routine and suppression of autonomy, first imposed by the despotic monarch and the army, is now the 'invisible machine' of the modern technocratic state... Mumford described how the utopian ideal of total control from above and absolute obedience below had never passed out of existence, but was reassembled in a different form after kingship by divine right was defeated.[27]

From the nineteenth century onwards, city planners began to take note of the internal social control function that cities could display. Policing took place in city streets, the location of possible criminality and unrest. Law and order was pursued at once architecturally and through rational planning, strategically. Embryonic forms of street surveillance within the 'urban fortress' began life well before the era of wall-mounted video cameras.

The other face of surveillance has to do with social participation or 'citizenship'. Just after the Second World War – the experience of which stimulated much of the transition from the 'warfare' to the 'welfare' state, as we noted above – T. H. Marshall published a small classic on *Citizenship and Social Class*.[28] He argued that modern welfare systems 'abate' the worst effects of capitalist inequalities and are an outcome of citizenship. Earlier citizenship gains are the foundation on which welfare states are built.

According to Marshall, civil rights emerged first, having to do with individual liberty and equality before the law. Subsequently, political rights developed in the form of widening franchise and the right to seek political office. The third, 'social rights', are somewhat more vaguely defined, but comprise, for Marshall, 'a modicum of economic welfare and security' and the 'right to share in the full heritage and life of a civilized being according to the standards prevailing in society'.[29]

From this point of view, the surveillance systems of advanced bureaucratic nation-states are not so much the repressive machines that pessimists imply, but the outcome of aspirations and strivings for citizenship. If government departments are to treat people equally, which is the starting point for the first of Marshall's rights, and from which other rights follow, then those people must be individually identified. To exercise the right to vote, one's name must appear on the electoral roll; to claim welfare benefits, personal details must be documented. Thus as Nicholas Abercrombie *et al* insist, the individuation that treats people in their own right, rather than merely as members of families or communities, means 'freedom from specific constraints but also greater opportunities for surveillance and control on the part of a centralized state'.[30]

The Marshall account of citizenship rights has been criticized on several counts, one of which is that the process of establishing 'rights' took place in different ways in other countries than England. In the USA, for instance, democractic participation extended only slowly beyond the confines of a white, male, landowning élite. Blacks in some Southern states continued to be excluded by means of poll-taxes and literacy requirements right up until the civil rights movements and subsequent court action in the 1960s. However, the essential point of discussing Marshall stands; modern surveillance is simultaneously a means of social control *and* of guaranteeing rights of social participation. Surveillance has two faces.

The rise of the 'surveillance society', then, is inextricably bound up with the growth of the modern nation-state. As the range of necessary administrative tasks expanded, bureaucratic organization evolved as a means of co-ordinating activities. People's daily lives were thus increasingly subject to documentation within the all-encompassing files of the bureaucratic state. All this may be seen from two perspectives; as an attempt to impose new forms of order, to control situations that threatened to breakdown into chaos as the now-familiar urban-industrial world came into being, and as the result of the quest of full citizenship and democratic participation in the new order, which required for fair treatment that individuals be identified, registered and documented in proliferating dossiers.

Capitalism and Modern Surveillance

It is important to remember that these different dimensions of modernity, seen in the rise of the 'surveillance society', are really somewhat artificial analytical distinctions. Each is actually intertwined with the others in complex ways. Military organization gave clues about civilian; Weber was influenced, some say overinfluenced, by his study of the Prussian army.[31] The bureaucratic organization is found in settings as diverse as the capitalist enterprise, the army, and the government department. Marshall's account of the widening of citizenship rights similarly takes us through different social spheres, each of which carries with it implications for the monitoring and documenting of individuals.

The appearance and development of the capitalist enterprise, however, gives another angle on the significance of surveillance in the modern world. As we noted, Marx observed how control was maintained through the enclosed space of the factory, and subsequent theorists have shown how the process of management serves to co-ordinate and direct the activities of workers, not least through monitoring and overseeing their behaviour. Weber also examined the ways that Frederick Taylor's scientific management' apparently induced a mechanical discipline into the labour force.

The capitalist system introduced new ways of disciplining workers who, in traditional societies, had often enjoyed a far greater degree of control over their labour. Where workers had previously been under the sway of a landowner or other employer, physical forms of coercion were available to deal with recalcitrance. Feudalism did involve force. But when it was accepted that workers had a right to dispose of their labour-power as they chose, however circumscribed that choice might turn out to be, other means had to be found of keeping people at work. One, of course, was sheer necessity; the need to survive with no other visible means of support but what an employer might give in a pay packet. The other was surveillance, through the timing, placing, observing, and checking of work, seen above all in the factory.

The contrast between working life in traditional societies and in modern capitalist-industrial societies is illuminated by considering time and daily routines. Whereas in settings that are primarily agrarian daily routines are constrained by season, daylight, and tide, modern work routines are geared to the clock. As E. P. Thompson says in a now-classic article, milking cows, shearing sheep, ploughing fields, fishing, spinning, and weaving are activities governed largely by 'natural' factors. These older rhythms of labour are replaced by the 'clock-work' routines of the factory and workshop within industrial captialism.[32] For Thompson, the accent is on time as a commodity; this gives it its specially capitalist flavour.

Giddens takes issue with Thompson for this, pointing out that the clock has a more general significance for life in the modern world; it serves to synchronize human activities in 'time-space'.[33] While he concedes that selling one's labour as abstract units of time – the 'nine-to-five' – is part of the alienation experienced by workers under capitalism, he also stresses the place of clock-time in co-ordinating all aspects of social life in modern times.

This theme is worth pursuing, not only with respect to the clock, but also to the computer. For while the clock clearly became a vital part of the mechanism of modern surveillance, especially in the capitalist factory, today the computer also coordinates activities in time-space, including activities well beyond the productive sphere. From the bar-coded plastic cards that admit workers to different parts of the plant and record when they were there, to the store-cards that take customers to their favourite brands of breakfast cereal and keep note of their purchasing patterns, the computer has a vital co-ordinating role today. Does the consumer capitalism of the late twentieth century depend on the computer, as once commodity-production capitalism depended on the clock? This question is addressed in Chapter Three.

The new clock-bound routines and reliance on management rather than force were major contributions of industrial capitalism to modernity. Control persisted, of course, but it was a control mediated more pyschologically than physically. This 'demilitarization' of production is one component of the more general process of 'internal pacification' taking place within early modern societies. It connects capitalist practice with the use of prisons rather than brutal and public punishments, with policing rather than the use of militia for the maintenance of law and order, and with the general growth of the administrative state.[34] In each case, moreover, surveillance activities become a more significant aspect of power relations, but not merely in the sense that the power of capital is enhanced. Closer surveillance could also ensure that workers were protected from unfair accusation and rewarded for appropriate work.

What remains unclear in this account is just how far the asymmetrical class relations between capital and labour actually define surveillance. A Marx-Weber tension remains at this point.[35] This tension is not unimportant because, as subsequent discussions will show, the character of surveillance has rather different connotations in the hands of Marxists and Weberians. The question boils down to whether surveillance power operates along the axis of class relations, or in relation to bureaucratic divisions, including those relating to occupation and employment. Another possibility, introduced by Foucault, is that power is ubiquitous, operating both at the two levels just mentioned and at every other micro- and macro-level of society.

Undoubtedly modern capitalist surveillance induced a crisis of control. As Marx rightly concluded, struggle is built into the capitalist labour contract. Workers resist the imposition of new disciplines and regimes that remove their autonomy and responsibility within the workplace. However, their struggle to regain some control is expressed within the labour movement and trade unions, which have succeeded in securing many rights during the twentieth century.

At this point we should recall Marshall's three-stage schema of citizenship rights. Giddens would modify this by saying that Marshall underplayed the role of 'economic rights' in his discussion of how 'citizenship' has 'abated class struggle' in modern times.[36] Giddens claims that the economic element of citizenship, seen in labour unions and in legislation supporting workers' rights, is 'double-edged'. It may be seen both in relation to surveillance and the control of subordinate classes, *and* as a lever of struggle to counter that control. Surveillance, in other words, is again shown to be more complex than a purely Marxist – class power – reading might lead one to expect.

While Giddens' comments are in some ways a timely corrective, it is also worth pointing out that *social* rights, so important to Marshall, seem to have been absorbed into Giddens' *economic* rights. Yet they too exhibit the 'double-edged' character of surveillance systems. Welfare benefits may be claimed to alleviate poverty, but at the price of 'prying' by social workers. Perhaps the problem lies in too narrow a definition of these spheres of surveillance and of citizenship rights.[37]

All this is important background to more recent discussions of surveillance. The theoretical position one takes is closely connected with political possibilities for change. Whereas Marx was fairly sanguine about the chances of a revolutionary transformation that would restore autonomy and dignity to workers, Weber was anything but. He warned that 'the dictatorship of the official is on the advance, and that this would be true even where the reins of state control might be taken over in the name of socialism. As for Foucault, we shall see in subsequent chapters that it is even harder in his work to discern anything but negative conclusions about surveillance and control. For him, any dreams of a democratic future seem foreclosed by ubiquitous power.

Putting pessimism on one side for a moment, it is a crucial message of this book that things have changed. In this chapter we have looked at the growth of surveillance as an inescapable dimension of modernity. But in the closing years of the twentieth century it is abundantly clear that character of capitalism is altering, as is its relation with the nation-state. Marx's original insights applied to the liberal era of Victorian capitalism. Since then, capitalism has become increasingly organized, and its activities articulated with those of the nation-state.

The liberal state facilitated capitalism with laws of property and contract, and by providing checks on currency and monopoly.[38] But in the middle of this century, capitalism maintained a closer relation with the state, which for a while diminished market forces through the intervention of bureaucratic administration. This galvanized the growth of surveillance practices, especially within large-scale business enterprises. By the 1980s, however, it became evident that another change was in train, variously conceived as 'restructuring' or 'disorganized capitalism'.[39] What does this mean for surveillance?

It is doubtful whether the reorganization or disorganization of capitalism spells the end of surveillance. Indeed, this is also the era of the commodification of information; data, including personal data, has a price tag. Within the capitalist business employees are still monitored, now through a new panoply of electronic technology. But it is still not obvious that this is simply a management ploy to secure subordination through surveillance. Equally interesting, however, are the activities undertaken to monitor and direct *consumption*, which now use computer techniques of tremendous power and sophistication.

In both administrative and economic spheres, moreover, surveillance is increasingly globalized. This process, facilitated by the rapid deployment of electronic information and communication technologies, has fascinating and significant ramifications. Administrative surveillance, which once occurred predominantly within the borders of the nation-state, now spills over old territorial boundaries, most obviously in the form of international intelligence networks.[40] Commercial surveillance, similarly, forgets frontiers when data on consumers is sought in the global marketplace. At the same time, the emergence of countervailing forces is simultaneously globalized. Data protection in one country becomes the model for (or in certain circumstances is imposed upon) another country,[41] while social groups concerned with privacy also mount more international operations.[42]

Surveillance, Modernity and Beyond

Surveillance is a central feature of modernity. The rudimentary practices of traditional and feudal societies were vastly intensified and made more thoroughly systematic in the modern era. The surveillance capacities of organizations were constantly enhanced, while the routines of everyday life became transparent as never before. What conclusions may be drawn from this which may yield clues for the further analysis of surveillance today?

Firstly, the question of power. We have seen how surveillance progressively replaces physical coercion as a means of maintaining order and co-ordinating the activities of large populations, especially in the contexts of capitalism and the nation-state. Surveillance also connects closely with knowledge, expressed variously in the special tasks of the bureaucratic official or the business manager, both of whom are increasingly separated from those whom they oversee. Being 'in the know' clearly has consequences for discipline and power. But if modernity may not be reduced to one of its dimensions, then we should beware of seeing surveillance power as exclusively related to any one aspect.

Secondly, there is the experience of surveillance. Part of the answer to the question of power is that surveillance power is patently not absolute. Surveillance originates in a paradoxical fashion – being the outcome of the quest for citizenship, and also of greater centralized state control – and is experienced with ambivalence. We are both grateful for protection or the procurement of rights which it affords, and simultaneously irritated and defensive when meddlesome bureaucracy invades what we see as our private space, or angered at the threats posed to our autonomy. Perhaps Foucault is right to say that power is a strategy; certainly scope exists for 'answering back' in at least some surveillance situations. Surveillance seems to enable as well as to constrain.

Thirdly, the political question; does control of information become the key issue in a 'surveillance society'? We have begun to see how surveillance capacity has grown systematically in modern societies. Rule suggests that this has to do with four things; the size of files, their degree of centralization, the speed of information flow and the number of contacts between administrative systems and subject populations. If we contrast the personal and indirect control involved in, say, the Domesday survey with the direct control that we have with multiple organizations today, we begin to appreciate how surveillance capacities have grown.[43] It is not hard to see why questions of information control are indeed highly significant, if not (yet) politically central.

In the late twentieth century, microelectronic technologies have been widely introduced in order to augment and sustain surveillance activities on an even broader basis than that known in the era of typed documents, printed regulations, and index cards. But as we have seen, while the advent of new techniques has in times past had a significant impact on surveillance practices, they themselves did not create an entirely new situation. In any case the impact of electronic technologies began to be felt in the surveillance sphere well before the 1980s. Telephone communication, for instance, considerably strengthened policing, government administration, and commercial enterprise from the early twentieth century.

At the same time, we cannot afford to ignore ways in which old forms of surveillance have declined or disappeared during the modern era. Likewise, we cannot deny that in some cases new technologies enhance the ability of workers, citizens or consumers to 'answer back'. Less than legal uses of new technology also widen scope for fraudulent activity, which has to be placed against any monolithic or hegemonic interpretations of how such technologies tighten social control.

What electronic technologies facilitate is the deeper penetration of surveillance. We must now explore the ways in which those technologies are actually used, how they help to augment, supersede or diminish the importance of already existing practices. The big sociological questions remain: what kind of power is involved? How is surveillance experienced? What political difference is made? But the context is crucial. Today's surveillance is constituted historically, and is thus the outcome of choices, struggles, beliefs and aspirations of the past. Whether or not the introduction of computer technologies portends a 'new' surveillance situation remains to be seen.

3

New Surveillance Technologies

From Papermongers[1] to Databanks

One thing features more frequently than any other in discussions of contemporary surveillance; the computer. Whether it is a massive new Australian databank called the Law Enforcement Access Network (LEAN), eventually intended to contain all of Australia's corporate data and land-ownership details and accessible to Social Security, Taxation, and Federal Police Departments, or a Louisiana company known as the Employers' Information Service, which prospective employers may use to find out about prospective employees' prior job injuries or worker compensation claims, the machine that makes it possible is the computer.[2]

Computers, or, more precisely, that combination of computer-power with telecommunications often referred to as 'information technology', seem to lie behind the huge expansion of personal data gathering in the later twentieth century. I say 'seem' advisedly, because, as this chapter shows, what information technologies actually do is make more efficient, more widespread, and simultaneously less visible many processes that already occur. In particular, computers in tandem with advanced statistical techniques help inaugurate a new dimension of surveillance. Alongside computers, new telecommunications networks facilitate remote contact between surveillance nodes. For instance, they enable the links to be made between different databases in Australia's LEAN, and allow employers in one American state to find out about workers previously employed elsewhere.

While organizations may crow about the tremendous strides made in information management, this exapansion is not always welcomed by those whose details are sucked away to circulate in distant digital libraries. Workers in Idaho sued that state's industrial commission to prevent records of their injuries and claims being sent to the Employer's Information Service. In Australia, where a national electronic identification card scheme was rejected as recently as 1987, many fear that LEAN's use of a single identifying number may turn out to be the proposed ID (identification) card by another name.

So it comes as no surprise that several commentators see computers as central to questions of surveillance. Duncan Campbell and Steve Connor's British study, *On the Record*, 'reveals a startling spectrum of threats to privacy posed by personal records on computer'.[3] Canadian David Flaherty's massive account of privacy protection begins by noting that 'individuals in the Western world are increasingly subject to surveillance through databases in the public and private sectors ... the technical feasibility of a world without privacy is fast approaching.[4] And in Australia, Simon Davies asserts that 'the introduction of new technologies' has the 'potential to erode liberties and freedoms because those technologies changed the balance of power in our society'.[5]

However, mass surveillance itself is clearly not a novel phenomenon. It emerged as a vital aspect of the growth of modern societies; indeed, it helps to define such societies. So while the scale and pervasiveness of contemporary surveillance would be impossible without computer-power, computers have not created the situation that citizens of the advanced societies find themselves in today. We were 'data-subjects' long before any supposed technical revolution occurred. So what difference, if any , do computers make?

In his seminal work *Private Lives and Public Surveillance*, James Rule contrasted the two worlds in which we exist. One is the 'ordinary world of events, people, relationships and so on as they directly impinge on experience. The other is a 'paper world' of formal documentation which serves to verify, sanction and generally substantiate the former ...'[6] Although, as he observed, the paper world – comprising marriage or degree certificates, for instance – may seem to offer a poor reflection of the realities they are supposed to represent, at times they may weigh more heavily on people's lives than the experienced realities. Rule's book relates this directly to the growth of bureaucratic control in modern societies.

By the early 1990s, however, the world of experience was increasingly contrasted not with paper but with digital or electronic worlds. Mark Poster, for instance, argues that databases constitute a kind of extra self, which leads a life of its own largely beyond the ken of the supposedly 'real self.'[7] Poster is less concerned with matters of privacy and bureaucracy than was Rule, but both agree that the issues relate to maintaining social order. The question here, however, is whether the dramatic shift from 'paper' to 'electronic' surveillance makes a significant difference and, if so, how that difference may be characterized.

The Difference Technology Makes

Fears that technology may be a runaway juggernaut[8] tend to appear *after* certain advances have been set in train. Judge Jack Love of Albuquerque, New Mexico, who is taken to be the originator of the practice of electronic tagging of offenders, is a case in point. Initially Love spotted the kernal of his innocent cost-saving idea in a *Spiderman* comic. In the fateful sequence 'Kingpin' clips an electronic bracelet to Spiderman's arm, warning that he can now zero in on Spiderman's location whenever he wishes. However, tagging took on more sinister tones, according to Love, when Japanese companies offered the added benefit of TV monitoring of tagged offenders. Suddenly the whole scheme seemed Orwellian, and he began to express his concerns publicly.[9]

Judge Love's worry was that 'the new technology is making it easy to infringe people's rights'. That he did not seem to entertain such doubts with tagging itself suggests that it is the *level* of technological development that is, for him, crucial. There is a limit, beyond which lies an 'Orwellian' scenario where civil liberties are threatened. It is not clear why TV monitors should be thought more oppressive or intrusive than wearing an electronic anklet, but for Love an unacceptable technological threshold has clearly been crossed.

As we noted in the first chapter, a variety of views exists on the interaction between 'technology' and 'society'. Even to put the matter thus is to fall into the trap of implying that the two can somehow exist separately. This view is most often associated with technological determinism, the idea that the important thing for sociology to study is the 'impact' of technology upon society. Perhaps its strongest form is seen in the hype of book or TV titles like 'The Computer's Threat to Society'.[10] Such a perspective would tend to exaggerate the significance of computers to contemporary surveillance.

Reacting against such views, however, other commentators seem rather to underplay the difference made by new technology. David Held's analysis of power and legitimacy in the modern state, for instance, virtually dismisses the idea that information technology may have a significant role in its own right; the computerization of information adds little that is qualitatively new to these [surveillance] operations, he states.[11] However,

The original *Spiderman* comic strip which inspired electronic tagging.

as we shall see, this account misses some important features of computerized surveillance. New technology – specifically information technology – does indeed make a difference.

Understanding the difference made by new technology involves some careful thinking. For a start, we should not focus exclusively on the supposed *effects* or *impacts* of technology. Computers and telecommunications used in today's surveillance systems arise in political, economic, and cultural contexts that help to shape and direct them. That is to say, they also have *origins* that we ignore at our peril. They are in this sense social constructions.[12] But they are not mere social constructions, as if it were somehow possible to reduce them to 'social relations'. Such social relations are undoubtedly present, but they do not comprehensively or essentially describe what those technologies are. The artefacts themselves have capacities that seem to invite use for surveillance purposes. To emphasize the social at the expense of the technical is as shortsighted as to do the reverse.

It makes much sense to think of technology as an *activity* that has social, political, economic and cultural dimensions. Seen in this way, as something that is *done*, technology may be understood both in the technical dimension of what tasks can be performed using this or that artefact or system, and in the dimension of social origins and consequences. Moreover, if technology is a human activity then it also relates to political purposes, personal preferences, and even religious commitments. In short, technology must also be viewed normatively if it is to be understood properly.[13]

In his classic study of the social role of technology, *The Bias of Communication*, Innis gave some important clues for understanding the changes occurring today. In a long-term historical analysis, he insisted that all forms of communication have an inherent 'bias'. Innis was sceptical of the common belief that developments in communications technologies are necessarily conducive to greater democracy. The invention of printing, which stimulated widespread literacy and undergirded modern notions of an informed electorate, also threatened the very existence of 'public' life. Innis' insight was that newspapers actually created monopolies of information. The emergence of the 'audience' spelled danger for public life, as it transformed people into essentially private readers and listeners.[14]

Beyond this, though, Innis has much to offer to our analysis of the social implications of electronic technologies. His studies of the Ancient World convinced him that the media of communication contained inherent biases. Commands inscribed in stone were likely to be 'time-binding' because of the heaviness and permanence of the medium, whereas the more lightweight and portable papyrus allowed the promulgation of rules over wider geographical space, as well as their easy alteration. These were more 'space-binding'. Without succumbing to the potential determinism of this outlook, we can see that computers, with their huge capacity for storage and instant, untraceable erasure or modification of data, considered along with the vast networking power of new telecommunications, could plausibly be viewed in the same light as space-binding, even imperialistic, technologies.

Although Innis' work ended before the advent of computer-power as a major contributor to organizational life, it is still highly suggestive for today. Who knows what about whom is increasingly a matter of computer databases. Who runs those databases, and who may or may not have access to them, relates closely to the distribution of power. Monopolies of information are evident here also. Moreover, the economic analogy implied by the term 'monopoly' becomes more appropriate because information has rapidly become articulated with the market.

On the one hand, with technological advance the cost of processing information has plummetted, so that gathering, storing, and disseminating data on a large scale is increasingly feasible. On the other, information previously thought trivial, such as consumer preferences, now has a high market value and is eagerly sought by thsoe wishing to gain a competitive edge over others. Beyond this, indeed, information generated by the machines themselves, such as where geographically people with those consumer preferences are located, becomes vitally significant to contemporary niche-marketing. Such data is often both unknown and invisible to its subjects. Thus many kinds of information that once circulated outside the market are now commodities, bought and sold at a price.[15]

But the economic perspective on its own is inadequate. Innis also indicates how different communications technologies 'bind' time and space in varying ways. Within oral cultures, where the spoken word still predominates, local, face-to-face relationships are vital. Story-telling is a means of transmitting tradition from one generation to the next. Writing serves to 'bind' time, by making possible a tangible record of history. Printing, in its turn, contributes to the 'binding' of space, by facilitating the widespread dissemination of ideas. The coming of the telegraph and telephone accelerated this process by splitting transport from communications. Messages no longer have to be carried on horseback or by stagecoach.

Such binding of space and time is visible in many other contexts as well. While Romantic histories of the Industrial Revolution concentrate on inventions such as the steam-engine or railroad locomotive, sociology suggests a different story. It was not so much the triumphant railroad as the humble timetable and the mechanical clock that actually served to co-ordinate human activities in time and space in the early indsutrial era.[16] These also have much to do with surveillance. The timetable and clock, together with the accumulation of coded information, give order to relationships within bureaucratic organizations of both the nation-state and the capitalistic workplace. They enable monitoring and supervision to occur on a day-to-day and even minute-to-minute basis.

So surveillance may be seen on the one hand in the hefty ledgers of the Victorian clerk, and on the other in Henry Ford's automobile assembly line, constantly paced by the clock. In the later twentieth century, however, computers augment those older technologies, co-ordinating social activities in time and space in ways more profound than any clock or timetable could ever do. Indeed, while Giddens distinguishes the two processes of direct supervision (as seen in the workplace) and administrative control (as seen in the government department), it could be argued that information technology is facilitating an increasing convergence between the economic and the administrative. In order to substantiate this, however, we must take a look at the technologies themselves.

What Do Computers Do?

Computers differ from other machines because they possess 'memory' and because they can 'talk' with each other using telecommunications. Using such human language of machines is misleading, of course, because it almost implies that computers can 'think'. However, it also draws attention to an important aspect of computer-power, that it does enable human beings to do more easily many tasks that requires brainwork. Unlike the machines of early industrialism, which multiplied muscle-power, computers can be programmed to perform functions associated with mental power.

When we speak of a database, on which surveillance systems depend, we refer to the machines themselves, the software and the data. A database is the whole system for processing data, which allows selective retrieval from memory. Thus when an officer in a police cruiser keys in details of a suspected stolen vehicle, she calls up on her screen not every car registered in Canada, but only those with the same or closely similar registration sequences. The data are all-important to a database, and may be updated at will; they are organized so that one fact is in one file or field, and consistently coded so that facts appear in a regular pattern. Many people may use a database; this signals the need for security if the data is sensitive. Many of the databases discussed here are also relational, that is to say, they take the form of tabular lists and can therefore be compared with each other. This is another example of 'computer matching' or 'record linkage'.[17]

If one thinks only of the workings of a database it is possible to see a number of potential issues that might relate to the 'monopoly of information' or the 'bias of communication' mentioned above.[18] As far as gathering data is concerned, many people are becoming annoyed about the apparently indiscriminate way that their personal details are amassed, for instance by companies anxious to sell. Filling in a guarantee form for a wahing machine may turn out to be an invitation for other appliance advertisements to come through the letterbox. Data storage also brings problems with it. There may too much, too little, inaccurate or dated data. Police records, as we shall see, notoriously contain much data 'just in case', which can easily prejudice the legal process. Added to which, people may not be aware of records held on them, or may be unable to check them.

Similar comments could be made about the actual processing of data, its retrieval – again, how far can the data-subject gain access? – and the use of data. On this last point, much data, such as that gathered for employment screening, is used in a covert fashion. It could also be used by the wrong people, and therefore quite inappropriately. This fear fuelled the outcry against Lotus Marketplace software, in 1991, that would have placed personal details of millions of householders in the hands of anyone, acting legally or not, who bought the relevant disks.[19]

The great attraction of databases, of course, is that they are very compact and, after the initial capital outlay, cheap to run. To store and gain access to, say, five million index cards each containing 100 words of personal data you need the space of a tennis court. The card index boxes would have to be in five 14–metre rows, two metres high and half a metre deep. A computer disk storage system, on the other hand, need only be in a cabinet two metres high and one metre square.[20]

Techniques such as Free Text Retrieval vastly speed up the process of searching databases, and other technical advances such as Optical Character Recognition, Speech Recognition Systems and Artificial Intelligence (AI) are also used to enhance efficiency in other ways. In Ontario, highway scanners are used routinely to check details of vehicles travelling past them, comparing registration plates with stolen-car data or simply monitoring traffic-flow. AI systems have been tested in Britain for determining welfare benefits and have even been proposed for automating the British Nationality Act, which determines who is and who is not a *bone fide* British citizen.[21]

The term 'dataveillance' is used by Australian computer scientist Roger Clarke to highlight the ways that the convergence of new technologies has confronted the advanced societies with a series of very rapid changes in the quantity, if not the quality, of surveillance. Referring to the Orwellian scenario, he says that 'ubiquitous two-way television *à la 1984* has not arrived even though it is readily deliverable. It is unnecessary because dataveillance is technically and economically superior'.[22]

The potency of dataveillance lies not merely in the computers or telecommunications systems, but in the plethora of new configurations available. The technologies can be combined in numerous novel ways, each magnifying the initial potential of computer-power. Clarke and others see Electronic Funds Transfer (EFT) systems as being particularly significant because they can be linked with many other facilities. Shoppers in the British grocery chain of Sainsbury's may now have their accounts debited directly at the check-out (or Point Of Sale, giving us EFTPOS). In this way, records that locate us in time and space are constructed with ever-increasing precision. Sainsbury's also uses the till records as a means of automatically checking stock, so they can know when cereals or fruit are in special demand, or when floor cleaners and face creams are likely to be sought. In Canada, A&P supermarkets have reduced their reliance on distributing coupons for groceries 'on offer' and now depend instead on plastic bar-coded 'supersaver' cards carried by each shopper. Similar systems are in use in all the advanced societies, including stores in the USA where shoppers are led from aisle to aisle by a small screen on their shopping cart that uses previous purchase data to guide customers to favourite brands and this week's bargains.[23]

EFT may now be linked with air, bus and train travel systems, telephone charging, or in Hong Kong, with road traffic toll-charging (and thus monitoring). But computer-telecommunication links also enable potential and actual contacts between drivers' licensing, police and court records, and even social security and taxation systems, the integration of property ownership records, as in Australia's LEAN system mentioned at the start of this chapter and so on.

Once upon a time, people feared the power of some great central computer that stored huge personal profiles of subject populations. But things have changed. Systems software overheads are high in central operations and single sites are risky, so local and networking standards have emerged, enabling much easier communication, while techniques have evolved for organizing distributed database management and operating system. Networking and dispersion have become far more common and economical. As Clarke observes , however, a 'dossier society' does not need centralization, only dataveillance. All that such a surveillance society requires is a range of personal data systems, connected by telecommunications networks, with a consistent identification scheme.[24]

The first two of these requirements is already in place in all the advanced societies. Government and commercial organizations run a range of personal databases, and a variety of telecommunications from modems and telephones to dedicated fibre-optic cables, and satellites link them together. The third requirement, a consistent identification scheme, is eagerly sought as a means of maximising efficiency and minimizing costs.

Any high integrity system calls for an elimination of the arbitrariness of traditional methods that rely on data such as names with date-of-birth. In countries such as the USA and Canada, where resistance to identity numbers is very strong, social security/insurance numbers tend to be used as *de facto* IDs, or, in the jargon, UPIs – Universal Personal Identifiers. However in Australia the New South Wales Police Department, whose bureau operates nationally, implemented in 1987 a fignerprint record system based on Japanese technology, and efforts to make such IDs socially acceptable are expected to continue.[25] In the UK, a national electronic identification scheme including DNA fingerprinting for males was proposed during 1991. If it were ever accepted, such as scheme would offer exactly the kind of high integrity identification that would be a dataveillance dream.[26]

Clarke distinguishes between personal and mass dataveillance. With the former, individuals have an explicit relationship with the organization, as clients. They pay taxes or purchase good. The organization in question may integrate its records on an individual in order to check a suspect transaction such as tax evasion, or it may screen an appilcation for new transactions, whether welfare benefits or a driver's licence. This may involve the use of further databases, beyond the particular organization in question. This process is called 'front end verification.'

A recent family experience of buying a washing machine may serve as a familar example of front end verification. Having chosen the appliance from Sears we asked to open an account. Among the other databases from which Sears wished to obtain reassurance of our creditworthiness were those of our credit card company and Employment and Immigration Canada. We granted the former but witheld the Social Insurance Number, a move not greeted with much enthusiasm on the part of Sears. The process was delayed and a number of protracted 'phone calls occurred before we could all have clean clothes again.

Beyond this, personal dataveillance may involve cross system enforcement', which makes the individual's relationship with one organization dependent on performance in another. Within small-scale systems like a university, students may well find that they cannot graduate until their library fines have been paid in full. In Australia, when the national ID card was proposed in the mid-1980s, it was suggested that free medical treatment under Medicare be refused to anyone reluctant to carry the electronic ID card.[27]

Mass dataveillance, on the other hand, has less to do with any specific suspicion or transaction. It occurs routinely, to identify people who may be of interest to the organization and who thus qualify for more focused attention. As an individual you do not have to *do* anything. Rather, as Gary T. Marx puts it, you simply come under 'categorical suspicion'[28] by virtue of possessing certain characteristics. The kinds of categories in mind here are very diverse. Applicants for shares in privatized British utilities such as Telecom and Gas have been subjected to 'file analysis' to ensure compliance with the 'single applications only' rule. Would-be blood donors in Canada may be refused not because they are HIV positive as such, but because their lifestyle may make such positivity possible. And couples expecting babies will receive special offers on diapers or babyfood simply because their names and addresses came up within that category.

By the same kinds of techniques, 'profiling ' may be done, in which a number of different factors are brought to bear on records of transactions with a given organization. The US Internal Revenue Service, for instance, has worked out a model of infraction which they apply routinely to all taxpayers. It follows the common pattern of a 'simple laundry list of "red flag" characteristics'.[29] Persons claiming deductions beyond a certain percentage of their income and certain more detailed deductions are likely to trigger more detailed inquiry, according to Marx and Reichman. Such profiling can help identify buildings with a high risk of arson, and a pool of persons believed to be potential highjackers may be refused tickets at airports through the same technique.[30]

Computer matching is also promoted by just the same kind of logic. In this case previously separate data within different databanks is merged in order to gain a fuller picture of a given set of individuals. The largest early implementation of such computer matching took place within the then US Department of Heatlh, Education and Welfare over a decade ago. Information technology advances made possible the comparison of files from different databases containing information gleaned for quite different purposes. In essence, as John Shattuck notes, a 'dragnet investigation' is initiated.[31]

That the first major use occurred in the USA is curious, because such dragnet operations contravene the spirit of existing law. The Fourth Amendment is violated, in that computer matching constitutes a 'fishing expedition' for persons for whom no evidence of wrongdoing has been produced. The presumption of innocence, enshrined in many laws, is overturned. One is presumed guilty until shown innocent. Welfare claimants in Massachusetts who were 'hits' in a computer match for fraud had to fight for reinstatement on the basis of information ignored by the state. The Privacy Act is not deemed to cover such cases because they can be construed by matchers as 'routine use'. People who are computer match hits are denied the due process of law, which would give them the chance to confront their accusers with contrary evidence before steps are taken to apprehend wrongdoers.[32]

New Technology and Surveillance Capacity

The concept of 'surveillance capacity', first suggested by James Rule, is intended as a means of measuring the effectiveness of surveillance systems. Rule takes a kind of worst case scenario of an Orwellian total surveillance society'. He argues that modern surveillance systems have only a limited ability to achieve such a state. Specifically, they are limited in terms of four factors: the size of files held in the system, the degree to which they are centralized, the speed of flow between points in the system and the number of contact points between the system and the subject.[33]

These four criteria may be used to gauge the surveillance capacity of any system, and thus, in Rule's terms, to judge how near is the total surveillance society.[34] In Rule's original study of British policing, driver and vehicle licensing and National Insurance, American consumer credit reporting, and the Bank Americard System, the overall conclusion was that, by these criteria of capacity, surveillance was increasing. This was true of both countries, and of all the various dimensions. Among them, increase was most dramatic, in nearly all the organizations he studied, in the pace of centralization of files. He also noted that speed of flow had quickened, largely due to computerization.

As we have seen, however, tremendous strides in technological sophistication have been taken since the 1970s, when Rule's research took place. In the 1990s, information technology has facilitated further expansion along all four dimensions. Firstly, the size of files has grown, and they are far more fine-grained, precise and discriminating, as a result of amplified storage capacity combined with the decreasing physical size required of machines.

Secondly, what Rule meant by centralization was that, by storing data in a central location, evading detection by moving around was made more difficult. Today, networking makes that comprehensivity of reach even more sophisticated, but as the databases are more dispersed, perhaps 'centralization' is not the single best term for this dimension of surveillance capacity. What seems to be happening in many countries is that both greater centralization and increased decentralization is occurring. Surveillance is indeed more dispersed, but the same technical systems make it easier for individuals to be traced by central institutions such as government administrative departments or the police.

Speed of data-flow has been enhanced by the use of advances telecommunications, and this affects especially the organization's ability to respond quickly to altered circumstances. The police cruiser terminal example reminds us that 'command and control' functions can be made much more efficient[35] with greater speed. Again, this squares with the perspective derived from Innis, that computer technologies are 'space-binding', and thus contain greater potential power because of the ease and pace of communication.

Lastly, with regard to points of contact between surveillance systems and their subjects, over previous examples clearly indicate how once again information technology developments facilitate big changes. Front end verification, cross system enforcement, profiling and computer matching, all of which have both government and commercial application, point up the increased capacity of surveillance systems, and the ease with which they can maintain numerous points of contact between themselves and their subjects. What might be called subject transparency is augmented. Ordinary citizens, workers and consumers are more visible to largely invisible 'watchers' who subject them to increasingly constant and profound monitoring.[36]

The notion of surveillance capacity to gauge the effectiveness of surveillance systems is thus shown to be most helpful. However, our comments suggest that the very categories proposed by Rule have themselves to be modified in the light of technological changes, even though the significance of each remains important to the overall strength of surveillance systems. In what follows, then, we shall work with the four dimensions of surveillance capacity as, one; size of files, two; comprehensivity of reach, three; speed of flow, and four; subject-transparency.

Other factors arising from technological development are important but do not necessarily affect surveillance capacity. I have in mind the tendency for surveillance systems increasingly to depend on their subjects to trigger their activity, by means of the trail of transactional information left behind as we make purchases or phone calls, submit claims or state preferences. A second process, also noted by Rule, is the tendency for surveillance systems to 'feed on themselves.'[37] This refers to the way that organizations depend more and more on checking personal details from other records rather than asking the data-subject himself. Herein lies a paradox. We collude more and more with our own surveillance, while for many routine purposes the systems themselves depend less and less on direct requests to us for data. At the same time, our personal data details are still demanded of us with great frequency. Thus, consciously or not, we continue to interact with surveillance systems, which weave their web ever more finely.

New Technologies: New Surveillance?

Our preliminary survey of what computers do has shown that along with telecommunications they permit considerable and sometimes dramatic growth in surveillance capacity. The question remains, though; does the wholesale absorbtion of information technology by surveillance systems mean that surveillance itself is qualitatively altered, or do we simply have more of the same? This is clearly a very important question for sociology, already grappling with the debate over whether the advanced societies are shifting into a 'postmodern era,' because it means that here too the adequacy of old analytical tools is in question. But it is also a pressing political question. In Rule's book, weakening the limits on surveillance capacity brings us closer to the 'total surveillance society,' so if new technology does just that, then what lies in the path of tyranny?

The strongest recent statement of the view that the new technologies portend a new surveillance comes from Gary T. Marx; 'Computers qualitatively alter the nature of surveillance – routinizing, broadening and deepening it'.[38] Marx's research on surveillance focuses on police undercover work in the USA, but broadens out to a general discussion of current trends in surveillance and social control. Marx questions the common assumption that the 'problem' of computerized surveillance arises only if the technology 'falls into the wrong hands'. On the contrary, he argues, the very way in which new technologies are being used today in liberal democratic societies has increasingly strong totalitarian potential. The new surveillance is already here, without a coup or a revolution.

Marx lists ten characteristics of the new surveillance that set it apart from traditional forms of social control. It transcends distance, darkness and physical barriers. It transcends time, and this can be seen especially in the storage and retrieval capacity of computers; personal information can be 'freeze-dried', to use Goodwin and Humphreys' term.[39] It is of low visibility or invisible; data-subjects are decreasingly aware of it, a theme explored in the following chapter. It is frequently involuntary, as we noted above. Prevention is a major concern; think of bar-coded library books or shopping mall video cameras, which are there to prevent loss, not to teach the immorality, of theft. It is capital- rather than labour-intensive, which makes it more and more economically attractive. It involves decentralized self-policing; again, we noted above how we participate in our own monitoring. It triggers a shift from identifying specific suspects to categorical suspicion. It is both more intensive and more extensive. In Stanley Cohen's metaphor, the net is finer, more pliable, and wider.[40]

One important virtue of Marx's book is that he discusses a range of technological innovations affecting surveillance. These include the bio-technological, like DNA fingerprinting. It is worth stressing, however, that in terms of surveillance capacities, information technology deserves particular attention. Genetic fingerprinting certainly does allow some intimate forms of surveillance to occur. But the actual location of individuals in time and space, and the co-ordination of their activities, depends on the peculiar capabilities of computer-based technology.

Biotechnological social control techniques, highly significant though they are, depend upon information technology. The converse does not hold. It is therefore hardly surprising that the British Parliamentary committee proposal mentioned above advocates both a national electronic ID system and genetic fingerprinting. Genetic fingerprinting on its own has limited use for the detection of crime. Only when such data are electronically stored, transmitted and retrieved do they become a powerful tool for criminal or other investigation.

Gary T. Marx's view of computer-power and surveillance has much to commend it. It does not suggest that technology on its own is capable of some mysterious 'effects', but nor does it allow us to imagine that all can be explained by reference to the kinds of organizations the technologies serve. Marx resists the stance that we are merely the 'hapless victims of technological determinism'[41], but his work also implies that we are not hapless victims of 'social forces' either. The account given by Frank Webster and Kevin Robins sometimes comes close to this latter position in their discussions of 'cybernetic capitalism'. Through new technologies, they say, everyday life is 'transformed and informed by capital'.[42]

In what follows we shall pay attention both to the technologies themselves, particularly in terms of their surveillance capacities, and to the social processes that shape and direct them. Capitalism is one of these processes, of course, but the perspective taken here is that other processes, institutions, persons, and events must also be seen as contributing to the mushrooming of electronic surveillance. We have already seen how influential an individual like Judge Love can be, and as for events, data privacy became a major headline issue in the US following Watergate, while a British football crowd disaster delayed parliamentary discussion of the feasibility of electronic identity cards.[43]

During the 1980s, the rise of 'New Right' policies within the advanced societies encouraged the growth of new surveillance technologies. On the one hand is the emphasis on the 'strong state' which seeks both external and internal security, for which new technologies provide a natural ally. The augmentation of the massive American National Security Agency (NSA) with its vast tracking stations in Yorkshire, England, and Australia, is a case in point. On the other hand, the drive towards 'free enterprise' paradoxically harnesses the mighty mechanisms of information technology in an attempt to control consumer behaviour. In fact, as we shall see, these surveillance systems are not as different as they may appear at first sight.

The pressure to increase survillance capacity may also originate within specific organizations. As an example, the propensity for direct checking of records is both technologically facilitated and simultaneously encourages the development of more technology. Opponents of data protection law have successfully retained loopholes – using catch–all terms like 'national security' or 'routine use', which condone exemptions – to ensure the unimpeded evolution of surveillance systems within government departments. Advanced technology is sought to ensure adequate future capacity, but this in turn can become a self-fulfilling prophecy. When Britain introduced a system of Numbercards for National Insurance, the machine-readable strip had a capacity considerably in excess of present use, which hinted that perhaps this would be the vehicle for an eventual national electronic ID.

New Surveillance: Evidence and Debate

The debate over a 'new surveillance' cannot easily be resolved. Moreover, quibbling over the precise meaning of 'new' would in the end be a distraction from the very real and urgent issues confronting us in the development of contemporary electronic surveillance. Clearly, the shift from paper-based to digital documentation heralds several profound changes in the nature and extent of surveillance.

The 'data-image' circulating within and between organizational databases both requires our participation and has increasing impact on our life-chances, but as the same time is less visible and accessible to us. Computer power facilitates new convergence between formally distinct surveillance systems, but this does not necessarily spell centralization. Indeed, dataveillance relies on networks of computers interconnected by telecommunications, plus a consistent means of identifying individuals. These information technologies enables surveillance capacity to grow substantially and at an accelerating pace in all its dimensions. All sorts of novel combinations become possible, giving rise to computer-matching, profiling, cross-system enforcement, and so on.

Having said all that, we are still not in a position to say under what conditions, for which social groups, in which countries and at what rate of acceleration surveillance is on the increase. What we have alluded to is an excedingly rapid *quantitative* expansion of surveillance, which simultaneously raises questions of a *qualitative* shift. The former will be illustrated in subsequent chapters by means of case-studies and by reference to a growing body of empirical social research.[44] The latter becomes visible as older concepts and theories of surveillance reveal their frayed and threadbare state. New ways of understanding surveillance are required in an era of information technology, which take account of the historical development of surveillance systems and also accomodate the new configurations and combinations that constitute the challenge of surveillance today.

But if there *is* a new surveillance, as I am arguing, does this necessarily mean that there is tighter social control, or that what Gary T. Marx calls the 'maximum security society' is around the corner? This question is addressed more fully in the following chapter, while the operation of the 'new surveillance' in different social spheres is analysed in more detail in Part Two of this book. We shall be in a better position to revisit this question after that ground is covered.

4

From Big Brother to the Electronic Panopticon

The Police State and the Prison

When I tell people that I am studying surveillance, and in particular investigating the ways that our personal details are stored in computer databases, the most common reaction is to invoke George Orwell; 'This must be the study of 'Big Brother'. A perfectly understandable response, given that *Nineteen Eighty-Four* is about a state that uses a huge bureaucratic apparatus, 'thought police', and the figure of 'Big Brother' on the ever-present telescreen to intervene in the smallest details of its citizens' daily lives.

Back in the early 1970s, computer enthusiasts James Martin and Adrian Norman noted that 'a surprising amount of what George Orwell imagined now looks plausible'.[1] Such sentiments were repeated routinely by both the complacent and the concerned. Political scientist Theodore Lowi warned that 'a *Nineteen Eighty-Four* type of scenario will be the most likely outcome if things are let go at the present rate and no attention is paid to the information revolution'.[2] As we have already seen, in the 1990s Judge Love worries about the 'Orwellian' aspects of his electronic tags for offenders.

Within sociological analysis proper, James Rule's work on surveillance also takes its cues from Orwell. Starting from a 'total surveillance society', he argues that the only limits to the present day realization of the Orwellian, nightmare lie in the level of available 'surveillance capacities'. As we saw in Chapter Three, those capacities are massively augmented by information technology. Some qualitative differences to surveillance come in the train of new technology. Does this bring *Nineteen Eighty-Four* closer?

Apart from the obvious – but banal – rejoinder that 1984 is now well past, others have begun to question how relevant is the image of Big Brother for the analysis of contemporary electronic surveillance. For instance, in the previous chapter we saw how Roger Clarke's work indicates that 'dataveillance is technically and economically superior' to the ubiquitous two-way television of *Nineteen Eighty-Four*. Total control in Oceania was also made possible by centralization. Now, it is true that the governmental and commercial 'centres' of contemporary states still have access to files on major populations, but extensive computer networking also decentralizes operations. Indeed, the old dichotomy between decentralization and centralization is itself now questionable. Today's surveillance society certainly needs nothing as cumbersome as the administrative machinery of *Nineteen Eighty-Four*.

In this chapter I argue that, while *Nineteen Eighty-Four* has in many ways been superseded technologically, limited but important aspects of its account of a surveillance society still remain relevant today. At the same time, Orwell never imagined how rapidly surveillance would extend its global reach, nor did he conceive of a situation where anything but the state would be its chief perpetrator. Today, surveillance is both a globalizing phenomenon and one that has as much to do with consumers as with citizens.

But now another model, another image, is gaining ground in the analysis of surveillance; Bentham's Panopticon prison plan. Much impetus for this comes from the fashionable flurry of Foucault studies that began in the 1980s, but now sufficient empirical work has been done to show the relevance of at least some aspects of the Panopticon to electronic surveillance.[3] The remainder of the chapter is thus taken up with the question of how far the Panopticon provides a useful model for understanding electronic surveillance. I shall suggest that while it is undeniably illuminating, analysis based upon the Panopticon image also retains some serious disadvantages.

It is worth paying considerable attention to both the Orwellian and the Panoptic model, in order to understand contemporary surveillance and to seek better or alternative models. I want to make it very clear that that both models are firmly rooted in normative and critical stances. Ironically the Panopticon, now the main alternative to Big Brother, started life as a utopian scheme for social reform, and a long time before Orwell. Indeed, Orwell wrote *Nineteen Eighty-Four* partly as a *dystopian* critique of such enterprises.[4] Analysis of what is happening in today's society is inextricably and inevitably bound up with questions of the desirability of what is happening.

Orwell's Dystopia

George Orwell wrote *Nineteen Eighty-Four* as a dystopia, that is, an account whose intent is the opposite of utopia; a literary depiction of an undesirable, avoidable but conceivable future state of society. Winston Smith, who attempts to think for himself, is eventually crushed into conformity by the surveillance state. Electronic media – limited of course to what Orwell knew about in 1948 – are the chief tool for manipulating the masses through unremitting propaganda. But forms of electronic surveillance also allow the Though Police to maintain constant vigilance over the intimate lives and relationships of each citizen.

The figure of Big Brother, who would appear on the telescreens in buildings public and private, claimed to monitor everything. Hence 'Big Brother is watching you!' which is now one of the most readily recognized catch-phrases in the English language. Here is Orwell's description:

> The telescreen received and transmitted simultaneously. Any sound that Winston made, above the level of a very low whisper, would be picked up by it; moreover so long as he remained within the field of vision which the metal plaque commanded, he could be seen as well as heard. There was of course no way of knowing whether you were being watched at any given moment.[5]

Nineteen Eighty-Four is often taken to be about the power of technology for social control and about the loss of privacy resulting from living in such a transparent society. So it is not surprising that his work has been so readily translatable into the language of microelectronics and information technology, with their supposed threats.

Orwell was astoundingly prescient, which is of course the reason why his work has not only survived but maintained its interest. He noticed the growing centrality of information in the operations of the nation-state. In Oceania there was even a 'Ministry of Truth' ('Minitrue') to deal with such matters as the creation and destruction of information. Today, computer technology facilitates the construction of new categories of data, a process that is encouraged by the penchant for statistical analysis within organizations. Moreover, the same technologies make possible the electronic erasure of data, either without trace, or traceable only by experts. Both processes are significant to the 'surveillance society'.

For one thing, the malleability of data may render Weberian confidence in the reliability of the record somewhat naïve. The electronic trail may be eradicated without trace, which leads to big questions about how far 'data' may be trusted. For another, sauce for the goose is sauce for the gander, and the malleability of data may also be seen in the phenomenon of 'fraudulent IDs'.[6] With the twentieth-century rise of credentialism and the constant demand for identification, the temptation to invent or enhance personal documentary details has for some been too hard to resist. Obtaining goods, services, benefits or employment may all be facilitated by a variety of ways of distorting identity or biographical details. Technology is not simply a tool of dominant social groups.

The focus on novel techniques for handling information also rings bells in the context of computing and administration. As we have seen, it is information *technology* that is especially significant for surveillance. The national databank, for instance, is exactly what one would expect to find in an Orwellian surveillance society. Recognizing this, American officials denied during the 1970s that such a databank would be created. Big Brother would be kept at bay.[7] Yet all American federal government employees are now listed in a single database that is used for matching.

Another significant feature of Orwell's 'Big Brother' surveillance is that it was imperceptible. Those under surveillance were unsure whether there was any time when they could relax. Like the Panopticon – and indeed as in other literary treatments of the surveillance theme, such as Franz Kafka's *The Castle* or Margaret Atwood's *The Handmaid's Tale* – this model of undetected surveillance keeps those watched subordinate by means of uncertainty. You simply comply, because you never know when 'they' might be watching. Information technology enables surveillance to be carried out in ways even less visible than those available in Orwell's, let alone Kafka's, day.[8]

Two further points, to do with dignity and division, may be made that underscore Orwell's relevance for contemporary surveillance. I mentioned above that *Nineteen Eighty-Four* has been used to connect transparency of behaviour with the theme of privacy. Yet there is a sense in which Orwell's focus was less narrow than that. For him, privacy was an aspect of human dignity. Winston Smith finally caves in, betraying his girlfriend Julia and declaring his love for Big Brother, not when his privacy is invaded but when deprived of his dignity by a confrontation with rats.[9] From that moment his identity merged with Big Brother's. His very personhood was impugned. The challenge of electronic surveillance is missed if it is reduced to a concern merely with privacy.

As for division, Orwell shows clearly how power is maintained at a broader level through the divisive character of surveillance. In his *Visions of Social Control*, Stanley Cohen stresses this facet of Orwell's work.[10] The middle-class and Party members needed careful thought-control and surveillance. Inclusionary controls reign here. But the proles, who formed 85% of the population, could safely be left in their ghettoes, 'working, breeding and dying'.[11] Their lot is exclusion. The important point here is the role of surveillance in different modes of social control, rather than the details of Orwell's analysis.

Things have changed since Orwell's time, and consumption, for the masses, has emerged as the new inclusionary reality. Only the minority, the so-called underclass,[12] whose position prevents them from participating so freely in consumption, now experience the hard edge of exclusionary and punitive surveillance. Anyone wishing to grasp the nature of contemporary surveillance must reckon with this fact. Whereas the major threat, for Orwell, came from the state, today consumer surveillance poses a series of novel questions which have yet to find adequate analytical and political answers. A perfectly plausible view is that in contemporary conditions consumerism acts in its own right as a significant means of maintaining social order, leaving older froms of surveillance and control to cope with the non-consuming residue.[13]

Having said that, however, some further qualification is called for. While consumerism may correctly be viewed as a means of social control, it differs from other types of such control. Those targeted for direct mail and other forms of personalized advertising are objects of an attempted channelling of behaviour. Companies wish to include rather than exclude them. The important distinction between exclusionary and perhaps punitive forms of control, which may be coercive, and more subtle ones, which rely on creating desired behavioural conduits, should be borne in mind as we proceed.[14]

This in turn also ties in with a more general theme in the history of social control; the progressive uncoupling of violent and non-violent methods. Orwell tended to keep the links. Both jackboots and Big Brother have their place in Oceania. But as Gary T. Marx, among others, observes, more subtle, less coercive means have become increasingly prominent in the advanced societies since the Second World War.[15] The use of electronic means for less conspicuous surveillance he takes to be an important instance of this shift.

Orwell's own experience and observations, after all, were of the Spanish Civil War, Stalin's Soviet Union and Mussolini's Italy. Many have imagined that he had only these obviously totalitarian regimes in mind in writing *Nineteen Eighty-Four*. However, it is more than likely that he intended its application to be broader. As a democratic and libertarian socialist, he was quite aware of certain authoritarian tendencies within capitalist societies. What he may not have foreseen was that new technologies might eventually permit surveillance tending towards totalitarianism with democratic processes still neatly in place. As Gary T. Marx notes, the velvet glove may hide the iron fist.[16]

Sociological analysis of surveillance that begins with Big Brother produces some useful insights. The fact that electronic technologies have been augmented considerably since Orwell's day does mean that his account needs some updating, but it does not render it irrelevant. Much of what Orwell wrote still stands, and deserves attention, but we should also explore the specific ways in which we must go beyond Orwell. At this point, then, we may turn to the Panopticon and ask whether as a model it can compensate for the shortcomings of Orwell's dystopia.

The Panopticon from Bentham to Foucault

The Panopticon has been used for analysing surveillance in a number of different settings; the workplace, government administration, and consumer contexts. We shall examined some of these below. It should be remembered that the Panopticon does not come to us directly from Bentham but recently mediated through the work of Michel Foucault and critics who have debated it.[17] Though many historians of ideas or of systems of punishment have recognized the importance of the Panopticon, it is really only since Foucault that interest in it has become widespread.

Foucault illuminates the connections between the Panopticon and modernity by showing that it forms the watershed between punitive and reforming disciplinary practices. Enlightenment reason, concerned with empirical observation and classification, and related to the rational reproducing of social order, is neatly expressed here. The theme of exploiting uncertainty as a means of of controlling subordinates reappears here as well, having obvious resonance with the unobtrusive monitoring of which new electronic technologies are capable. However, this in turn propels us into the debate over postmodernity. A hallmark of modern thought is the way individuals are placed centre-stage in history. But postmodern discourse pushes such actors into the wings, and this seems to echo what happens with electronic surveillance. If the supposedly 'personal' details of intimate everyday life circulate beyond our control within remote databases, where now is the human 'centred self?[18]

Jeremy Bentham, the British philosopher and social reformer, published his plan for the Panopticon penitentiary in 1791. Essentially, it was for a building on a semi-circular pattern with an 'inspection lodge' at the centre and cells around the perimeter. Prisoners, who in the original plan would be in individual cells, were open to the gaze of the guards, or 'inspectors', but the same was not true of the view the other way. By a carefully contrived system of lighting and the use of wooden blinds, officials would be invisible to the inmates. Control was to be maintained by the constant sense that prisoners were watched by unseen eyes. There was nowhere to hide, nowhere to be private. Not knowing whether or not they were watched, but obliged to assume that they were, obedience was the prisoner's only rational option. Hence Bentham's Greek-based neologism; the Panopticon, or 'all-seeing place'.[19]

The Panopticon was to be a model prison, a new departure, a watershed in the control of deviance and a novel means of social discipline. Bentham invested more time and energy in this than any other project – and 'mourned its failure more passionately'.[20] He saw in it 'a great and new invented instrument of government' and believed the panoptic principle held promise of 'the only effective instrument of reformative management'. In a closing eulogy he made the famous claim, 'Morals reformed – health preserved – industry invigorated – instruction diffused – public burthens lightened – Economy seated, as it were, upon a rock – the Gordian knot of the Poor Laws not cut, but untied – all by a simple idea in Architecture!.[21]

Bentham's apparently utopian enthusiasm for the Panopticon had personal, political, and cultural origins. Personally, he hoped to reap financial benefit from an entrepreneurial stake in the project, and to to raise his status profile through being its first director. Indeed, when shown the plans, Edmund Burke saw straight through them; 'There's the spider in the web!' he exclaimed.[22] Politically, the Panopticon promised local, non-religious prison reform over against the Evangelical and transportation-to-Australia alternatives currently on offer. And culturally, the Panopticon epitomised the kind of 'social physics' so popular with the *philosophes* of his day. It neatly translated the clockwork image of being human seen in La Mettrie's *L'Homme Machine* into an architectural reality.[23]

Ironically, while it appears that no prison was ever built exactly along the lines Bentham had in mind, and he certainly failed to persuade the British government to invest in it, the principles embodied in the Panopticon were to have a widespread influence. The key principle was inspection, through inspection of a specific kind. Bentham's Panopticon represented a secular parody of divine omniscience, and the observerd was also, like God, invisible. Thus '. . . the more constantly the persons to be inspected are under the eyes of the persons who should inspect them, the more perfectly will the purpose of the establishment be attained.[24] And if such constant supervision proves impossible, prisoners should be given the *impression* that the gaze is unwavering.

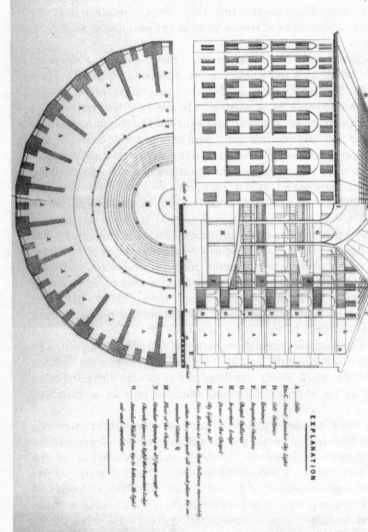

A General Idea of a *PENITENTIARY PANOPTICON* in an Improved, but as yet, Unfinished State. See Postscript References to Plan, Elevation & Section; being Plate referred to as N.º 2.

EXPLANATION

A — Cells
B — C. Small Annular Sky Lights
D — Cell Galleries
E — Entrance
F — Inspection Galleries
G — Chapel Galleries
H — Inspector's Lodge
I — Dome of the Chapel
K — Sky Light to D.º
L — Store Rooms &c with their Galleries immediately within the outer wall; all round; place for an annular Cistern; Q
M — Floor of the Chapel
N — Annular Opening in ditto; open except at Church times; to light the Inspection Lodge
O — Annular Wall from top to bottom; for light air and inspection

Bentham's innovation, then, was not just to inspect, or even to ensure that the gaze is asymmetrical, but to use uncertainty as a means of subordination. The asymmetrical gaze created uncertainty which in turn produced surrender. Asymmetrical surveillance became part of the whole modern project of destroying the certainties of alternative powers, the supposed hangovers from traditional societies, wherever they still lurked.[25] This is why the Panopticon *principles* were so significant.

The inspection principle suited other purposes than prisons, according to Bentham. Of courses they did! Indeed, he got the original idea of the Panopticon from his brother's workshop in Russia. And he advertised the virtues of the panoptic as being appropriate for any context in which supervision was required; for '. . . punishing the incorrigible, guarding the insane, reforming the vicious, confining the suspected, employing the idle, maintaining the helpless, curing the sick, instructing the willing in any branch of industry, or training the rising race in the path of education'.[26] Foucault argues that panoptic control has indeed become significant in many of these spheres.

Two other principles attached to the panoptic[27] in the specific context of the penitentiary. One was the 'solitude' or isolation of inmates, the other was to allow the prison to be run as a private enterprise by outside contractors. Solitude would extend even to having private toilets for prisoners, and to holding chapel services from a central position above the inspection lodge, without prisoners moving from their cells. Inmates were to be atomised, secluded. As for running the prison by contract, this would possible enable profit to be made and prison governors to be held in unaccustomed esteem.

Bentham cheerfully defended his Panopticon from any misplaced liberal attack. Might it be thought 'despotic', or might the result of 'this high-wrought contrivance . . . be constructing a set of *machines* under the similitude of *men*?[28] Let people think so if they wish. Such criticisms miss the point, namely, 'would happiness be most likely to be increased or decreased by this discipline?' Here is control, and clean control at that. Much better, he commented, than something like Addison's bizarre-sounding proposal to 'try virginity with lions'. There you saw blood and uncertainty: here you see certainty without blood'.[29] Of course, uncertainty still exists for those subjected to the Panopticon regime. Indeed, the 'machine' depends on it. Certainty resides in the system, and, one might add, with the inspector, the one 'in the know'.

This kind of certainty, sought by Bentham in the Panopticon, epitomises for Foucault the social disciplines of modernity. Whereas in earlier times the failure of social control would result in punishment that was public and brutal, modernity introduced clean and rational forms of social control and punishment. The unruly crowd is rendered manageable; no plots of escape from prison, no danger of contagion if they are sick, no mutual violence if they are mad, no chatter if schoolchildren, and no disorders or coalitions if workers. The crowd is replaced by a 'collection of separated individualities'.[30] As Foucault says, Bentham made 'visibility a trap'.

In the following important quotation Foucault summarises his understanding of the major effect of the Panopticon:

> to induce in the inmate a state of conscious and permanent visibility that assures the automatic functioning of power. So to arrange things that the surveillance is permanent in its effects, even if it is discontinuous in its action; that the perfection of power should tend to render its actual exercise unnecessary; that this architectural apparatus should be a machine for creating and sustaining a power relation independent of the person who exercises it; in short, that the inmates should be caught up in a power situation of which they themselves are the bearers.[31]

In the Panopticon, discipline crossed what Foucault calls a 'disciplinary threshold' in which the 'formation of knowledge and the increased of power regularly reinforce each other in a circular process'.[32] Older, more costly, and more violent forms of power fell into disuse and were superseded by 'a subtle, calculated technology of subjection'.[33]

Recall for a moment our previous discussion of *Nineteen Eighty-Four*. Though the older forms of power are still present there, the later concern with power for power's sake and the 'subtle, calculated subjection' clearly predominates in Orwell's mind. On the other hand, Orwell places less emphasis on subjects being the bearers of their own surveillance and of the power relation connected with it.

Sociology is indebted to Foucault for his theory of surveillance, touching as it does on both aspects of its power; the accumulation of information, and the direct supervision of subordinates. The former is found in the detailed files held on each Panopticon inmate, the latter in the architectural potential of the building itself. Acknowledging Foucault's contribution, Giddens observes that in modern times 'disciplinary power' is characterised by 'new modes of regularizing activities in time-space'."[34] Observation is central to these modes, and thus the Panopticon epitomises such disciplinary power.

However, Foucault also insists that such power is typically present throughout the institutions of modernity, in all kinds of administrative contexts. 'Is it surprising', asks Foucault rhetorically, 'that the cellular prison, with its regular chronologies, forced labour, its authorities of surveillance and registration, its experts in normality ... should have become the modern instrument of penality?' But not only that; he goes on,

'Is it surprising that prisons resemble factories, schools, barracks, hospitals, which all resemble prisons?'[35] What for Bentham was an aspiration is for Foucault a social reality – the panoptic principle diffusing different institutions. This assumption, often questioned within the sociology of administrative power, must be re-addressed in the context of electronic surveillance.[36]

The perverse irony is that Foucault himself seems to have made no comments about the relevance of panoptic discipline to the ways that administrative power has been enlarged and enhanced by computers, especially since the 1960s. Yet surely we see here nothing less than the near-perfection of the principle of discipline by invisible inspection *via* information-gathering. Or do we? Today no shortage exists of social analysts prepared to complete Foucault by making the connections explicit. Thus we turn next to explore the extent of that link; may we think of electronic surveillance as panoptic power?

Electronic Surveillance: Panoptic Power?

In what ways, and in what contexts, might electronic surveillance display panoptic features? No consensus exists about either question. Different analysts focus on different aspects of panopticism that reappear or are reinforced by computers: the invisibility of the 'inspection', its automatic character, the involvement of subjects in their own surveillance, and so on. Equally, different analysts emphasize different spheres of operation of the putative panopticon: in workplace organization and especially, electronic monitoring, in criminal records and policing, in consumer behaviour and transactions, and in the myriad administrative activities of the state.

Giddens makes a distinction between two major axes of surveillance, which we shall use as an initial framework for our analysis. He proposes that sociology consider two levels. Firstly, surveillance is the accumulation of coded information, seen in what he calls the 'internal pacification' of nation-states. This is bound up with the growth of bureaucratic administration, defence, and policing. Secondly, surveillance refers to the direct monitoring of subordinates within the capitalistic workplace that has become the key to management in the twentieth century.[37]

Giddens admits that the two senses of surveillance belong quite closely together. Indeed, only when thought of together can the twin processes of surveillance illuminate the tying-up historically of the capitalistic labour contract with the state monopoly of violence. Still, he maintains that they should be analytically distinct. We shall begin by following this distinction, looking first at the treatment of criminality and deviance as a central aspect of state surveillance. Secondly, we shall examine the putative Panopticon of capitalism, starting with the workplace. This obliges us to rethink Giddens' distinction, for two reasons. Capitalism in the late twentieth century focuses at least as much 'management' attention on the marketplace as the workplace; and, the application of information technologies may be encouraging a convergence between different surveillance activities.

The persistence of panoptic principles in contemporary society has been noted by those studying general trends in social control, such as Stanley Cohen, and by others examining specific practices involving new technology in policing. Cohen, for instance, investigates the later twentieth-century shift towards crime control 'in the community' that includes rather than excludes offenders. He notes the ways that panoptic ideas are present in methods of 'technological incapacitation'.[38] Radio telemetry, or electronic tagging, allow relatively minor offenders to live 'freely' at home, or even to go to work while wearing a computerized device on the ankle. This tag involuntarily obliges him or her to remain in touch with some central control. Cohen relates this to the panoptic in that the wearer is (potentially) constantly supervised and participates in the process, but cannot verify it.

Gary T. Marx's analysis of American undercover police work takes this much futher, noting numerous ways in which electronic technologies portend the 'new surveillance'. Particularly relevant here are these characteristics: they are invisible (or of low visibility), involuntary, capital rather than labour intensive, involve decentralized self-policing, introduce suspicion of whole categories of persons rather than targeting specific individuals, and are both more intensive and more extensive. He sees the state's traditional monopoly over the means of violence giving way to new controls: manipulation not coercion, computer chips not prison bars, remote and invisible tethers, not handcuffs or straitjackets. He cautions that these panoptic shifts may be 'diffusing into the society at large'.[39]

In another American study, Diana Gordon subjects the National Crime Information Center (NCIC) to analysis as a panoptic 'machinery of power'.[40] Her central concern is simply expressed; 'With the national computerized system, the entire function of crime-control, not just the prison, becomes a 'panoptic schema', with the record a surrogate for the inmate and all of law enforcement as warden'.[41] Gordon is at pains to argue that the presence of panoptic tendencies spells dangers often unperceived by those working closest to the NCIC. Certain structural social changes may be occurring, she suggests, and therefore it is mistaken to see the issue as merely one of infringing civil liberties. For instance, in many states at least a third of criminal record requests are for non-criminal purposes, mainly employment and driving licences. Like Gary T. Marx, Gordon believes that the effects are societal; 'and then we are all enclosed in an electronic Panopticon'.[42]

The distinctions between criminal record databases and more general computerized systems for government administration have become increasingly blurred over the past few decades, especially as computer-matching has become a more widespread practice. This refers to the linking of records from different databases to track offenders or to limit abuses such as tax evasion or welfare fraud. Employment records may be checked, for example, to prevent welfare claims being made by people receiving salaries.[43]

Oscar Gandy, who makes extensive use of the Panopticon model in his work on modern surveillance systems, suggests several other ways that new technologies extend its reach within a government context. Apart from the massive databases of the Department of Defense, the Central Intelligence Agency, the National Security Agency and the Federal Bureau of Investigation, the US Internal Revenue is a major collector of personal data, used to identify non-reporters and under-reporters. Political parties also seek to strengthen their position by using computerized surveillance methods to affect public opinion.[44]

Turning now to the second area, we find that the Panopticon has also been rediscovered in capitalism. The debate over whether or not the adoption of new technologies represents intensified workplace control within capitalism is complex and inconclusive. Shoshana Zuboff's ethnography, *In the Age of the Smart Machine*,[45] takes the view that computers in the workplace have a transformative capacity. Paralleling authority as the 'spiritual basis of power', she examines technique as the 'material basis of power'. The key to contemporary management technique, she argues, is panopticisim, enabled by the use of new technologies.

The extremely precise computer systems of today's organizations permit minute monitoring of events and performances within the workplace. At one of the workplaces investigated by Zuboff, a highly automated pulp mill, a small explosion occurred in the early hours of the morning. By scrutinizing the 'Overview System', a bird's-eye view of the whole operation which was constantly recorded at five-second intervals, management could determine the exact cause of the accident; equipment failure, poor decision-making, or a sleepy operator?[46] Workers at such sites are thus highly transparent to management even in the apparently small details of day-to-day routine. This heightened visibility – recall the prison blinds and lighting – also noted by researchers looking at computerization in much smaller contexts such as ordering in restaurants and taxi-calling systems,[47] – Zuboff connects with the panoptic.

Zuboff also discusses the allure of panopticism for management, which is the 'promise of certain knowledge'. Increased reliance upon the 'facts' produced by the computer systems generates new management styles, in her account. Employee performance appears as 'objective' data, which often correlates with another panoptic feature, the certainty of punishment. Apparently, any dismisal process tends to be shortened from around a year from the start of the dispute to something much more immediate.[48]

Operators within the ubiquitous digital 'gaze' of such computer systems, and without the more familiar face-to-face relationships with superiors, may seek modes of resistance, but compliance appears more common. Information systems 'can transmit the presence of the omniscient observer and so induce compliance without the messy conflict-prone exertions of reciprocal relations'.[49] Zuboff comments that in workplaces where workers as well as management have access to the personal data collected on the systems, workers exhibit 'anticipatory conformity', showing that the standards of management are internalized by workers. This again seems to be a case of Foucault's 'normalizing discipline' of the panoptic.

Interestingly enough, Zuboff does not try to generalize her findings to a societal level. She sees no need to; for her, the transformations within the workplace are striking enough. Her modesty may be wise. Others, however, have argued that some of the kinds of management strategies made possible by the use of information technology are now being applied in the marketplace as well as in the workplace. In this way, it is suggested, the panoptic power of surveillance spills over into society at large, but now the vehicle is commercial organization, not government administration.

The link is made directly by Frank Webster and Kevin Robins, for instance, who argue that information technologies facilitate the massive extension of Taylorist principles of scientific management from the realm of production into the realm of consumption. As they say, '"teleshopping" global and targeted advertising, and electronic market research surveillance all combine to establish a more "efficient" network marketplace'.[50] In this case, surveillance is accomplished by means of gathering transactional information such as itemized telephone bills, credit card exchanges and bank withdrawals. The whole process of using transactional information to try to influence consumer behaviour is sometimes called 'social management'.[51] Oscar Gandy takes up the same themes, focusing particularly on ways that personal consumer data has become a vital 'information commodity' within contemporary capitalism.[52]

As with the electronic extension of criminal records systems mentioned above, social management is the springboard for considering society itself as panoptic. 'On the basis of the "information revolutior", assert Robins and Webster 'not just the prison or the factory, but the social totality comes to function as a hierarchical and disciplinary Panoptic machine'.[53] Gandy refers to this as the 'panoptic sort'. The so-called wired city renders consumers visible to unverifiable observers by means of their purchases, preferences and credit ratings. Private, sequestered, decentralized activities, the mundane routines of everyday life, are as it were in view, continuously and automatically.

Following Foucault, Webster and Robins point to no single power source, although the capitalist system of discipline is what they see being panoptically augmented. There is, they say, 'no single omniscient inspective force'. Nonetheless, 'society as a whole comes to function as a giant panoptic mechanism' in which, to pursue the analogy, hapless consumers find themselves in atomized – designer? – cells at the periphery.

This picture is very similar to one painted, in richer Foucaldian colours, by Mark Poster. For him the world of consumer surveillance amounts to a 'Superpanopticon'[54] because the panoptic now has no technical limitations. The Panopticon was invented for a new industrial capitalist society. Today the 'population participates in its own self-constitution as subjects in the normalizing gaze of the Superpanopticon'.[55] Poster's analysis occurs in the context of a study of the 'mode of information' which, he explains, 'designates social relations mediated by electronic communications systems which constitute new patterns of language'.[56]

The technology of power in Poster's Superpanopticon does two things. It imposes a norm, disciplining its subjects to participate by filling in forms, giving social insurance numbers, or using credit cards. But it also helps to constitute complementary selves for those subjects, the sum, as it were, of their transactions. New individuals are created who bear the same names but who are digitally shorn of their human ambiguities and whose personalities are built artificially from matched data. Artificial they may be, but these computer 'selves' have a part to play in determining the life-chances of their human namesakes. Thus are subjects constituted and deviants defined within the Superpanopticon.

Evaluating Electronic Panopticism

The Panopticon offers a powerful and compelling metaphor for understanding electronic surveillance. The prison-like society, where invisible observers track our digital footprints, does indeed seem panoptic. Bentham would surely smile wryly if he saw us complying with institutional norms as we use barcoded library books or note telephone-callers' IDs before accepting a call. The familiar distinctions between public and private life dissolve as both government and corporation ignore old thresholds and garner personal data of the most mundane and intimate kinds.

Beyond the metaphor, a model of power also lies in the concept of the panoptic, and it takes us well beyond the Orwellian jackboots and torture, or even the rats. The normalizing discipline, the exaggerated visibility of the subject, the unverifiability of observation, the subject as bearer of surveillance, the quest for factual certainty – all are important aspects of the panoptic as model of power. The question is, to what extent are all these necessarily present in each context? Sociologically, is electronic surveillance panoptic power?

To answer this question satisfactorily, three others must be addressed. First, can the panoptic be generalized over different social spheres? Several analysts using the panoptic image think of electronic surveillance as a process that transgresses conventional social – and thus sociological – boundaries. Diana Gordon remarks that because diverse databases, found in government and commerical organizations, are enabled to 'talk' to each other, crime control affects all of us; hence her comment that we are all 'in an electronic Panopticon'. Robins and Webster, likewise, focus attention on ways that management styles developed in the workplace now encroach electronically on the daily domestic lives of consumers. For them, this is one crucial factor that makes the Panopticon an appropriate 'central figure for understanding the modalities of power in the 'information society'.[57]

Electronic technologies facilitate convergence of practices over different and once-distinct institutional areas. Zuboff notes that within the workplace alone older divisions are fading as information technology is applied. 'Continuous process' and 'discrete parts' manufacturing, which developed separately to address different problems of production, now find work-tasks and work-organization becoming more alike with the coming of computer integrated manufacturing.[58] Again, similar techniques are used for matching disparate data for targeting tax-evaders within government administration as for targeting potential consumers with income-and-lifestyle-specific direct mailing.[59] Incidentally, members of both groups are frequently unaware that they are under surveillance.

For Foucault, the Panopticon epitomises the disciplinary network of society seen not only in prisons but also in the capitalist enterprise, military organization, and a multitude of state-run institutions. It does not wait for offenders to act, but classifies and situates before any 'event', producing not 'good citizens' but a 'docile deviant population'.[60] Despite Foucault's opposition to what he calls 'totalizing', he frequently gives the impression that the panoptic prison has been made redundant through the development of a disciplinary network on a societal scale; the Panopticon-at-large. Analysts of electronic surveillance may be forgiven for picking up a relatively undifferentiated view of power from Foucault.

But it is one thing to say that boundaries may be blurred in new technology contexts, and another to suggest that the Panopticon should be central to our understanding of contemporary surveillance. Giddens, for instance, differentiates between the means of economic production and the political means of administration, and also insists that prisons are qualitatively different from other social organizations. With respect to the first, the fact that during the nineteenth century locales were established in which regular observation of activities could take place with the purpose of control makes the workplace and state similar, but not the same. Hidden exploitation rules the workplace, whereas state power depends ultimately on force.

Regarding the nature of prisons, Giddens points out that inmates have to spend all their time there; they are what Goffman calls 'total institutions'. Contrast schools, business firms, or other civil organization, where only a part of the days is spent and where disciplinary power is far more diffuse. So Giddens correctly concludes that 'Foucault is mistaken in so far as he regards "maximized" disciplinary power of this sort [i.e. panoptic] as expressing the general nature of administrative power within the modern state.'[61]

Nonetheless, the neat theoretical distinctions – between government and commerce, between collecting data and supervising – do begin to blur when confronted with the realities of contemporary electronic surveillance. Increasingly, disciplinary networks *do* connect employment with civil status, or consumption with policing. Moreover, the characteristically modern geographical and temporal 'stretching' of social relations, facilitated by changes in transport and communications, is also undergoing change.[62] Now the advent of information technologies enables novel configurations. The worker could once leave the capitalistic enterprise behind at the factory gates. Now it follows him home as a consumer. The same home was once regarded as a private haven. The computerized 'king' may now enter the 'Englishman's castle', at will. Indeed, the householder carries him in, disguised as a social insurance number.[63]

Even if new technology does facilitate not only a novel penetration of the mundane routines of everyday life, but also a blurring of conventional boundaries, it is still not clear that this in itself augurs a general societal panopticism. For Bentham and the other bearers of modernity have in a sense done their work. Citizens of the advanced societies are already expert-dependent in a radical sense. We cannot but rely upon those 'in the know, the experts.[64] Electronic panopticism may equally turn out to be a vestigial residue of modernity's – Benthamite – utopian hunger for certitude.

The ghost of the unseen inspector may continue to haunt specific milieux, such as Zuboff's pulp mill, courtesy of computer-power. It may even contribute to new forms of categorizing subjects across different spheres and thus serve to sustain social control, but this still does not add up to the more apocalyptic vision of a societal Panopticon. Nonetheless, even such 'panoptic residues' raise significant sociological queries.

This discussion of historical changes and of consumerism in particular brings me to my second question; does the panoptic do justice to the realities of social order in capitalist societies today? Numerous plausible answers have been given to the classic sociological query of how social order is maintained. To be worth anything, the answer must connect directly with contemporary realities.

Today, consumerism contributes heavily to the maintenance of social order; the Panopticon deals with those left out of the market. Zygmunt Bauman points to a duality between what he refers to as the 'seduced' and the 'repressed'. People become socially integrated – seduced – by means of market dependency. Though Bauman makes little reference to the fact, this is powered in part by commercial surveillance. But its strength does not lie in a panoptic 'imposing of norms'. Surveillance supplies a structure to channel behaviour, but one within which real choices still are made.[65]

Rather, social skills and economic capacity entitle the seduced majority to consume. Some panoptic methods may well underlie the surveillance techniques used to seduce. But the minority, the new poor or the underclass, is subjected to tight normative regulation, where the excluding capacities of the panoptic come into their own. This would explain why modern life is experienced by the majority as pleasure and not – as the 'social Panopticon' theorists see it – as a prison sentence. In fact, according to Clifford Shearing and Philip Stenning, a similar distinction is already present in the work of Foucault. They say he worked with both a generic concept of discipline and a (more fully worked out) 'historically specific examination of it in the context of carceral punishment'.[66]

Foucault's physics or anatomy of power, technology' represents the generic mode of discipline, of which the panoptic is merely a type. Discipline is dispersed throughout the micro-relations that constitute society. It is not, for Foucault, 'from above', like monarchical power. This embeddedness of power, say Shearing and Stenning, is what makes the Panopticon the exemplar of discipline. They go on to contrast the *moral* discipline of carceral punishment – for example in the Panopticon – with the merely *instrumental* discipline manifest in other locations such as factories, hospitals or workshops. Their own investigations of private security companies in Canada reveal a discipline that is strictly instrumental, not moral in basis. As they say, 'within private control the instrumental language of profit and loss replaces the moral language of criminal justice'.[67]

The distinction between moral 'soul-training' of carceral discipline and the instrumental discipline of private security systems is a useful one, though how far it reflects what Foucault wanted to argue is debatable. Rather like Bauman, Shearing and Stenning see 'the dominant force in social control' as consumption, visible in microcosm – they offer a charming vignette – in Disneyworld. Less like Orwell's nightmare, much more like Huxley's *Brave New World*, here is consensually-based control in which 'people are seduced into conformity by the pleasures offered by the drug 'soma' rather than coerced into compliance by threat of Big Brother, just as people are today seduced to conform by the pleasures of consuming the goods that corporate power has to offer'.[68]

Here then is a plausible answer to the question about the reproduction of social order in the capitalist societies of the late twentieth century. Paradoxically, the panoptic may not be an appropriate image on account of its capacity to make 'society like a prison' so much as because of the embedded nature of its discipline.[69] However, this does not mean that we can safely forget the panoptic. Carceral discipline, perhaps relating to residual moral categories, may well still be experienced by Bauman's 'repressed', the underclass. But, as I stressed above, this is a residual and not a general, let alone an expanding, category.

But as the repressed are frequently, as Bauman puts it, 'flawed consumers', a question arises as to how far even the normative discipline meted out to them is actually moral and not merely instrumental. The norms from which they deviate are essentially rooted in consumer skills. It is primarily participation in society as consumers from which they are excluded, through lack of credit-worthiness, welfare dependence, and so on.

As it could be argued that the application of information technology encourages the extension of instrumental discipline, the question of whether the dominant trend is towards instrumental discipline becomes even more pressing. In a postmodern context, says Lyotard, the (moral) 'metanarratives' of modernity are replaced by, among other things, the (instrumental) categories of computerized control.[70] If he is right, perhaps Max Weber's worries about a completely 'rationalized' world[71] will turn out to have been justified.

The idea of a dual system of control raises further questions about political power, democratic institutions and citizenship. This brings us to the last question about the panoptic qualities of electronic surveillance. Does the panoptic yield a complete picture of the origins and nature of surveillance?

Of course, this question has already received a partial – and negative – answer, but what follows serves as a reminder of the ambiguities or paradoxes of surveillance. It involves our looking not only at where Foucault obtained his conception of the panoptic, but where Bentham got it from in the first place.

We may grant that Foucault theorized a more general view of disciplinary power than that embodied in the Panopticon. But he certainly gave the impression that citizens of modern nation-states find themselves increasingly to be the subjects of centralized carceral discipline. And, for someone who spent precious little time considering how the warm bodies of which he wrote might respond to such discipline, he made a curious closing comment in *Discipline and Punish*; 'In this central and centalized humanity, the effect and instrument of complex power relations, bodies, and forces subjected by multiple forces of "incarceration", objects for discourses that are themselves elements for this strategy, we must hear the distant roar of battle'. [my emphasis][72]

What did he mean? It is not clear that the roar of battle was as loud as Foucault predicted, or so distant. If the 'battle' is one of revolt against discipline, then this assumes, further, that discipline is viewed by subjects in an entirely negative light, and that there would be a considerable time-lag between the imposition of discipline and the battle. However, one could equally argue, on sound historical grounds, that changing processes of social control always occur in the context of struggle, and that the contest is confused, ambiguous and recursive.[73]

As we noted in Chapter Two, the much-prized achievement of welfare citizenship in modern societies could 'only become effective if accompanied by the growth of a state bureaucracy capable of enforcing these rights in practice'.[74] In other words, the burgeoning panopticism of nineteenth-century institutions emerged hand-in-hand with growing commitments to social rights. Recognizing people as unique identities to ensure that each is treated equally simultaneously makes their control that much easier.

This may be seen as a more general phenomenon which Giddens calls the 'dialectric of control'. In this view, all strategies of control 'call forth counter-strategies on the part of subordinates'.[75] It is a sociological theorem about the ways that 'the less powerful manage resources in such a way as to exert control over the more powerful in established power relationships'.[76] Of course, Giddens hangs onto human agency here, a premiss abandoned in Foucault's work. So the build-up of administrative power is accompanied by expanding reciprocal relations beteween rulers and ruled. Modern management practices can be viewed in the same light. Strategies and counter-strategies are in constant tension with each other. In this account, Foucault's battle is neither distant nor, necessarily, roaring.

To put the idea of the dialectic of control in a slightly broader context, it must be understood that Giddens uses it as part of a more general argument that forms of contestation and conflict take place on many levels. A key element of his critique of Marxism is that class struggle is not the archetypical, let alone only, kind of struggle that takes place in modern societies. Struggles over what he calls 'authoritative' resources are also extremely significant.[77] According to this theorem we would expect to find attempts countervailing power in all situations where surveillance is experienced negatively as constraint. While the careful study of surveillance may oblige us to explore more precisely just how this occurs,[78] as a guiding assumption it has much to commend it. Indeed, the present analysis owes much to this insight, as well as to the commitment to the significance of action within sociology.

Fears and anxieties about electronic surveillance, and critiques of or resistance to it, arise from – among other things – specific aspects of its panoptic character. Opponents of the 'new surveillance' deplore the fact that it depends upon categories, that no knowledge of the individual is required, that it is increasingly instrumental, that areas of personal life once thought to be inviolably private are invaded, and that it effectively erodes personal and democratic freedoms. Foucault offers little help at this point, not only because he did not comment on computer technologies, but more profoundly because he never examined the basis of his own 'moral outrage' against the Panopticon.[79] In my view, the basis of moral objections should rather be explored and worked out in relation to a critical theory of the Panopticon.

In the Panopticon itself the issues are sharply etched. What contemporary commentators object to is both prefigured there and emphasized by electronic technology. Bentham, following the Cartesian logic that regarded human beings as machines whose activities could be measured and controlled, wrote impersonality, abstract classification, and automatic power into the Panopticon. Precisely these features reappear, now digitally inscribed and intensified, in the new, computer-run surveillance.

Bentham's project was nothing less than a secular utopia, a model society-in-miniature, cut loose from any theological moorings that might complicate his claim that the Panopticon stood as the solution *par excellence* to the human condition.[80] In the crucial principle of inspection he explicitly parodied the doctrine of divine omniscience, taking it to be an unsurpassed means of moral control. What he conveniently ignored, though, was the personal character of knowledge present even in the biblical quotations with which he ironically epigraphed his text. It is hardly surprising, then, that the Panopticon excludes the personal, and slips almost imperceptibly from moral to instrumental categories.[81] It is equally unremarkable, given this backdrop, that today's actors in the surveillance drama have started to focus their criticisms on these aspects of electronic panopticism — perceived control by inspection, and impersonal categorization.

Beyond Orwell, Bentham and Foucault

No single metaphor or model is adequate to the task of summing up what is central to contemporary surveillance, but important clues are available in *Nineteen Eighty-Four* and in Bentham's Panopticon. Orwell's nightmare, though technologically rather dated now, correctly spotlights the role of information and technique in orchestrating social control. Its focus on human dignity and on the social divisions of surveillance also remain instructive. But the shift from violent to non-violent methods has come a long way since Orwell, and is given much greater scope by the advent of information technology for surveillance. Moreover, Orwell's dystopic vision was dominated by the central state. He never guessed just how significant a decentralized consumerism might become for social control.

The Panopticon, on the other hand, offers scope for social analytic interpretation in precisely such contexts. Studies referred to here illustrate the broad sweep of potential relevance, in administration, policing, the workplace, and the consumes marketplace. The Panopticon points to the role of subordination *via* uncertainty, and to ways in which power pervades social relations. It does seem to hold some promise for the age of subtle, computer-based surveillance.

Yet its use is also fraught with difficulties. While the adoption of computers does blur the distinctions between surveillance spheres, and thus poses questions for surveillance theory, this does not mean they are dissolved altogether. The Panopticon offers no neat 'total' explanation of surveillance. In addition, the Panopticon as a means of exclusion may well be in eclipse, leaving the advanced societies under the superior sway of consumerism, with only a minor role left for the harsher panoptic regimes.

In what follows, these themes are further explored. However, Orwell's 'Big Brother' and Foucault's understanding of the Panopticon should be in no sense be thought of as the only, let alone the best, images for yielding clues about surveillance. Powerful metaphors lie relatively unexamined in various films as well as in novels such as Franz Kafka's *The Castle* or Margaret Atwood's *The Handmaid's Tale*. In the latter, the gendered dimension of categorization, and its implications for a stunted citizenship for women, is vividly portrayed.[82] At present, however, the majority of studies is informed by either Orwellian or Foucaldian ideas, which is why it is to these writers that the following pages contain most reference.

The surveillance society is examined, then, through the critical use of sociological analyses deriving mainly from the imagery present in Orwell and the Panopticon, mediated by contemporary figures such as Anthony Giddens, James Rule and Gary T. Marx. The ethical edge of the present analysis, however, emerges not only from the democratic and 'human agency' orientations of such figures, but also from a conviction that the philosophical and religious discourse obscured by theorists such as Foucault requires rediscovery and re-emphasis within contemporary social thought.

Part II

Surveillance Trends

We now turn from situating surveillance in various contexts – historical, theoretical, critical – to examining actual trends taking place today. In four areas in particular the contribution of new technology to surveillance, alongside certain political, economic and cultural developments, has been tremendous. These areas, which define the general scope of each of the next four chapters, are government administration, policing and security, the capitalist work situation and the consumer marketplace.

The analytical distinction between the four spheres follows a fairly conventional pattern, although one important question is how long it will continue to be workable when the deployment of information technology makes such a huge contribution to the erosion of such distinctions in practice. Data collected for government purposes, for instances, increasingly finds its way into the digital repositories of commercial organizations, and *vice-versa*. Thus even these chapter divisions may start to appear somewhat arbitrary.

While these chapters represent a discussion of significant trends, it must be noted that, in the main, they are based upon secondary research materials. Wherever possible, I make clear where further empirical details may be discovered, but I use cases to illustrate important points rather than as part of a systematic empirical study. My aim, after all, is to place current debates over computer-power and social control in the contexts of historical development, social theory, ethical reflection and the politics of policy-making and social movements.

In the 1990s, the backdrop to surveillance includes global recession and accompanying economic restructuring and the consequences of events such as the collapse of Communism in Eastern Europe and processes such as the growth of high technology industries in countries of the Pacific rim. Simultaneously, consumption may be making a subtle but crucial shift to the centre of contemporary social existence, within the technologically advanced societies, with long-term implications for social order. That much of this takes place in many societies at once – globalization is a reality to be reckoned with – makes comparative study imperative. But it also means that empirical exhaustiveness sometimes has to be sacrificed for the sake of highlighting consequential new directions.

5

The Surveillance State:
Keeping Tabs on You

You and Your Data-Image

Imagine you heard that in a certain country, where the population was twenty-six million, the central government operated 2,220 databases, containing an average of twenty files on each citizen. The names of ten per cent of that population are contained in the national police computer. A state in pre-1989 Eastern Europe, perhaps, or maybe South Africa? Wrong. This is Canada.[1] It is not until one stops to consider just how much personal data is held by administrative, police and security departments that the realization dawns that 'surveillance society' may be a good way to describe what has been created. But the introduction of computers alone does not account for its creation.

Surveillance concerns the control of information, which is why computer-power is significant. The question is, in what ways is it significant? New microelectronics-based technologies make possible a massive expansion of information storage capacity and processing potential, and facilitates data retrieval enormously. Applied to the business of personal information, this enchanced capacity has major implications for surveillance. Then new technological mediation of data, and the computerized construction, communication, and use of personal files raises a number of questions that are either new, or at least more urgent than they were a few years ago.

The crucially important way that information technology makes a difference to surveillance is that integrated profiles of individual citizens become increasingly available. Organizations using information technology for surveillance purposes are now able to obtain a detailed picture of the ongoing everyday lives of individual people relatively easily. Data referring to matters such as financial standing, health records, consumer preferences, telephone transactions, welfare eligibility, residence, nationality and ethnic background, educational experience and criminal activities are readily available in ways that go far beyond what was possible using manual – that is, non-computerized – systems of surveillance. In other words, surveillance capacity is augmented by the use of new technologies.[2]

It is not merely that records may be kept in greater detail or for longer, but that records can be retrieved and compared with each other with astonishing ease. And this is true not only within the organization that originally collected the data, but between organizations that are both geographically and functionally remote. Who would have guessed that the call to military service could be associated with the enjoyment of ice-cream sundaes? But that is just what happened with Farrell's Ice Cream Parlour in the USA, mentioned in Chapter One. The key technique goes under various names, computer matching being the most common.[3]

It is the particular ways that information technology makes possible these concatenations of data that must be explored. Computers make it possible to bring together in one place otherwise discrete and scattered data, and manipulate them into novel configurations. Stated simply, these concatenations relate to the means of identification on the one hand, and the means of comparison on the other. When computer-power and sophisticated statistical technique come together, all sorts of profiles of persons and populations can be built.

One or two other aspects of the putative difference made by using information technology to run surveillance sysetms should be recalled at this point. Rule and others have argued effectively that the growth of bureaucratic surveillance during the twentieth century has produced a 'new category of relationships between ordinary people and large centralized organizations'.[4]The category of relationships they have in mind is mediated by the data collected. Decisions about data-subjects are closely tied to available information about those subjects. Computerization, they suggest, intensifies this trend. Specifically, what Kenneth Laudon calls a 'data-image'[5] of individuals is built up and conclusions – or judgements – are drawn from it. For instance, 'this person is creditworthy' – recall my own experiences buying a washing machine. The data-image could suggest that 'she is a prime suspect', 'he is a bad insurance risk' or 'she'd make a poor tenant'.

Intensified trends is not necessarily the same thing as newness. Seen from another angle, however, such data-images may well be part of a qualitatively different situation. This position depends on a distinction between written texts, like the one before you, and electronic language.

Unlike books and index cards the latter is not limited by paper and print. This is what Mark Poster sees as an aspect of a new 'mode of information'; electronic language imposing itself on top of others.[6] Poster suggests that the electronic language of databases in particular is a very limiting grid of categories and fields, lacking all the nuances and ambiguities of everyday talk or writing. For Poster, electronically mediated languages constitute a new social region distinct from but overlapping with, the capitalist economy, the welfare state, and the nuclear family. Structurally distinct from face-to-face interactions and from printed communications, they emerge into technically advanced societies, undermining the boundary between public and private space.[7]

In this view, not only the nature of surveillance but also the modes of resistance to its negative effects will have to be rethought. The data-image, which may include details of name, address, phone number, age, sex, ethnic origin, plus consumer preferences, traffic violations, creditworthiness and educational achievement, 'constitutes individuals according to these parameters' says Poster.[8] This 'other individual' enjoys an existence separate from the individual whose data comprises it, although the latter could be disadvantaged as well as advantaged by the former. How far this view is correct, to the extent that we would be warranted in distinguishing sharply between previous forms of bureaucratic surveillance and electronic surveillance, can be judged only in relation to the kinds of situations described in this and the following chapters.

The Surveillance State

Let us look more closely at how enhanced technical power contributes to the intensification of surveillance in the sphere of the state. The twin issues of identification and comparison are of central importance here though they also form a link between this chapter and the next one on policing and security.

As we saw in Chapter Two, the modern state is best thought of as an advanced form of organization whose administrative bureaucracies are concerned above all with surveillance and maintaining social order on the one hand, and economic management on the other. These tasks embrace a wide spectrum from registering births, marriages and deaths, through collecting and redisbursing taxes, to maintaining armed forces to defend territory and interests. Nation-states thus play a major role in manipulating the settings in which human activities occur and thus controlling their timing and spacing.[9] At the same time, however, such states themselves are increasingly implicated in a global system that allows some personal data to be even more remotely dispersed outside them than within them.

In Sweden, arguably that technologically most advanced surveillance society in the world, the relationship between state functions and the manipulation of settings for social life is clearly perceived. The social democratic state that places so much emphasis on the comprehensive provision of health, education, and welfare services also produces what one Swedish newspaper called the 'computerized Swede, from head to toe.'[10] By 1987 it could be said that a well brought-up, unmarried adult probably appeared in about one hundred personal information systems of administrative agencies, whereas a married person might appear in twice as many.[11] It is noteworthy in the light of Poster's 'additional self' that some members of the Swedish Data Inspection Board believe that state databases 'know' more about individuals than they know themselves.[12]

Evidence suggests that Swedes are now reacting negatively to what is often perceived as state control of their 'timing and spacing. Progressively lower response rates are obtained by Statistics Sweden to all requests for personal data except the obligatory census. This relates to a crisis that occurred in the mid-1980s, even though government bureaucracies such as Statistics Sweden were not directly involved in the most publicized case, a project known as 'Metropolit' based at the University of Stockholm. This was a historical study of 15,000 Stockholmers, born in 1953, covering their experiences of background, education, employment, social mobility, physical and mental health, drug or alcohol abuse, and criminal records. At the age of thirteen, data-subjects were informed while in school, but most had forgotten by 1986 when the newspaper *Dagens Nyheter* carried reports of the 'public scandal' of this 'Orwellian' project.[13]

It transpired that some government departments – the National Police Board and the Central Bureau of Statistics – had passed data to Metropolit researchers,[14] and this fuelled fires of controversy. Amid the commotion that followed, in which the Data Inspection Board Director Jan Freese said Metropolit treated subjects like rabbits and the senior researcher Carl-Gunnar Janssen asserted that data subjects do not own information about themselves, several important issues were aired. These related to the extent to which personal data should circulate, even for sociological research, without informed consent, and the appropriate role for the Data Inspection Board.[15]

The state represents, of course, the classical locus of Orwellian anxieties. For many people, connecting computer power with surveillance in the realm of the state is a sure way to activate the hairs on the back of the neck! While there do turn out to be somewhat chilling aspects of contemporary surveillance by the state, it should be stressed that the emerging picture is far uniformly totalitarian. To detect totalitarian tendencies in specific practices is a far cry from declaring that the 'total surveillance society' has finally arrived. It also assumes that the fear of political domination is the most appropriate concern of those considering this new surveillance.

This tendency to exaggeration is not merely 'Orwellian' either. Frederick Jameson, for instance, deplores what he calls 'high-tech paranoia' in which the circuits and networks of some putative global computer hookup are 'narratively mobilized by labyrinthine conspiracies of autonomous but deadly interlocking information agencies in a complexity often beyond the capacity of the normal reading mind'.[16] But does the evidence really point towards a state of affairs as conspiratorial as this?

A number of counter-examples could be used to show that such high tech paranoia is misplaced. Just to take one instance, the 'circuits and networks' of computer systems worked decisively *against* an attempted reassertion of totalitarian power in the Soviet Union during August 1991. Messages from Boris Yeltsin and others circulated widely throughout the world *via* the electronic mail facilities of Compuserve and Internet, the latter of which is a network of universities, military facilities and businesses. Following the example of the Tiananmen Square protesters in China, who used similar tactics to keep the outside world informed of their activities in June 1889, opponents of the abortive Soviet coup worked constantly to keep electronic communications channels open. Though the old guard in the Soviet Union had been implacably opposed to the widespread use of microcomputers the perpetrators of the coup were apparently unaware of the 'GlasNet' system and its international links, which contributed to the rapid demise of the coup.[17]

Even this example may be misleading, however, because it still focuses on the use of new technologies. While the question of the supposed difference made by information technologies is of tremendous importance, several other matters should not be forgotten. One is that information technology augments the already existing techniques for monitoring everyday life that characterize modern societies in general. How far does this increased monitoring mean increased social control by the state?

It is striking that the most complete attempts at totalitarian social control have occurred in low technology states such as Stalin's Russia, Pol Pot's Cambodia and Mao Zedong's China. Another open question is how far electronic surveillance limits the extent to which its subjects can 'answer back.' If it does, then this would indeed indicate a difference made by technology, because, as we saw in Chapter Two, most surveillance in modern societies has been both constraining and enabling. Do computers really swing the process decisively in favour of constraint? Even to the liberal, the answer may well be negative. But as I say, it is not clear that this is the right question.

Caution about premature judgements on the 'computer state' should not be read as an apology for complacent social analysis, however. One of the underlying quesions running through this book is whether the apparently innocent mushrooming growth of surveillance in contemporary society, accomplished today in the name of efficiency and by means of electronic technologies, actually changes the name of the game. Scepticism about high tech paranoia is one thing; realism about authoritarian potentials resulting from information technology *within* democratic societies is another.[18] Such authoritarian potential, though present for all citizens, is especially likely to be realized in relation to political dissidents, minorities, and the poor.

By examining a series of factors relating to surveillance capacity in a number of different organizational settings, we shall be in a much better position to assess just how far information technology is indeed making a difference to the practices and experiences of surveillance within government administration. Different historical and cultural conditions have given rise to a variety of surveillance systems in the advanced societies, so it should not surprise us if similar variety is also found in relation to the advent of information and communication technologies. One important question to ask is how far the use of similar technologies on a global level induces similarities in surveillance.

The Political Economy of New Surveillance

While electronic technologies undoubtedly facilitate a massive augmentation of surveillance capacity in contemporary states, the last thing I want to do is give the impression that some kind of technological determinism is at work. Far from it. The fact that information technology provides the instrument or means of this strengthened surveillance does not mean that surveillance capacity is an outcome of technological pressures. They play a part, as we shall see, but within the broader context of political, economic, and cultural processes that give them their chance.

Michael Rubin states the issue bluntly. The 'forces of change' that he discerns behind the recent massive expansion of administrative surveillance in the USA boil down to one factor: 'money'.[19] Though this is not hyperbole, it may be misleading. It might be more accurate to use the term 'profit', which once again indicates how social relations are implicated here. And it should also be stressed that the quest for profit is displayed in different ways, some of which – like quality control, mentioned below – affect surveillance indirectly.

Undeniably, though, fiscal preoccupations characterize the modern state. What Rubin means is that, with an acceleration in the pace and size of financial transactions in the post-War period, limitations on the risks involved are increasingly sought. Georg Simmel described classically how modern society is characterized by a growth in the extent of relationships between strangers,[20] the institutional result of which is that it becomes harder and harder for organizations to judge what risks may be entailed in transactions. Hence the perceived need to monitor accounts more closely. Such monitoring of accounts means increased demands for data and information, which rapidly becomes an almost self-propelling process and leads directly into the complexities analysed classically by Max Weber and more recently by Jacques Ellul.[21]

This phenomenon applies equally, of course, in both government and commercial contexts. Governments face greater demands and bills relating to health, welfare, and safety, not least as a result of sheer population growth. Education, highway maintenance, and police protection are three obvious areas where costs escalate steadily. Hence the tendency to be more and more aggressive in cost control and debt collection, the vehicle for which is improved surveillance. In the commercial world, it is rather the squeeze of global competition that makes for greater defensiveness and a quest for higher productivity and more rapid cash-flow. This translates into a desire for more accountability from workers, reluctance to grant credit to 'problem customers' and, again, aggressive debt collection.

During the 1980s the political preference for monetarist policies and their balanced budgets contributed further to the search for better methods of control. The impact of this was felt earliest and most keenly within the US Internal Revenue Service, where new methods of computer matching were utilized to try to contain tax evasion. The direct results were not impressive, although in the longer term the effect was to contribute to the institutionalizing of such methods. Their matches compared tax returns with reported income files, an activity which aroused considerable ire on the part of taxpayers.[22] Indeed, Rubin observes that the 'computer dragnet of the two-thirds of the population that had taxable income under $20,000 would be very hard-pressed to detect enough tax cheating to reduce the federal budget deficit by as much as one per cent'.[23]

Parallel with this development is the renewed attention paid to the verification 'transfer payments', That is, of the redistributive systems that provide welfare payments and social security to those unable to maintain their position in the consumer marketplace. In the USA, social security expenditure has risen from one-half of one per cent of the 1946 federal budget to almost twenty per cent in 1986. (Given the inequitable tax system this does not of course mean that the poor are necessarily better off.) Medicare, Supplementary Security Income and Food Stamps display a similar growth curve. With the economic recession of the 1980s and 1990s, and its associated job-losses, welfare systems at both national and local levels are financially stretched, so that any means of rooting out fraud or checking expenditure levels is welcomed by those charged with operating such systems. Indeed, it seems that greater energy is expended here than in attempting to establish a fairer system. Surveillance efforts are redoubled as the price of state welfare.

One tangible result of this is the setting-up of an Income and Eligibility Verification System, which operates in all fifty states in the USA. Interfaced with non-government data regarding education, payrolls, credit reporting and so on, the system is designed to provide maximum administrative access to personal data that will assist in checking reported financial transactions. As with systems run directly by government, margins of error may be high. Credit reporting bureaux, for instance, who are in the business to sell information gleaned from one source to interested parties in any other field, obtain their data by all manner of means, including hearsay and other third-party reporting, and often find ways of evading responsibility for incorrect data. At this point, however, it is less the reliability than the mere existence of such systems that is worthy of note.

Alongside the drive for fiscal control, another tendency is discernible; the search for quality control within organizations, not least those involved in government administration. Quality control depends on traceability and is best known from the productive context. To take a trivial example, when I complained to the makers of a muffin mix that my breakfast had been rather flat they could immediately tell from the barcoded serial that the offending mix had lain on the shelves far too long. Applied to any kind of personal services, traceability is still crucial to quality control. So-called relational databases ar used to link bits of data back to a specific individual, much as the tiny serial number found in the wreckage of the bombed plane that crashed at Lockerbie in Scotland located the bombers. Unique identifiers for individuals will be sought more and more in the quest of better quality control, which in turn spells more surveillance.

All these examples show how the political-economic context of the late twentieth century encourages the growth of specific kinds of surveillance systems. The comparison of records through computer matching represents the fastest growing surveillance trend in government throughout the industrialized societies. The overriding aim, in recessionary times, is to ease fiscal crises, especially by means of conspicuous strategies such as cutting down supposed welfare fraud and improving quality control.

Personal profiling by computer becomes more intimate and tends to focus attention particularly on the less well-off.

Of course, variations occur from country to country, and these should be borne in mind when attempting to assess this trend in any given context. To contrast the American and Australian situations, for instance, while around a quarter of US federal government expenditure is on each of defence and welfare, in Australia only ten per cent goes to defence but thirty-five per cent to health and social welfare.[24] As we shall see in the next chapter, this means for example that greater incentives exist to find consistent general means of identifying persons in Australia than in the USA; this has stimulated several attempts to establish a national personal data system in Australia, while Americans tend to fall back on existing systems such as those centred on the Social Security Number.

The growing links between government departments and credit-reporting bureaux also means the surveillance net becomes more comprehensive. If government seems to operate more by commercial criteria, it seems that, equally, certain corporations appear to act in a quasi-governmental role. This kind of technologically-facilitated convergence between functions that once were separate has already been noted; it also appears to be a general trend. The whole process illustrates once again the mushrooming of surveillance capacity.

New Technologies and Surveillance Capacity

Organizations employ surveillance systems for two purposes: to keep track generally of who is observing and who is disobeying rules, and to identify and locate more precisely those in the latter group.[25] This may be seen in the sphere of taxation. In the USA the Internal Revenue Service (IRS) is the largest civilian collector of personal data. Huge efforts have been mounted over the past decade in applying computer-power to identify non-reporters and under-reporters. Controversially, this has even included searching private databases to find out about citizens' income and expenditure.[26] The rule of organizations thus depends upon the existence and the efficiency of the surveillance system.

As I noted in the Chapter Three, the term 'surveillance capacity' refers to the efficiency of a system whose task is to gather data on or monitor subject populations. The four criteria for gauging surveillance capacity, identified originally by James Rule, and modified here are: one, the size of files; two, the comprehensivity of reach (Rule considered this in terms of centralization); three, the speed of flow; and four, subject transparency (Rule referred to the number of points of contact between the system and its subjects). These should be borne in mind in relation to the case studies illustrating this and following chapters.

When a sophisticated dossier on an individual citizen may be constructed with relative ease, the question of file-size comes into its own. Rule's work in the 1970s related generally to files built within specific surveillance systems. Now that files from different systems may be integrated with relative ease, a new picture emerges. Technological limits on file-size are steadily being removed. In most Western societies, the full potential of new technology to create megafiles is curbed by law. But in Thailand, where no such laws exist, personal data on sixty-five million Thais will be stored within a single integrated network by the year 2006.[27] Even with Data Protection laws in place, however, Western societies are witnessing tremendous growth in file-size within government systems.

The phenomenon of networking computer databases that are geographically remote from each other means, secondly, that 'comprehensivity of reach' is facilitated without there necessarily being a central computer operation. On this criterion, information technology has also made possible greater surveillance capacity within government administration. Similarly, speed of flow has been increasing rapidly during the past two decades, and the impact of this is especially marked within the command-and-control aspects of police systems.

Thirdly, information technology tends to intensify the transparency of data-subjects. Such transparency was a feature of Bentham's Panopticon; computer-power enhances the 'visibility' of those whsoe details circulate within and between databases on a scale unimaginable to those whose 'gaze' relies merely on window-light, blinds and uninterrupted vision. It is important to remember, however, that such deepening penetration of daily life does not necessarily have negative consequences for those thus 'observed'. It is a mistake to see surveillance as automatically reducing the power of certain people or groups; transparency may be a condition of liberty in some cases.[28] It is worth recalling our earlier discussion of the limits of 'panoptic' power.

This last point also relates back to Chapter Two, on 'Surveillance and Modernity'. Surveillance capacity depends not only upon measurable items such as speed of flow and comprehensivity of reach, but on what sort of surveillance system is in question. I suggested earlier that while surveillance in traditional societies was local, depending on proximate relations but not very intensive, in modern societies it is more remote but also much more intensive. Christopher Dandeker observes that surveillance in the modern world has shifted from 'personal and patronage systems of indirect control to direct control through bureaucratic systems of administrative power'.[29]Modern systems are extensively 'depersonalized', making it harder to 'name' the person, and even sometimes the agency, behind the surveillance.[30]

Beyond this lies the issue of whether information technology simply intensifies existing patterns, or whether it is implicated in a new kind of – postmodern? – social ordering. If the language – or discourse, to use Foucault's term[31] – of databases constitutes individuals in fresh ways, unrecognisable within the theories of capitalism or the state, then the challenge is to find ways of articulating what this means for power and for justice today.

Today's computerized administrative systems also vary in the extent to which data-subjects are aware that they are such, whether they have access to their files, and what they can do to curb the power of the surveillance system or, in other words, affect its capacity. Thais may thus find themselves in a different position from Canadians, whose opportunities for 'counter-surveillance' may in turn be different from those of Swedes.

However, since one of our main concerns is to indicate ways in which information technology is augmenting surveillance capacity, it is worth pointing out that the above four criteria may be affected by the processes of technological innovation and bureaucratic expansion. Moreover, in some cases these processes are linked together in a somewhat symbiotic fashion. Recall Rule's remark that mass surveillance through documentary identification, as practised by today's organizations, 'feeds on itself'. He goes on, the more important events in life entail production or consumption of personal documentation, the more feasible it is to institute effective surveillance through direct checking based on such data.'[32] What he means is that, as the range of documentary identification has grown, so it becomes increasingly possible to find out about someone not by asking them (self-identification) but by direct checking from other records.

This process is facilitated, cheaply and effectively, by using computer systems linked via telecommunications. Once the (still relatively expensive) capital plant has been established, new uses are sought for data, and new capabilities of the technology are explored. Thus the question of surveillance capacity is affected progressively by system proliferation, which in turn is enabled by new uses for data and new ways of handling data. We turn next to two case-study examples of how surveillance capacity is enhanced by computerization.

Social Insurance Numbers are prime examples, in several countries, of data whose use extends far beyond the immediately obvious, but their use grew out of governmental health and welfare schemes. You now may have to present the relevant card to rent a car or obtain a loan for university studies. The idea that governments had 'cradle-to-grave' responsibilities for its citizens provides the first example. And so-called smart cards, part of the second case-study, provide an instance of technological innovation whose potential is highly attractive to those running surveillance systems. Whether for medical use, where doctors, pharmacists and insurance companies would be relevant users, or commercial, where banks, credit card companies and employers might be users, the storage of data from multiple agencies driectly affects surveillance capacity.

From Crib to Coffin: Fine-grained Files

Integrated surveillance of citizens has become a reality in all societies where a so-called welfare state exists. In post-war Britain, for instance, initiatives were taken on several fronts at once, establishing a National Health Service and a National Insurance (Social Security) scheme, and extending provisions for education, housing, and unemployment relief. All these necessitated massive bureaucratic expansion, connecting citizen to state by the tissues of personal records.

The administrative machinery to run such a complex, interrelated system was vast, and within a few decades strategies were being sought to avoid collapse. While reforming the system might have been an administratively appropriate move, politically it was impossible. So the advent of computer power appeared as a godsend, a technological fix that would not only avert crisis but simultaneously streamline the systems and demonstrate a progressive commitment to the social application of advanced high technology.[33] Various uses were made of computers, mainly to ease the burden of keeping track of records, but by the 1970s it became clear that more co-ordinated effort was required.

Just such a coordinated effort materialized in 1977, in the twenty-five-year plan of the then Department of Health and Social Security, as an 'Operational Strategy'. By 1985 it was claimed that this represented the 'biggest computerisation programme in Europe', and Secretary of State Norman Fowler stated forthrightly that 'A fully integrated computer network is the government's policy'.[34] The entire social security system will eventually be run through a central index, much of which is already in place at the time of writing. This means that information on almost every citizen of the United Kingdom is available to a wide variety of agencies and people, structured around a 'whole person concept'.

The justification for the 'whole person concept' is that citizens should not be made to feel that their records are fragmented between numerous different departments which may make contradictory or ambiguous use of them. It thus holds an intrinsic attraction for many claimants, especially those who feel like pawns, pushed from one counter to another only to hear conflicting messages. The situation of claimants suffering from the use of differing procedures and being unfairly subject to varying rules would be eliminated. Rather, a full data image should be available that approximates as closely as possible to a correct overall picture of each citizen. This could mean that more attention is paid to full entitlements, and to the elimination of embrassment and pain over matters such as the dispatch of letters to dead people.

In practice, the 'whole person concept' means that a wide range of data on each citizen is available to numerous agencies, and at remote geographical locations, through computer terminals situated at local offices. People are known by their data-image. Thus matters of income, employment, education, health, housing, expenditure, dependents and so on are recorded and stored within a central system. The system is accessible though the National Insurance Number, which appears on each citizen's plastic, machine-readable card. Moreover, the system is deliberately sensitive to the needs of other government department especially the Inland Revenue, within what has emerged as a *de facto* government data network.

The integrated network appraoch was regarded with considerable scepticism and hostility by the government committee on data privacy set up in 1978 (the "Lindop Committee"), but was justified in the end by the criterion of efficiency. If a cumbersome and unwieldy bureaucracy could be cut down in size – at least in terms of costs and personnel – this was a palpable advantage. Indeed, great benefits were to accrue through cost cutting. Staff could be reduced in the Civil Service, and fraud and overpayment prevented. The political economy of surveillance may be seen in clear profile here.

The case of the Operational Strategy for the British Department of Health and Social Security illustrates well the enhancement of surveillance capacity. On all four criteria, file-size, comprehensivity, data-flow speed and subject transparency, the Operational Strategy show distinct gains. It also provides a case-study of the interplay between technological innovation and bureaucratic imperatives within the context of recessionary fiscal restraint and neo-Conservative policies.

Not surprisingly, critics have observed that they system may also serve to perpetuate existing policies, just at a time when reformers were arguing for a comprehensive overhaul. The new system, it was said, 'could come to be seen as rendering reform unnecessary. If computers can handle the mathematics of the myriad of benefits which are available some of the pressures to get rid of the poverty trap for example might die down.[35] Fiscal restraint, not social justice, appears to have been the prime mover in this case.

Whatever the precise reasons given for constructing this massive new database, the fact remains that it represents a hugely augmented surveillance system. Capacities are expanded in each respect, while the legal right to self-protection from potential errors and abuses is all that the British Data Protection Act affords to data-subjects. Such inflated surveillance capacity means in turn that a higher proportion of British people are 'known' more by their data-image than through personal contact. We must not forget that this 'knowing' directly affects life-chances. It is above all those who are less well-off whose personal details are processed so minutely and who thus have least access to skills and resources for ensuring that what is 'known' is correct and fair.

Managing Health Care Spending: The Ontario Health Card

Another instructive example of the relationship between new technology and surveillance capacity is provided by the changeover, in 1990, from the Ontario Health Insurance Programme (OHIP) to a Health Number system. Prompted by the same kinds of factors as the much larger British Operational Strategy, for example that management efficiency is a key criterion, the Health Number system is also intended to make it easier to plan for long-term health-related needs and to facilitate the further introduction of new technology.

The old OHIP system used a family number, in which the family head was registered, and in whose name others obtained benefits. Certainly it seems that gross inefficiency resulted. Up to twenty-five million individual records were created for a population of only nine million.[36] Charges could be inaccurate when several people used the same number, yet one can only have an appendix removed once, and only give birth if one is a woman. A more complete health service picture of each individual was sought, including for example details of hospital care and prescription drug use. These were kept separately under the OHIP system.

Behind this, however, lay the fiscal issue, as the rationale for seeking more accurate personal data; 'The Ministry of Health has responsibility for an annual transfer payment of $15 billion, and while it has in the past been a relatively passive payer, it is now moving to an active role in managing health care spending'.[37] Such information was required to 'survey health status of Ontarians, analyse use of health care, determine requirements for health services, redirect health resources, fund new programs, take action when services are overutilized or unnecessary, and identify disease patterns at an early stage."

Various benefits of the new system were claimed, including improved customer service and confidentiality of records. Public concern was expressed, however, about the potential for abuse; some newspapers perceived the outline of a police state in the new plastic cards.[38] Many feared that the non-health-care use of the card would escalate, just as use of the Social Insurance Number had since its introduction in 1964. This would mean that computer matching, or record linkage, as it is often called in Canada, would occur more frequently between different government departments. The news media also focused on fraud prevention as a major reason for the health cards, and were natuarlly delighted when one Toronto family managed to register family pets for the Health Number.

Two of the promised benefits in particular may be singled out for attention. One is the enhanced ability to relate disease and treatment patterns to geographic and demographic profiles, and another is to prepare, using the plastic card, for further technological augmentation of the system. The epidemiological and innovative advantage promised fit in neatly with surveillance capacity.

As we saw earlier, surveillance systems developed in the modern world in tandem with the growth of citizenship rights. Personal and social advantages attend the spread of surveillance. The case of epidemiology demonstrates this in the later twentieth century. Two obvious areas for potential gain are cancer research and AIDS research. Determining which population groups are at high risk in order to prevent disease and death is a project with which few would quibble. If Health Numbers are a means to that end, then let us have them. Acknowledging this does not mean that epidemiological research is problem-free, however.

For a start, AIDS-related personal information is extremely sensitive. Epidemiologists may not intend to stigmatize high-risk groups – especially homosexual and bisexual men – but such stigmatizing and discriminatory practice is part of the social context in which the AIDS epidemic has occurred. Thus their demand to collect, use, and disclose personal information as part of an effective public health response to AIDS is bound to be controversial. Risks relating to carriers of Human Immunodeficiency Virus (HIV) mean that they may be refused employment or entry into a country, or disadvantageously or abusively treated, if their condition is known.

Add to this the relative imprecision of testing methods and it becomes clear that the social advantages of such surveillance are far from unambiguous. It would be easy to conclude from newspaper reports that testing for HIV is a cut-and-dried affair. Far from it. Epidemiologists struggle with several issues here. The first is sensitivity; how well does the test pick up HIV? The second is specificity; does this test show only HIV positivity or does it actualy reveal the presence of other, unrelated conditions as well? The third is predictive value; if the test result shows up as positive, how reliable is that as a guide to whether or not the individual tested really is infected?[39]

To take a different kind of case, the benefits of epidemiology may in some instances be withheld. In some countries, where certain holders of information are prevented by data protection law from disclosing what they know, yet other problems may arise. In France, controversy has arisen over the incidence of a hereditary form of glaucoma, which, among other things, may cause blindness. 30,000 people in Northern France are at risk, all of whom are descendants of a fifteenth-century couple who had the disease. The results of a study begun in 1988 by the Institut National d'Etudes Demographiques have indicated to doctors that many young people are at considerable risk. Their vision could be saved if they were told in time, but the Commission Nationale Informatiques et Libertés has warned that this would be illegal.[40] The dilemmas of surveillance for epidemiological research run deep.

To return to Canada, the other benefit in the Ontario individual record system worthy of note is the intention to let the Health Card pave the way for future, improved versions; so-called smart cards. The Ministry of Health says that 'it is possible to store important medical and drug history on future versions of the card so that providers can access important information in both emergencies and normal treatments'.[41] In this case, further anticipated technological developments are clearly part of the reason for the transition to the Health Card.

Smart cards look like any other plastic numbercard, but have embedded within them a memory chip and integrated circuitry. Information can both be stored within and added to such a card, which makes it ideal, say its proponents, for health care use. On one card, medical records and the use of health care services can be stored and made accessible to medical personnel, pharmacists, hospitals and insurance companies. Smart cards have been under trial for several years in the Canadian provinces of Saskatchewan, Alberta, Québec and Ontario. They provide an interesting case of commercial and technological push, in that high-technology companies are involved in partnerships with government departments for tests (and not only in relation to health care).

This provides a telling illustration of the ways in which conventional boundaries between surveillance spheres are being overridden using the capabilities of new technologies. While a government-related Department of Health would supply some data for the smart card, other agencies would also take 'space' on the same card. These may include insurance companies, employers, hospitals, pharmacists and so on. Among other things it is unclear how far checks could be maintained on the circulation of data held on the cards. While we are assured by enthusiasts that new techniques vastly improve existing security, even enthusiasts are unsure how far this could be trusted on the large-scale systems envisaged by government departments and corporations.[42]

In terms of surveillance capacity, smart cards offer an important in relation to all four criteria, while at the same time having some clear benefits for their users. Proponents claim, for instance, that lives could be saved at the scene of a highway accident if a medical record were immediately available. At the same time, many doctors and civil libertarians express reservations about smart cards. The Québec Federation of General Practitioners, for example, was unhappy about matters such as the violation of professional confidentiality.[43] Others have argued that smart cards could pose a threat to personal autonomy if they were linked with financial rewards or punishments for 'healthy or unhealthy' lifestyles as health care options were offered on an increasingly consumerist basis.[44]

Smart cards offer a good example of what Jacques Ellul calls the 'self-augmenting' character of new technology. Each phase of development calls forth further modification and enhancement in a never-ending tail-chase to 'complete the system', The chief danger is that technological and commercial criteria, suitably dressed in the discourse of social benefit, are allowed by default to drive administrative changes of considerable magnitude. In the case of the OHIP numbercard in Canada, the expectation of technical enhancement was explicitly written into the initial issue of the cards. Social, personal, political and ethical questions often come low on the agenda of technological 'progress'.

Administration, Computers and Beyond

It is apparent that the modern state not only keeps tabs on its citizens but does so with an astonishing array of highly sophisticated surveillance systems. The increasingly integrated profile of each person that constitutes his or her data-image is a complex concatenation of diverse bits of data. But while the data may be gathered in a remote, impersonal and scarcely perceptible way, the data-image nevertheless has definite consequences for the experience and life-chances of the person to whom it refers. Conclusions are drawn, and decisions and judgements are made on the basis of the data-image rather than by checking details with the individual concerned. Indeed, data gatherers often believe that they, not data-subjects, 'own' personal data.

Increased surveillance capacity comes as a result of specific political and economic circumstances that favour the use of technological systems of particular kinds, which invariably feature enhanced capabilities. This may vary in detail, depending on the type of society; whether for instance it is Swedish social democratic, or American entrepreneurial individualist. But at least two significant factors emerge from examples used here, and they appear to be somewhat general effects. One is that such increased capacities within the systems of government administration have a disproportional impact on the less well-off. The other is that the practice of integrating computer networks is facilitating a certain functional convergence between government administration on the one hand and capitalist corporations on the other. The boundaries are blurring once more.

We cannot, however, lay all this at the door of some 'autonomous technology'. True, surveillance systems seem to feed on themselves and new technologies to augment themselves. But are the consequences of this malign or benign? We have found no necessary connection between high-technology surveillance systems and authoritarianism – indeed, counter-examples may be found – but it does seem that as far as administrative systems are concerned, the conditions of democratic involvement are altering in favour of government, in part as a result of the use of computer technologies. Velvet gloves may hide iron fists. Totalitarian tendencies of a very subtle nature may expand with democratic process still in place.

At the same time, social benefit accrues from surveillance systems. Though none is exempt from ambiguity and dilemma – think of the Ontario Health Card and epidemiology – the advantages of modern state-run surveillance systems should not be sneered at. A more appropriate response would be greater public vigilance regarding the installation of such systems and the encouragement of a sceptical attitude towards technological capacities. The limitations and possible drawbacks of such systems ought equally to be in view.

In terms of our earlier exploration of models or metaphors for surveillance, we have noted a number of panoptic aspects of state-sponsored surveillance, particularly the 'unseen observer'. Surveillance is subtle but effective. The Orwellian aspect is also here; the systems described have strong implications both for social division and for personal dignity. The use of new technologies appears to reinforce already existing cleavages within consumer capitalism, conferring no obvious advantage on the non-consuming minority. And the data-image on which they depend raises more sharply questions of dignity. From a modern perspective, impersonality and diminished autonomy appear to accompany the surveillance trends noted here. But perhaps this begs further questions.

In the next chapter we turn our attention more directly to matters of policing and social control. However, in surveillance terms, the difference of focus is one of degree rather than kind. For if surveillance has to do with organizations keeping track of who is and who is not deviating from rules, and if this generates attempts to locate and bring into line those in the latter category, then welfare and policing look fairly similar. This does not of course mean that one can be reduced to the other, but it does mean that each may be subjected to scrutiny regarding enhanced surveillance capacity according to the same criteria.

In particular we shall examine more closely the ways that identification takes place and how comparison between files is facilitated by information technology. As we mentioned above, these two factors illustrate both the difference made by computers and the strong connections between the administrative and policing functions of the state. As in this chapter, however, the emphasis is not merely on new technology, as if current changes all hinged decisively on microelectronics. It is easy but misleading to exaggerate the social consequences of computers. New technology does have an impact, but it is an impact mediated by the particular circumstances already existing in each modern society.

6

The Surveillance State: From Tabs to Tags

Spiderman's Solution

'Don't send him to jail. Send him home'. So reads the glossy brochure advertising 'Justice Electronic Monitoring Systems Inc'. Starting from the innocent bed-time comic reading of a new Mexico judge,[1] the idea of keeping low-risk offenders at home and tagged with an electronic anklet has attracked attention in several countries.[2] Spiderman has much to answer for, it seems! Prison populations, especially high in the USA and Canada, present a number of pressing problems to government, not least expense. In Canada the daily cost of housing offenders in provincial or federal institutions is $127. On any day there are more than twenty-seven thousand prisoners, according to Statistics Canada. But up to thirty percent of these, and many others on probation, parole or supervision, could be eligible for home arrest programmes, whose cost, claim the high-tech companies, is a mere $20 per prisoner-day.

Advertising for these tagging schemes is worthy of Jeremy Bentham himself; 'A twentieth-century answer to a twentieth-century problem; Public protection similar to incarceration, at less cost; helps relieve jail and prison overcrowding; humane and unobtrusive; relieves probation/parole staff of time-consuming surveillance function; easy to install, simple to operate; provides accurate monitoring of offender's presence at a designated place; tamper-proof; safe to use and reliable ... ' claims the CSD Home Escort Electronic Monitoring System.[3]

The essential idea behind tagging is simple. A battery-powered device on a bracelet or an anklet gives signals, transmitted through a box attached to a telephone, to a control room that is constantly staffed. Police or other relevant authorities are alerted if ever the wearer moves out of range or fails to 'report' using the device. Proponents of such schemes argue that they are cheap and humane alternative to prison. Opponents argue that in practice they tend to be used in addition to prison, do not reduce stigma, and are a technical fix that both diverts attention from pressing social and political issues concerning justice systems and helps create a more intense surveillance society.[4]

As far as this chapter is concerned, electronic monitoring of offenders represents the sharp end of surveillance over individuals by the sate. If surveillance in general has to do with keeping track of who is observing and disobeying rules, then the main theme of this chapter is how those in the latter category are identified and located. Matters of policing and state security come to the fore here as manifestations of a modern concern with law and order and the containment of deviance. As we saw in Chapter Two, the use of forcible methods to keep social control diminishes dramatically in modern societies. The threat of physical force is steadily replaced by administrative control – 'keeping tabs' – and by new systems of codified law and policing. There is a constant quest for new techniques, including today the widespread use of information technology, to make these more efficient. Hence 'from tabs to tags'.

Three comments are in order regarding the use of new technology in this context. Firstly, With the shift to modernity, control within particular locales became important. Urban space in particular was seen as a special site for potential disturbance by criminals of varying stripes. Today, while urban crime is still viewed as a peculiar threat,[5] new technologies facilitate containment over much wider geographical terrain, international as well as national. Secondly, while the modern nation-state became the focus of attempts to create internal order, which gave rise to the police and prisons of today, the process of globalization now means that external order also requires a strong policing function.[6] This relates both to security and intelligence services and to the more mundane matters of policing borders. Information technology is increasingly sought to cope with the huge task of such globalized policing. Thirdly, modern societies have largely – but not completely – dispensed with the use of the military to deal with issues of internal order, but this does not mean that the influence of the military has entirely dissipated. New technology can actually encourage the adoption of military tactics within civilian policing.

The variety of 'new technologies' one encounters within this sphere is striking. While the particular focus of this book is on information technologies, because they enable many of the others to be effective, it is worth mentioning which others are involved. The US Office of Technology Assessment (OTA) lists five categories of surveillance technology.[7]

Audio surveillance includes miniaturized transmitters and wired systems like telephone taps and concealed microphones. Visual surveillance includes photography, television (such as cameras in streets and shopping malls), night vision devices, and satellite-based observation.[8] Data surveillance covers the familiar ground of distributed processing, computer networks, and software such as expert systems and pattern recognition. Sensor technology is of various kinds: magnetic, seismic, infra-red, strain, and electromagnetic. Other devices include citizen-band radio, vehicle location systems, magnetic strips, polygraphs, voice stress analysis, voice recognition, laser interception and cellular radio.

As I have stressed, my intention is not to indicate how new technology is somehow creating an unprecedented 'Orwellian' or 'panoptic' state of affairs. Rather, by bearing in mind the various trends that have characterized the growth of surveillance in modern societies, we hope to discover which of those trends is magnified and which diminished by virtue of adopting new technologies and what social consequences might follow.

As the single most significant item concerns how individuals are identified and different personal files compared, I begin by examining what I call 'electronic IDs'. These IDs, sometimes called 'Universal Personal Identifiers' (UPI), are vital to the process of pinpointing individuals believed to have broken or to be likely to break, given rules or laws. Not only do they enable such individuals to be pinpointed, they also serve as keys to unlock different files on those individuals, often stored elsewhere and collected for different purposes. In the remainder of the chapter we shall explore trends on policing and security respectively, and finally consider in a preliminary way the implications of the 'surveillance state' for the process of democratic involvement and for its contributions to the globalization process.

Electronic Identification

It matters little whether a UPI goes under that name or some other, such as 'electronic ID'. The important thing is whether or not a number which readily identifies an individual across a number of databases is available. Many organizations and agencies in the public and private sectors hold personal databases. The data is thus dispersed, and what has been collected for one databank cannot be easily utilized within another. A UPI, however, permits much easier access between databases. Imagine you wished to see all Van Gogh's surviving paintings. You would have to obtain catalogues, and spend much time and money travelling form gallery to gallery. But a ticket to see a rare exhibition of Van Gogh works loaned by the various galleries would save most of that tremendous effort. A UPI is the electronic equivalent of the ticket to see the exhibition, where the pictures represent personal data.

While the advanced societies use the huge computer-power of personal databases and have access to telecommunications facilities enabling in principle extensive contact between them, the linchpin of a 'dossier society,'[9] a consistent identification system, is generally not yet in place. But not for want of trying. Although in the USA, for example, Congress has consistently refused those who would create a National Data Center, arguably the National Criminal Information Center (NCIC) along with the Computerized Criminal History (CCH) system provides just that. With matching, screening and profiling, individuals can be identified and their activities tracked across many databases, albeit rather inefficiently.[10]

Several attempts were made in the 1980s to introduce national ID systems. In Germany, despite vociferous opposition, such a scheme came into being in 1987. All citizens will eventually be required to carry computer-readable identity cards. Some concerned German citizens shared the fears of Gunter Schroeder, a police union chairman, who believed the electronic IDs were 'secret police through the data door'.[11] They were hardly reassured by the insistance that the data is for 'internal use' only. As Social Democratic and Green Party opponents observed, 'internal' covers everything from traffic wardens to the state intelligence agency and border police.[12]

At about the same time, similar proposals were made in Australia, with the main purpose of reducing tax evasion, and fraudulent practices in social security claims. What difference could possibly be made by 'one more piece of plastic for your wallet'?[13] The Australia Card Bill was introduced in October 1986. Public opinion seemed at first to support the idea, but support waned as the debate proceeded. Threats to civil liberties, and the system's alleged technical deficiencies, were used as arguments against it, but the scheme was finally defeated through the discovery of a legal loophole which effectively halted parliamentary debate.[14]

In Britain debate has been sporadic, but the idea of a national ID card system has been increasingly mooted in Parliament over recent years. Although such electronic identifiers have yet to be introduced, the strongest argument for them appears to be the opening of the European Community borders for unhindered travel and trade, which occurred in 1992.[15] Several EC member states already have ID card systems, though only in a minority are then fully electronic. Britain once operated an ID card system as a war-time exigency (indeed the National Health Service took over these numbers when it was created in 1948), but abandoned it in response to complaints about police abuse of the system in 1951. At the time few were sorry to see it go. Of course, that ID card was a mere cardboard ticket. How the experience of possessing a bar-coded or similar electronically operated card would differ from this, or how far new forms of domination might appear with such systems, is as yet unclear.

A major argument for an electronic ID system in Britain is the hindrance to criminals[16] it would present. Greater international police cooperation in Europe, consequent on opening the Channel Tunnel between England and France and the borders between all members states, would be greatly facilitated by such a card. But, at a more mundane level, electronic IDs would be a weapon against soaring crime rates, both to prevent and to trace criminal activity. The police themselves are divided on this, fearing that public relations might be further damaged by the use of such IDs, which would render them counterproductive. Police hesitations about ID cards also grew after the 1989 football stadium disaster at Hillsborough. Evidence of crowd movement suggested that it earlier proposals for a 'test-case' national football supporters' ID had been accepted, even more deaths might have occurred at the turnstiles.

Alongside such direct 'policing' concerns lie other bureaucratic and commercial pressures to adopt electronic IDs. Civil Servants in Britain, as elsewhere, seek more streamlined and integrated systems, encouraged on the one hand by the fiscal squeeze and on the other by companies eager to take advantage of lucrative government contracts. A general purpose identiciation system makes widespread dataveillance that much more straightforward.[17] Establishing an ID system might also be encourage by the thought of potential revenues accruing from the sale of certain kinds of data to interested organizations.[18]

Ranged against electronic IDs for the UK are several arguments under the 'civil liberties' banner. Opponents are quick to observe that Adolf Hitler made extensive use of ID cards. This objection is perhaps even stronger in North America, and in some continental European countries where direct memories of the Third Reich are more vivid, than in the UK.[19] Fear of misused police powers is closely bound up with this, and the British civil liberties group Liberty claims that minorities, dissidents and anti-government demonstrators tend to experience greater harassment and discrimination in countries where compulsory IDs exist.[20] Others fear not only that democratic involvement might be curtailed by the use of IDs but that privacy will also be at risk, with yet more personal data circulating without consent and beyond individual control.

It is clear that the quest for consistent ID systems is both national and international. The maintenance of internal order, characteristic of modern societies as national states, is matched in an increasingly global environment by a concern for co-ordination between different countries. The initiative, however, does not necessarily originate in policing or security departments, as is shown in the case of machine-readable passports. A May 1968 meeting in Montreal of the International Civil Aviation Organization (ICAD) faced the challenged of airport congestion in an era of huge air traffic expansion. One key solution that emerged was the machine-readable passport that would enable passengers to pass through lines more quickly.

The International Criminal Police Organization (Interpol) monitored the meeting for security checking purposes. The passports were to have the now familiar strip containing the issuing state and bearer's name on one line, and on the next line the passport number, nationality, date of birth, sex, date of expiry and, optionally, the national ID number. An Optical Character Recognition (OCR) device 'reads' this data at the immigration desk, allowing most travellers to continue with 'no trace'. For the minority, however, who for some reason have a computer record, a 'Subject Check' alerts the officer, who takes appropriate action. This is now standard practice internationally.

To reduce fears of any 'Big Brother' aspect, the ICAD agreed to use roman letters and arabic numerals (rather than, say, a barcode) so that people could read 'all' details on their passports. What few recognize, of course, is that the OCR brings to the screen a computer file corresponding to the name on the passport.[21] It therefore comes as a surprise to some that they are stopped at the immigration desk. The unkown factor is how broad is the spectrum of suspicion. Hence, to take a notorious example, the consternation of Canadian environmentalist Farley Mowat when he was prevented from entering the USA to give a lecture in 1985.[22] The machine-readable passport, like the electronic ID card, lends itself to the creation of potentially endless categories of suspicion. The comforting thought of safety in the skies may be partly offset by thoughts less comforting.

Computers that Converse: Record Linkage

The stretched spectrum of suspicion results not only from identification systems but also from their connection with the computer files held in databases. An electronic ID yields a definitive dataset relating to a specific individual. But even without such an ID, sophisticated personal profiles may be constructed using computer-matching or record-linking techniques. This is a means of direct checking made possible by the use of advanced computers and telecommunications. While the value for surveillance systems of electronic IDs is clearly enormous, in places where they are politically unacceptable the problem may be circumvented by the use of computer matching.

In Sweden, for example, where Personal Identification Numbers (PINS) have been in widespread government use for some time, worries about a new method for conducting the census surfaced in the early 1980s. Rather than ask individuals to complete forms, the idea was to collect data directly from existing registers of tax, health insurance, and so on.[23] This ill-fated innovation illustrates neatly the more general surveillance trend towards direct checking rather than self-identification as a means of obtaining what is held to be reliable data.[24] Although in the Swedish case this specific form of direct checking did not go ahead at that time, the general principle behind it has become standard practice in many countries.

Computer matching represents the greatest single contributor to an expanded spectrum of suspicion. Information from two or more distinct data sources is compared, often with the purpose of discovering violations through the creation of profiles of likely characteristics of offenders. As the costs of direct computer linkage through modems falls, so the practice of computer matching increases.[25] We mentioned in Chapter Three how the earliest large application of computer matching was a dragnet investigation intended to eliminate fraud in the then US Department of Health, Education and Welfare (HEW). When such authorities can triumphantly claim hits such as the California woman who received welfare payments for thirty-eight non-existent children,[26] such investigations appear to be vindicated. The reality, however, is somewhat different. HEW's "Project Match" was an abject failure – producing only thirty-five minor convictions and less than $10,000 in fines from an original 33,000 'raw hits' – although it 'success' was cited in the drive for further computer matching in the late 1970s and early 1980s.[27]

Traditional reliance upon witnesses to produce information about law-breaking becomes weak when citizens fail to speak up or when they simply do not know about certain offences. Under these circumstances, police may engage in undercover activities, colluding with criminals or acting as victims. Or official attention may turn to data searching by means of computer-matching.

Thus the practice of making welfare claims in more than one American state may be exposed with ease by matching claimants' rolls from different jurisdictions. A little more tricky at present is the prevention of cross-border fraud. In Canada, the New Brunswick health insurance programme has recently switched to using health cards that expire after three years in order to limit fraud among previous residents who have moved south of the border into the USA. Another example concerns insurance fraud discovered by the American National Auto Theft Bureau. It was once common for the registration document or title certificate of a wrecked car sold for salvage to be bought, and the car insured and subsequently reported stolen. Insurance could be collected on a non-existent car. Now the Bureau matches lists of cars bought for salvage and those listed as stolen, thus identifying fraud previously hidden in different files.[28] In Canada, the Comptroller General has used computer matching to perform a research project involving the collection of defaulted student loans by deducting outstanding amounts from tax rebates.[29]

While these could be dismissed as isolated cases or mere anecdotal evidence, they actually illustrate a more general expansion of numerous kinds of computer matching within large organizations throughout the advanced societies. For this there exists a considerable body of evidence.[30] Decreasing costs of technical equipment and increasing perceived requirements to keep fraud in check combine to encourage its rapid development. The growth of such networks of interconnecting information services has prompted concern, both within nation states and, in cases such as the European Community, between them.[31]

The two faces of surveillance appear again in the case of computer matching. Many matching purposes are laudable; few would quibble with their basic intent, when this has to do with preventing or limiting criminal behaviour. Eyebrows might be raised over welfare fraud and cognate cases, however. As Nancy Reichman observes, 'focusing the responsibility for budget deficits on a few relatively powerless individuals who may be defrauding federal programmes diverts questions about the structure of those programmes and the actions of those who administer them.[32] In the sphere of tax avoidance, fraudulent insurance claims and so on, most would sympathize with the intentions behind matching.

One of Canada's previous Federal Privacy Commissioners, John Grace, comments that 'it is precisely the goodness of the cause which makes matching both so attractive and so hard to stop'.[33] He refers to 'stopping' such programmes because in his view 'the invasive, indiscriminate use of the computer in gathering, storing, and comparing personal data for purposes either benign or malign reduces individuals to commodities, subjugates human values to mere efficiency'.[34] The fears expressed relate to the fact that the computer, and non any particular person or department appears as the informant,[35] to the loss of control of personal data, to the 'dragnet' that 'fishes' without prior suspicion of individuals thus searched, to the presumption that 'raw hits' are guilty until proved innocent,[36] and to the fact that when data subjects are 'raw hits' they may be unable to challenge authorities before decisions are made and thus lose any right to equal protection before the law.

Computer matching continues to be controversial, mainly because it encourages what Gary T. Marx calls 'categorical suspicion'[37] But it remains a vital tool of government surveillance, where policing of everyday rule-infractions is concerned. Indeed, in some countries where computer matching is practised, databanks have been created solely for matching purposes.[38] Information collected for one purpose has been copied or transferred, to be used, whenever required, for unrelated purposes. The processes of social control would seem to be strengthened by the enhanced ease of personal identification and of discovering violations through computer matching. Relations between individual citizens and regulatory organizations do seem to be affected by these applications of new technology.

This raises critical questions regarding the paradoxical nature of modern surveillance. If, as I have argued, today's surveillance systems developed in some respects symbiotically with the expansion of citizenship rights, then one might expect those rights to continue to grow, or at least to be maintained, as surveillance intensifies. The problem with the case of computer matching and its concomitant expanded spectrum of suspicion is that precisely those hard-won citizenship rights seem threatened. Maybe we should be less sanguine about the citizenship-surveillance link? If 'raw hits' diminish due process of justice and create a situation where data-subjects are 'guilty until proved innocent', then this makes a mockery of the basic right to equality before the law. The historical – but perhaps tenuous – symbiotic relation between surveillance and citizenship could be severed by this increasingly common use of computer technology.[39]

Police Computers: Command and Control

All the advanced societies possess large-scale computer systems for policing. Such systems develop in the context of practices reflecting the priorities and capacities of police and national governments. But does the use of police computers simply augment existing arrangements, power relations, and the processes of criminal justice? Or do they contribute in particular ways that help to shape policing, so that computers may be said to make some qualitative difference to the realities of relations between police, government and people?

The growth of police computer-power over the past few decades has been dramatic. The American FBI National Crime Information Center (NCIC) contained almost two-and-a-half million records in 1971. Today it stores or indexes over seventeen million, and handles a million transactions a day.[40] From 1970 to 1985 the centralized gathering of criminal history information in every American state occurred on a far greater scale and in a much more co-ordinated fashion than in any other area of criminal justice. Most files are turned up for arrests, bail-setting and sentencing purposes within criminal justice. But many records are now also used for employment, licensing, and even housing and financial purposes.[41]

The British Police National Computer (PNC) started life in 1974, its main task being to register vehicle owners and the stolen-and-suspect vehicles list. Now fifth million records are kept of these details, in addition to criminal names, fingerprints, convictions, wanted and missing persons, and disqualified drivers.[42] Routine police work now depends heavily upon the PNC: eleven million people and thirteen million vehicles are checked against it every year. Again, however, its brief is broad, and files may be maintained on persons or vehicles that relate to no 'substantiated suspicion'. Many records exist, in other words, 'just in case,' where there may be 'actual or potential' suspicion. Here computer matching comes into its own.

Similar growth of police computing is evidenced in other countries. The National Swedish Police Board handles centralized police registers and maintains a large automated 'Judicial Information System.' The German Central Police Computer, INPOL, keeps even more close watch on the movements of citizens than does the British PNC, largely because the linking of state-run computers is more advanced. In Canada, the Royal Canadian Mounted Police (RCMP) runs the Canadian Police Information Centre (CPIC), which like other national police computers also serves to link Interpol with local and regional forces such as the Ontario Provincial Police (OPP).

Focusing exclusively on the new technologies, their expense, or their scope may give the impression that computers are transforming police operations. The dazzling high-tech of police helicopters with their computer terminals, 'heli-tele' video cameras, and thermal imagers (heat-seeking telescopes) provides an 'eye in the sky' picture of contemporary police beloved by movie-goers.[43] Indeed, films such as *Robocop* feed the popular perceptions that today's policing is an automated, digital, technology-driven affair.

The reality is more mundane. Police use new technology in many ways like any other organization to enhance efficiency and to try to upgrade services. They too have to cope with budgetary constraints and to respond to the varied whims of national governments. They attempt to update their role to match current social realities while simultaneously maintaining their status. But their use of new technology is somewhat different from other organizations, even though it is not transformative.[44] And certain important consequences follow from 'techno-policing'[45] in specific social contexts that do contribute to altered social relations.

Policing in general represents an extension of state surveillance. From early modern times, when private policing waned in importance,[46] police were seen as a professional and bureaucratized body, paid for and answerable to the government. During the nineteenth and twentieth centuries, police in the advanced societies have been obliged to adapt their methods to increasingly mobile populations, and to find means of maintaining social order, especially in urban and industrial contexts. Although different emphases on national or local police agencies and different legal traditions have led to some variety, all advanced societies have seen significant growth of surveillance in the shape of policing during the twentieth century. National networks have been established, techniques of command and control within police units have produced structural tightening, and the information capacities of police organizations have expanded.[47]

All three of these changes have been facilitated by the introduction of information technology. As we have just seen, national police computer networks enable rapid communication between remote locations, nationally and internationally. Interpol makes extensive and increasing use of information technology to co-ordinate activities and track individuals such as those on extradition charges or listed as missing.[48] Globalized policing is thus facilitated.

Secondly, internal command and control – reflecting, in some ways, forms of military organization – means that police using computers have massive amounts of data at their fingertips, so that at least in principle much more appropriate and rapid responses may be made. Furthermore, higher management may more readily retain control and also engage more realistically in forward planning.[49]

Thirdly, computer-power vastly increases surveillance capacity in respect of subject populations. An older balance began to shift during the 1950s and 1960s between preventative policing, which depends on the visible presence of uniformed police, and deterrent policing, which relies on the fear of detection through applying science to monitoring criminal groups. They emphasis shifted towards more pre-emptive policing, both through rapid response to crises and crime detection and 'forecasting'. Gary T. Marx argues that this is part of a general trend in social control, in which new technologies are deeply implicated. His characteristics of 'new surveillance' include 'prevention ... decentralized self-policing ... categorical suspicion.'[50]

The changing relation between police and society may be most clearly seen here. Paradoxically, though, the slogan designating the shift is 'community policing', which does not immediately conjure up visions of abstract impersonal machines. 'Modern', 'contemporary' or 'progressive' policing is frequently depicted as 'community policing', and involves, among other things, a 'proactive approach to crime and disorder problems' and an emphasis on 'information management'.[51] Community policing initiatives have been sparked over the last decade above all by urban unrest, such as the riots in Liverpool and London in the 1980s. It remains to be seen what will occur following the Los Angeles riots in 1992.

Community policing tries to anticipate future calls by identifying local crime and disorder problems through scanning and forecasting based on demographic and other social data, including input from local communities. 'Hot spots' are brought to the attention of police officers and community-police commissions so that appropriate preventative measures can be taken.[52] Police work thus relies increasingly on the scrutiny of data gleaned from the surveillance infrastructure, and is geared to anticipatory, pre-emptive activity.

The paradox of community policing does however reveal some dilemmas. The professional model of policing is wedded to updated technology – some say is technology-driven – whereas community trust of police seems to depend upon personal contact. Technopolicing could thus portend more serious ruptures in police-society relations, reduce the liberty of citizens as categorical suspicion increases, and, ironically, deepen the dependence of police on subjective data, gleaned from 'the community', which then acquires an aura of objectivity as it appears on computer terminals.[53]

Those 'subjective data' which contemporary police practice includes in computer records may not be insignificant. In Britain, they can include racial orgin, political opinion, health, sexual life, and criminal convictions.[54] In the USA, complaints have been made about the quality of data in the CCH system and in particular that certain groups such as ethnic minorities and those on welfare are disadvantaged.[55] Such factors may be viewed both as the technological amplification of disadvantage and as part of a possible more general social change.

This chapter began with electronic tagging. Some British evidence suggests that those given the option of such monitoring are disproportionately weighted towards what might be called 'underclass' status.[56] (On the other hand, when tagged offenders in the USA are obliged to pay for their monitoring, and can use it as a means of evading the privations of jail, then the opposite may obtain.)[57] But much of the police computer data we have just discussed fits well with the thesis that modern societies use classifying surveillance as a major means of social control, serving both to include and exclude deviants. Inclusion might cover for instance the video surveillance of shopping malls, while exclusion – 'putting away' would be reserved for the 'hard' end of the deviance spectrum. In contemporary societies the gap between those who have a place in the socio-economic structure and those cut off from it – the 'underclass' or, in Steven Spitzer's telling words, 'social junk'[58] – is subject to technological definition.

Computerizing National Security

The twentieth century is the century of total war. For the first time, whole societies, not just armed forces were involved in war efforts. This meant, among other things, that intelligence services developed their capacities not only for 'spying' abroad, but for monitoring the population at home. Indeed, according to one commentator, by the end of the First World War British security services were more preoccupied with domestic subversion than was German espionage.[59]

The threat of atomic and nuclear warfare after the Second World War intensified security arrangements, which were often shrouded in secrecy. This is especially true of Britain, as witness the protracted fiasco over ex-security agent Peter Wright's 'revelations' about British intelligence services in the book *Spycatcher*.[60] For many months the British Government tried to preven publication of this book; this eventually served only to increase its sales and decreases the credibility of that Government.

The upshot of the growth of national security services is that certain civil liberties have been eroded in the effort to protect citizens from threats both internal and external. Once again the question must be asked whether that symbiotic relation between surveillance and citizenships is gradually being blurred. The question is made all the sharper, and should possibly be extended, because of the use of new technologies.

The world of security intelligence is one to which new technology has greatly contributed. At the same time, it is, by definition, one about which least is publicly known. In the USA, the huge international operations of the National Security Agency (NSA) are but dimly perceived by the American population, let alone by others whom it touches. Highly sophisticated satellite tracking stations are used to monitor domestic communications, for instance, and these are coordinated with the security arrangements of other countries.[61]

Britain's GCHQ (General Communications Headquarters) at Cheltenham and the facility at Fylingdales in Yorkshire are linked with the NSA, and are linked in turn with intelligence operations in Canada, Australia and New Zealand, as they have been since the Second World War. This UKUSA security and intelligence community itself is no small enterprise, as it represents more than a quarter of a million full-time personnel and a budget of sixteen to eighteen US dollars billion. Numerous other countries are also related to this network, in varying degrees of 'limited trust' or 'secret' relationships.[62]

Many sophisticated techniques are used, including electronically up-graded time-tested ones. Modern methods of telephone tapping often leave limiting legislation far behind. British Telecom's System X – digital switching that replaces older electro-magnetic systems – permits totally unperceptible tapping. GCHQ can intercept any communication going through the airwaves, including categories outlined in the 1985 Interception of Communications Act as 'interests of national security', detecting 'serious crime', and 'safeguarding the economic well-being of the UK.[63] According to the Act, taps may only be made after a minister has issued a warrant. But several different departments are involved, and there is no way of telling when taps are actually made.

The establishing of Integrated Services Digital Networks (ISDNs) in the advanced societies leads to the intercepting of all manner of messages. An old-fashioned wiretap involved unique messages flowing down one line, but the digital networks carry many signals simultaneously – multiplexing – and anyone attempting to listen in will pick up the whole range of messages. Once the need to wiretap for security purposes is accepted, as it is almost everywhere, then the number of signals captured is bound to exceed those required.[64] On the other hand, the adoption of fibre optics within ISDNs will make conventional 'wiretapping' more difficult because light rather than electrical impulses are involved and because of the packet-switching and compression techniques used in data transmission.

However effective security systems are for detecting major crises – and some doubt exists in this regard; 'information overload' can be a hindrance[65] – they do have big implications for the surveillance capacity of modern states. In Germany the *Verfassungsschutz* (Department for the Protection of the Constitution) keeps files on all who in any way criticize the government or endanger national security.[66] In Canada, CSIS (the Canadian Security Intelligence Service) has been taken to task for 'intruding on the lives and activities of too many Canadians' because of its observing of left-wing, peace-activist and environmental groups.[67] Its predecessor, the RCMP Security Service, employed a definition of subversion as broad as 'being militant against the status quo. . . on the left rather than on the right'.

The extent of internal surveillance by security agencies surfaces from time to time when it is revealed that ethnic or union leaders have had their phones tapped, or when a prominent individual is found to have been monitored. In Britain during 1991 a ninety-three-year-old start of silent films, Kathleen Tacchi-Morris, discovered she was a GCHQ phonetap target, no doubt because in the 1950s she founded Women for World

Disarmament.[68] What is revealed in such cases is the routine and generally undetected surveillance of all kinds of citizens for all kinds of reasons by agencies whose activities are usually only weakly restricted by law.

Undoubtedly, then, the use of information technology for the surveillance systems used in national security has massively augmented their capacities. Indeed, the American NSA is itself a world leader in telecommunications, and oversaw the development of IBM's encryption system for coding secret messages, which is now in general use, for instance, in electronic banking.[69] As with other areas in which new surveillance technologies have been adopted, it is worth asking how far the policies and priorities of security agencies are subject to democratic accountability. Such matters are highly controversial in most contemporary societies; the rapidly growing dependence of national security on new technology only makes it more urgent that these matters are confronted.

State Surveillance, Citizenship and Globalization

Societies that claim to be democratic imply by that term that there is a degree of involvement by the citizenry in the political process. Governments thus claim to be responsive to citizens, who are viewed as political equals.[70] This situation, in which the state relies less on force and more on administrative surveillance to keep order, assumes what Giddens calls a 'dialectic of control'; that is, citizens have the right to answer back, to make a difference, because the power of the state depends on the compliance of its citizens. In particular, citizenship since the Second World War has been articulated with full social participation in the sense of having certain 'rights' – and, recently, defending those rights – in the welfare state.

The question raised sharply by this chapter and the previous one is how far that dialectic of control still operates when the technologies used for surveillance seem in some instances to swing the balance of power in favour of the agencies of social control. Can citizenship be assumed and assured on the same grounds as it was in the halcyon pre-recessionary days of state welfare? But there is another question as well. Is it adequate to speak only of 'balances of power' when the use of databases seems to be blurring these very categories – such as state or individual citizen – with which we conventionally operate?

We have seen that in various ways information technology is implicated significantly in changes occurring in policing and security, from the establishment of national identification systems and computer matching programmes to pre-emptive policing and scarcely visible monitoring of citizens. Without doubt, surveillance has intensified in certain spheres, but is this really eroding citizenship? Again, in terms of conventional, modern analysis the answer would probably be yes. But my first caution is that gauging which 'rights' are augmented and which diminished as new technology systems proliferate is exceedingly hard. The second is that the categories within which discussion takes place are steadily losing their salience.

Take the first caution. One crucial feature of contemporary surveillance by government agencies is the broadening 'spectrum of suspicion'. A kind of paranoia seems to have gripped not only the agencies of social control, but citizens of the advanced societies themselves. The apparently arbitary suspicions of those involved in social control, discernible in the novel categories of deviance and the profiling of potential rule-breakers, spills over into public life. The phenomenon of 'video vigilantes' demonstrates this most clearly; in this citizens carrying camcorders record events from police treatment of tranffic offences to babysitters' handling of their charges.[71]

Precisely such 'video vigilantism' lay behind the charges of white police beating a black man – Rodney King – and the notorious acquittal that set the torch to Los Angeles in May 1992. All had seen the video film of the beating, made by an amateur bystander, and many were justly outraged by the judgement. One thing this indicates, however, is that even when the camcorder is in the hands of 'ordinary citizens' this is insufficient to swing the so-called dialectic of control back in their favour. Nonetheless, benefits of new technology are far from monopolised by dominant social groups, as we have seen. In the ex-Soviet Union, as we saw, information technology was used effectively against those in power. No simplistic zero-sum analysis is appropriate.

The range of issues raised, secondly, includes a well-worn list of the familiar categories of privacy, autonomy, secrecy, accountability, as well as the question of which metaphors and images help us most – Orwell's 'Big Brother', Bentham's Panopticon or yet others. But it also raises issues of what citizenship comprises – for instance in situations where the pursuit of national ID systems would also classify people by ethnicity – and of what consequences follow the increasingly global character of both surveillance and citizenship. With both intelligence surveillance and, as we shall see in Chapter Eight, marketing surveillance increasingly ignoring the territorial boundaries of the nation-state, the time has come for rethinking citizenship in the light – among other things – of surveillance.[72]

Some of the issues touched upon here are amenable at least in part to legal remedy, whereas others, such as the putative reinforcement of 'underclass' status or the processes of criminalization encouraged by new technology, call for social and political remedies. Others, that relate to less tangible but no less real matters like the definition of individual persons within their data-image, require not only fresh thought but also understanding and action at an international level. So far from there being any quick technical fix, it appears that the struggle to understand and where necessary regulate state and supra-state surveillance systems will be long and difficult.

7

The Transparent Worker

Chaplin and Chips

Movie-goers with good memories will recall the image of Charlie Chaplin meshed with the cogs and gears of an assembly line factory in *Modern Times*. The film epitomized one of the key themes of anti-modernism in the 1930s. In this attack against the mechanization of life, Chaplin parodied the breaking down of activity into its component parts for time-and-motion analysis and the subsequent detailed instruction to each worker – the system known as scientific management or Taylorism. He tried unsuccessfully to move faster than the line in order to get a break, ending in a whirl of wrenches. If ever a film depicted the desired – but incomplete! – compliance of workers within 'Fordist' mass production it was *Modern Times*.

Curiously enough, IBM recycled Chaplin in computer advertising of the mid-1980s. But now the dapper, bowler-hatted gent of the information age sits astride a high stool in a shiny-smooth environment before a keyboard and monitor, fully in control. Or so it appears. But how close to reality is the new image? The mechanized control of workers churning out cars, cookers or cabinets with standardized parts, undoubtedly represents an accurate picture of Fordism, the system inaugurated by Henry Ford in Detroit. Taylorism, its management method, achieved a high degree of supervisory scrutiny; workers were aware of being under its eye. Are things different now?

Today, capitalist activity is slowly moving away from mass production of standardized goods, and into the era of what some call 'post-Fordist' flexible production of designer commodities, with infinite consumer choice. Just-in-Time management and Total Quality Control devolve responsibility within the factory. Does this mean that the old supervision and control will become a thing of the past? Certainly, new technology is central to today's production, in the office as well as in the factory. But computers are also deeply implicated in the processes of consumption. They permit much closer attention to demand, much more scope for customized products.

For example, the system of daily supermarket ordering to meet the perceived desires of the day is transposed into a different key in vehicle production. Indeed, the founder of Toyota got the initial inspiration for a new way of making cars on a visit to an American supermarket.[1] What consumers see as more individualized products is merely the public face of a whole new system in which the circulation of capital speeds up, and labour control and organization undergoes quite radical change.[2]

But what does this mean, specifically, for surveillance? This chapter attempts to get at the heart of the question; does new technology help propel us into 'Postmodern Times' as far as workplace surveillance is concerned? Would Charlie Chaplin have discerned any continuities between his Fordist factory and today's flexible manufacturing – which now even extends to film-making itself? Or would he be forced to conclude that only a quite different analysis would be adequate? This chapter suggests, among other things, that it is as big a mistake to imagine that new technology produces new social relations as it is to think that it simply reflects or reproduces old ones.

In order to understand social relations, old and new, in the capitalistic workplace, several tasks confront us. We must start by recalling the centrality of surveillance to capitalist techniques; how indeed capitalist surveillance forms one of two dominant threads in the tapestry of modern surveillance systems. At the same time, it is clear from the empirical evidence that surveillance involving new technology cannot be reduced simplistically to the operations of capital. While in some ways it may express capitalist relations, the surveillance consequences of new technology are often unintended.[3]

Secondly, we must evaluate scientific management and explore the connections between 'Taylorism' and technology. Thirdly, we will examine the shifts to post-Fordism or flexible manufacturing, including service delivery. Information technology helps to extend surveillance across all economic spheres, and also increases its international impact, which was unknown in the days of print or even telephone media.[4] But it is not more extensive, it is more intensive too. In the fourth and fifth sections of this chapter we survey the variety of work settings in which surveillance and new technology ae implicated, and look at a number of cases of computerization to assess their lessons regarding surveillance. In each case, the increased depth of penetration of the 'gaze' is remarkable.

Lastly we return to the question of capitalism, what kinds of challenge, in surveillance and social control, are thrown up by post-Fordist times? Once again, it seems that the challenge of surveillance appears in its own right. Economic restructuring, and the use of new technologies in particular, make it less and less plausible to think of surveillance simply as a reflex of capitalism. It is a mode of power mediation which, while displaying some traits amenable to analysis in terms of Adorno's 'administered society', Foucault's 'disciplinary society', Marx's class-conflict society and so on, may not be reduced to any one of them.

The Watched Workplace

Nestling in the hills of West Yorkshire lies the model village of Saltaire. Sir Titus Salt, who founded this Victorian enterprise as a shining example of 'capitalism with a human face', knew just what he was doing. Apart from the entrepreneurially brilliant siting of the new town, well outside smoky industrial Bradford and at a point where river, railway and canal converged, he also paid close attention to internal order. Within the vast textile mill, which employed three thousand workers, machines lined the floor in long ranks, and were easily overseen by the foremen.

Outside the mill, the hierarchy of order was reproduced architecturally. The row of workers' houses, stretching up the street, was punctuated by slightly larger dwellings on the corners, occupied by those same foremen and their families. The bell that summoned the workforce could be heard from every corner of the town. While Salt supplied many amenities such as laundries, libraries and a hospital, he deliberately excluded any drinking from the town; no public houses appeared within its boundaries.[5]

Here we see clearly the collusion of surveillance and social control in the context of a capitalist workplace. The locale, the physical space within which productive action occurs, is carefully controlled by means of organizational supervision. The problem faced by early industrial employers was how to control large numbers of people in the workplace without using the kind of physical force that characterized, say, the building of pyramids in ancient Egypt.[6] The answer lay in new modes of industrial management. Labour entered into a contract with employers in order to gain a living. Employers in their turn kept close watch over workers' activities; monitoring was a means to discipline. Imposing sanctions, and later offering financial incentives ensured their control. The benefit to workers lay in the formal freedom to dispose of their labour-power in whatever situation they chose. The benefit to employers was a productive, and, they hoped, docile labour-force, under their eye.[7]

A familiar starting-point for the analysis of surveillance within the capitalist workplace is the work of Karl Marx. He realised that locating workers under one roof was a key means of keeping control. He also anticipated that new technologies would be developed to maintain that control, quoting Andrew Ure to make his point: the self-acting mule was 'a creation destined to restore order among the industrious classes. . . when capital enlists science into her service, the refractory hand of labour will always be taught docility.'[8] In the later twentieth century Harry Braverman revived Marx's account and attempted to bring it up to date with reference to new technology, arguing that capital constantly subordinates labour through a division between the 'conception' and 'execution' of labour. In other words, capitalism encourages control by those 'in the know' over those who merely carry out predetermined tasks. According to Braverman, the latter thus become a de-skilled and increasingly homogeneous group.[9]

For Max Weber, on the other hand, the process of bureaucratic surveillance in the workplace had as much to do with the socially distinct impetus to rationalize production as with control by a capitalist class. If bureaucratic social organization proved itself technically superior to other means of discipline, it was likely to be adopted in situations of growing competition. Organizational imperatives were at work, according to Weber, that pointed logically to the 'visible hand' of management supervision as the most efficient way of shaping economic life.[10] A hierarchical bureaucracy allows managers to predict, from a knowledge of files, that their wishes will be carried out. Knowledge and discipline are thus fused.[11]

Going beyond bureaucracy, Michel Foucault argued that surveillance in the capitalist workplace is just one instance of the rise of the kind of disciplinary society that characterizes the modern world. The timing and spacing of human activity is a prime means of regulating social life. Power and knowledge are chronically wrapped together. The Panopticon, which was elaborated by Bentham as prison architecture, not only derived from but, for Foucault, reappeared in the capitalist factory. The very architecture of the workshop made workers highly visible and thus amenable to attempts at complete control by their supervisors. In this perspective, however, if 'techniques of power are invented to meet the demands of production' then such 'production can include the production of destruction, as with the army'.[12]

This connects back to Dandeker's interesting observation, often neglected in the history of capitalist enterprises, that business benefits from military experience and that workplace discipline derives in part at least from military discipline. Dandeker notes the familiar case made that military competition between nation states can galvanize capitalist activity, but emphasises as well that military-style organization *within* firms lay behind much scientific management. The splitting of military organizations into ranks and divisions in the quest of greater efficiency, for instance, reappears in the structure of the business firm. The system of 'Command, Control, Communication and Intelligence' or '3CI' may be discerned in internal management strategy and, as we shall see, in the realm of consumption.[13]

Certain crucial changes occurred in the managerial control of labour during the nineteenth century. Sir Titus Salt stands at the watershed between the older, more personal systems of control within the workplace, and the newer, less personal managerial style that was to emerge in the twentieth century. According to David Dickson, textile factories were set up for four reasons: to control and market everything produced and thus avoid being embezzled, to oblige workers to labour longer and faster, to allow technical modifications to take place in ways that would maximize profit and minimize worker resistance, and to make the role of the employer indispensable.[14] An interesting illustration of items two and three is a work-timing clock, now in Bradford Industrial Museum, that adjusted its pace according to the flow of stream-water feeding the mill. In this case even external factors over which the capitalist had no control could be overcome by technical means!

Similar but more subtle processes are discernible in the development of American companies in the second half of the nineteenth century and until the 1920s. During this period, as Joanne Yates has shown,[15] railroad and manufacturing companies altered their management communication style, moving away from the use of quills and pigeonholes to typewriters and telegraphy. Small firms were unable to grow without such innovations, simply because the older methods imposed strict limits on communication needed to hold together more complex enterprises.

However, the technological change was simultaneously a social change, replacing oral and informal management style with more formal bureaucratic written documentation. The meaning of management also altered as the quest, for internal efficiency and 'system' became paramount. Thus the technical innovation was intrinsically bound up with the increasing importance to management of written communications for the control and co-ordination of the expanding companies.

Elements of the Marxian, Weberian, and Foucaldian accounts of surveillance in early capitalism help illuminate what occurred as the discipline of management came into being. One factor they have in common is that workers experienced a major alteration in their daily experience. From toiling in relative independence, and according to the traditional rhythms of seasons, day-and-night, and holy days, workers found themselves labouring to an increasingly rigid timetable, within enclosed spaces, ever observed by a supervisory eye.

Taylorism and Technology

Much hangs on the question of how far new technology extends Taylorism, or scientific management. For Taylorism developed from early industrial management and was tightly tied to the introduction of new techniques for standardization of products, cost reduction to remain competitive, centralization of planning, hierarchical authority, and rigid organization based on highly specific job descriptions. Henry Ford's car production lines examplified such scientific management. Just as hand-loom weavers were undercut in the 1830s, so Ford undercut craft-built cars. His Model T sold for less than a tenth of the normal price in 1916, and he took fifty per cent of the market.[16] To understand today's debate over computers and management, therefore, we must first grasp what was going on in Ford's factories.

Scientific management essentially involves three processes: controlling and evaluating what workers actually do from day to day and from moment to moment so that costs can be counted accurately, integrating this with detailed control of production, and planning and monitoring production by means of new central management staff, who also gather and distribute information in new ways.[17] From the 1880s onward, such scientific managing developed apace. Cards or tickets were used to transmit order requests from the engineering office to the foremen and workers, who would send back work-tasks and cost estimates which soon included detailed breakdowns of parts required. Machinery, used above all in automobile production lines, increased the speed of production flow. This is turn meant heavier capital–intensity and a growing complexity of administrative tasks.

F.W. Taylor, who gave his name to scientific management, initiated systems of central management control over a hierarchy of workers, each of whom had specific tasks. Much energy went into planning and careful deployment of resources. Hence the concern with what each task involved, how long it took, and how much it was worth. Harry Braverman took up just these issues in the 1970s, arguing that they paved the way for tightening management control of labour through the adoption of new technology. He focused on the transformation of knowledge involved in work-tasks, from traditional rules-of-thumb and informal guesswork to formal 'scientific' procedures, the widening divide between those who plan and those who actually do the job, and the precise specification and monitoring of workers engaged on each task.[18]

In this account, new technology figures prominently as a key means of bureaucratizing labour management. Indeed, it has also been referred to as 'technical control'.[19] Although Braverman's work sparked a vigorous controversy, in which several of his ideas on de-skilling and management control have successfully been refuted,[20] his work still stimulates or informs further study.

David Noble, for instance, argues that computerized automation is seen by employers as a means of reinforcing managerial power. In his study of machine tool operations he argues that managers tried to maintain their control by keeping crucial decisions in the central office rather than on the shop floor. Faced with a technical choice they opted not for 'record playback', which would have left more autonomy on the shop-floor, but for a 'computer-numerical' system that did not. To their chagrin, however, managers not only experiencd sustained resistance from machinists, but also found they still needed skilled machinists on the shop-floor.[21]

Others have drawn upon Braverman to show how gender relations are also important in understanding the role of new technology on workplace supervision and control. In the UK, for instance, Jane Barker and Hazel Downing proposed that automation – in this case word-processing – is designed to eliminate the non-productive time lost in the personal relations of a 'social office'.[22] The machines themselves can be used for supervision – counting keystrokes, for instance – and can also contribute to de-skilling of tasks. This kind of analysis has given rise to a general impression among commentators that production and clerical workers are the most likely candidates for technologically-intensified surveillance.

How far is this justified? Braverman's work tends to oversimplify matters. He has justly been criticized for romanticizing the traditional craft-worker to contrast with the 'de-skilling' of workers in automated settings, exaggerating the adoption of a 'pure' Taylorism across firms and within them, overstating the distinction between the 'conception' or 'planning' of tasks and their execution, wrongly assuming a singleness of vision of capitalist employers and managers, and failing to acknowledge the knowledgeability of workers and the extent of their resistance. Much variety attends the introduction of new technology , in different countries, in different industries and within different managerial and industrial relations traditions. It is by no means clear that changes are uniform or as predictable as Braverman and his disciples might imply.

What we can say is that new styles of management are progressively more bound up with the use of new technologies and that employees are subjected to intensified forms of surveillance. Workers typically find themselves more watched, not just by managers but by workmates and, in a sense, by themselves. This does not necessarily entail greater control of workers by management, or mean that new technologies render particular group less powerful, still less that information technology is deployed in order to subordinate the workforce or that it has a determining effect on social relations. It does seem to help maintain the position of capital within the workplace, keeping the basically unequal relations between it and labour in place when older methods of management have started to fail. But to see it merely in this light is to miss its broader significance.

Towards Disorganized Surveillance?

Fordism attempted to make production predictable, and in management, to ensure certainty through surveillance. But Fordism failed. From the 1960s on, demand became more specialized, fragmented and volatile. Industrial strife struck productivity levels. Investment fell with profits. Oil prices soared. And culturally, Fordism was felt to have put everyone in 'little boxes, just the same'. Governments tried to shore up the old system with Keynesian buttresses and then, mixing metaphors, to dose it with monetarist medicine. Meanwhile the economic system itself adjusted by using new technology and new production methods. Fordism became flexible.

One important aspect of Fordism's failure was the increasing levels of difficulty experienced by older bureaucratic management in the workplace. Especially in large enterprises, the problems of supervision grew to unwieldy proportions as more and more layers of management were required to monitor labour. They cost more, the flow of information slowed down as the conduits became clogged with data, and some managers appeared to forget the ultimate aims of the enterprise in their concern to keep the whole system running according to the rules. Both workers and managers could lose any sense of motivation, becoming dissatisfied and alienated, with resulting further costs to capital in terms of absenteeism and resistance.[23]

This is the backdrop to the changing face of surveillance in the workplace and indeed beyond it. In several different kinds of contexts we shall see how new technology is implicated in the attempt to overcome the difficulties of Fordist surveillance and workplace control. As I observed earlier, new technology does not in itself produce new social relations, neither does it simply reflect or reproduce old ones. This is the error of an easy equation between surveillance by computers and a sort of neo-Taylorism. In many post-Fordist contests, surveillance transcends traditional Taylorism.[24]

Toyota car production, for instance, does not assume that management has or should have a monopoly of information needed for constant innovation. Toyota dispenses with de-skilling because producing quality goods depends on multi-skilled manual workers. On the other hand, this may mean that fewer workers are required for a given productive process, so that other problems – unemployment – are obscured. So while computers are certainly used for control, this often means control of processes rather than people. At the same time, people are still finding that their work activities are scrutinized, though they themselves might do the scrutinizing.

Not that there are no human costs in post-Fordism.[25] Most obviously, peripheral, non-unionized workers – in First and Third worlds – are disadvantaged in relation to the skilled, long-term workers. But this is better seen as part of a more general upheaval, in which management too undergoes considerable change. At least at Toyota, the rigid hierarchy of Ford's management system gives way to greater decentralization, horizontal teamwork and local autonomy. As far as surveillance is concerned, all manner of groups and positions are vulnerable to greater scrutiny.

The general upheaval I refer to gives new weight to consumption. Mass production systems always ran the risk that with too little stock they would lose market shares and with too much they could glut the market and be stuck with stagnant warehouses. By analysing consumption patterns, production is now geared to finding the market niche, the consumer cluster.[26] The accent is on customized quality goods. New technology enables small-scale batch production, whether in automobiles or the colours of Benetton sweatshirts.

In fact, the customer may take on an unaccustomed role of 'manager'. The customer ethos of the company may mean that workers receive data from customers as a means of retaining discipline. Bell Telephone operators in North America are routinely informed of customer responses. Supermarket check-out operators may get similar treatment or even be visited by supervisors posing as customers. Carefully recorded customer responses – compiled automatically by computer – are increasingly used to discipline workers.[27] A similar process is at work in universities. Professors are subject to the discipline of having citations of their work, recorded within the databases of journal scholarship, checked as a means of assessing their worth, which imposes a need to publish where citations count.[28]

At the same time, information technology also permits the sub-division of productive organizations into different countries and the free flow of capital from one part of the globe to another. Dispersed units can be controlled remotely, using the same technologies. Surveillance and control of subsidiary companies is made feasible by new communications technologies, however distant the parent company. American Airlines (AA), for example, pioneered a novel form a power relation with their SABRE reservations system in the late 1970s. From the early 1980s, each computer terminal installed by AA in a travel agent's office has captured an extra thirty per cent in ticket sales for AA. While data on the terminal relates to all airlines, they do so with a bias towards AA. This form of 'electronic handcuffing', which 'locks up' customers, has in some ways become more importnt than the airline itself. It has also been adopted by others including Cabbage Patch Dolls and the American Hospital Supply Corporation, which has used it damagingly against Johnson & Johnson.[29]

Such transformations of the way goods are produced and the parallel growth in the service sector has stimulated debate about how to characterize the new situation. Those discerning a decline in the centrality of capitalism see 'postindustrial society'.[30] Others, for whom capitalism still seems tremendously significant, write of 'disorganized capitalism'.[31] This debate is important for understanding workplace supervision, because clearly the previous changes in capitalism involved considerable expansion of surveillance systems such as scientific management.

Scott Lash and John Urry, for instance, trace what they claim is a reversal of bureaucratic and centralizing tendencies; hence 'disorganized capitalism'. Christopher Dandeker, on the other hand, for whom bureaucracy and surveillance seem inescapably linked, prefers the term 'reorganized capitalism'.[32] There is another alternative, however, which is to see one function of new technology as permitting a split between surveillance and bureaucratic methods of management. In this account capitalism retains its salience and its reliance on new technology, but within a flexible, post-Fordist framework, geared primarily not to production but to consumption. Are we witness to the coming of 'disorganized surveillance'?

It seems to me that a concept such as 'disorganized surveillance' would indeed begin to do justice to the complexities of contemporary practices. New technologies permit a relaxing of centralized, bureaucratic management supervision and monitoring. But they simultaneously make possible a new intensity of surveillance, penetrating much more deeply into the daily routines of workers. Random checking – for instance of telephone operators' dealings with customers – and the tracing of defective goods to their origins by quality control become the order of the day. However, within any concept of disorganized surveillance must also be scope for variety based upon the intrinsic differences between types of production, as the following examples show.

The Transparent Worker

In the mid-1970s, following a case of employee theft, closed circuit TV cameras were mounted around the Puretex Knitting Company in Toronto. Not only were production, storage, shipping, and loading areas covered, but even the women's washroom was now under the eye of the camera. Workers, to whom no explanation had been given, were upset. They filed a complaint about invaded privacy under the Ontario Human Rights Code. They went on strike. Three years later, the cameras were removed. Professor Ellis, the arbitrator, commented that 'electronic surveillance is the ultimate socializing device and the public controversy which always attends its use attests to people's instinctive identification of its fundamentally anti-human character'.[33]

By the early 1990s, the Puretex union victory notwithstanding, electronic surveillance in the workplace has become far more extensive and intensive. Indeed, the limitations of workplace are themselves less significant. Data-entry workers at keyboards in their homes or even in countries other than where their company is located may have their acitivity electronically monitored. And the long-distance truck driver's tachometer enables employers to know how long were the breaks taken, how fast the truck travelled, and so on.[34]

Even before one gets a job pre-employment screening is often very rigorous. In Britain, up to a million jobs are subject to security checks, not only for government positions, but also for employment within the BBC and British Telecom.[35] But many other companies use agencies such as the Economic League, which holds large personal databases and vets 200,000 job applicants a year. A worker on an induction programme at Ford in Essex, England was dismissed after three days due to 'unsatisfactory checks' on his work record. He had been dismissed previously from car-making rival Austin-Morris as an alleged political activist.[36] But not only political activism appears as a threat; so-called 'computer terrorism' in the form of hacking, virus-placing and high-tech secrets espionage is another fear that encourages candidate vetting.[37]

Once employed, workers may have to use an array of plastic cards to gain entry to their workplace, or to areas within it. Some of these feature biometric security systems, such as electronically stored fingerprints, retinal patterns or voice tests[38]; and some may ensure safety, such as those used in nuclear power plants. Forms of electronic tagging may perform the same function, for instance on off-shore oil drilling rigs.[39]

These techniques have developed from the time clock device mentioned earlier. Night watchmen were issued with keyed clocks, to prove they had completed their rounds and to allow companies to pinpoint times when break-ins might have occurred. Barcoding techniques now allow employers to break down employee days into minute-by-minute allocatable hours for billing purposes as well as to measure efficiency. Coded security locks are also used to limit access to specific parts of plant or offices.

Such devices help keep track of, and manipulate, the timing and spacing of work. They serve to pinpoint the location of workers to management at any given moment. The actual pace or quality of work done may also be subject to electronic monitoring. Keystroke counting is just one rather obvious example of such automated supervision. Others include data security systems, retail check-out clerks, telephone operators, and the checking of telephone calls and other communications. In a recent California lawsuit Epson, the electronics company, was accused of reading employees' electronic mail[40] messages.

Hardly surprising, then, that companies using new technology surveillance attract descriptions like 'the omniscient organization.'[41] New forms of surveillance in the workplace are often less obtrusive, but more invasive. Beyond the workplace, vetting techniques may permanently exclude certain classes of would-be workers.[42] We referred earlier to Shoshana Zuboff's conclusion that new technology produces a situation of panoptic transparency for workers, inducing 'anticipatory conformity'.[43] Her contention is that such transparency serves the purpose of 'total control'. But is this the only, or the best, way of understanding transparency in the 'omniscient organization'?

Accounts like the one I have just given have the virtue of indicating both the range of work-surveillance technologies available and the variety of settings within which they operate. No occupation, it seems, is immune from surveillance when computer technology is at work, and the significance of this should not be underrated. In a post-Fordist context, surveillance touches not only traditional sites of productive activity, but offices and informal situations like restaurants and taxi-cab companies. The space-binding capacity of electronic technologies even diminishes the significance of the location where work occurs.

On the other hand, the danger of accounts that begin with new technology and proceed to detail its supposed impacts is that sociology is effectively abandoned in favour of high-tech journalism. This spawns a lopsided emphasis on the novelty and capacity of new gizmos and gadgets, which may then jump straight to questions either of how you too may take advantage of this advanced computer-power, or of legal or other limits to technology, depending on the perspective taken. Even when sociology is brought back in, as in the rich ethnography of Zuboff's *In the Age of the Smart Machine,* panoptic imagery may mislead regarding management aspirations for 'total control', or assumptions about who is vulnerable to surveillance may divert attention from just who is being watched.[44]

Computer-Intensified Surveillance

A few years ago an article appeared in *Industrial Engineering* entitled 'Office Automation Provides Opportunity to Examine What Workers Actually Do'.[45] Information technology permits managers to scrutinize work tasks to a degree of detail undreamed by F.W. Taylor. But as a group of sociologists at the state University of New York (SUNY), Stony Brook, discovered in a systematic analysis of a variety of firms in New York State, such computerized scrutiny of workers itself requires closer investigation.

What the SUNY team found gives further content to the notion of disorganized surveillance, but this time in terms of its unanticipated consequences. They discovered that computer surveillance may not reflect the original intention of managers, and may affect workers on whom surveillance was not necessarily meant to be carried out. At the same time, they say, the use of new technology for surveillance may represent little more than 'computerized Taylorism'.[46]

The New York study indicates that computers allow managers to 'see' more clearly and precisely what occurs within their businesses. Among other things managers are better able to scrutinize exactly what workers are doing and how well they do it. Personnel surveillance is not necessarily the primary aim, but it turns out to be an important factor. Thus for instance in the 'Dockside Grill' mentioned in the New York study waiters and waitresses take orders and enter them discreetly onto a terminal, which is their only contact with kitchen staff. Customers get exactly, and only, what they ordered. But from this data the manager can discover who serves what, when, and how effectively compared with others. Thus deeper access or knowledge into processes, and potentially greater control over them, is yielded.[47] But achieving that greater control was not the objective managers originally had in mind.

In another example from the same New York study, 'Mercury taxicabs' computerized its dispatch service. The woman managing Mercury developed a system for requesting cabs that discriminated between the wealthy Manhattan lawyers, who paid for preferential treatment, and ordinary members of the public. The latter may be informed on a snowy night that no cabs are available when in fact prioritized customers get cabs in under ten minutes. But the same system generates reports on telephone operators and cab-drivers, indicating the number of calls handled or fares taken, thus again permitting deeper reach into working lives than is possible without the computer.[48]

Such workers become aware, of course, that individual performance is more closely observed, and this itself may have a disciplinary effect. Direct attempts at greater management control over workers, usng surveillance data, may be counter-productive in that they generate resistance. But awareness of individual accountability may have a self-discipling effect, rendering direct control superfluous. In Powerco, a British insurance company, for example, where clerks introduced to computer technology increased their interaction with the terminal at the expense of interaction with co-workers and managers, just this occurred. 'We've got no one else to blame for the backlog now', they admitted. Without adopting the new technology to achieve this effect, managers derive extra control without bureaucratic or mechanical help, owing to self-discipline.[49]

Zuboff's study comments mainly on computerized surveillance in large scale operations, and concludes that production and clerical workers are especially vulnerable. By contrast, the New York study looked at a far bigger sample of firms (184), but their average staff was fifty-seven employees, and this shows that predicting which groups are vulnerable to surveillance is tricky. In the latter study, distinctions were made between three areas of job surveillance; sales analysis, work-order tracking and inventory control. Whether in steel parts fabrication sales, or a veterinary clinic work order system, or warehouse inventory, managers obtain deeper knowledge of workers by computer monitoring.

As to the kinds of workers affected, the New York study showed production workers are certainly subject to surveillance, but clerical workers less than proportionally among all staff. Sales and marketing staff, on the other hand, who made up 8.6 per cent of all workers comprise 18.63 per cent of those subjected to computerized surveillance.[50] The explanation offered for this is that computer surveillance of work tasks is frequently a by-product of computerization for other purposes. In a printing company, for instance, means were sought of informing customers exactly where their orders were within the plant, and how long they would have to wait for delivery. As it turned out, this entailed closer examination of work tasks, and thus of workers, than was previously possible. Staff performance came under review as an indirect and unanticipated consequence of improving customer relations.[51] A case of 'disorganized surveillance' again?

For a final example, let us turn to 'Kay', a foreign-owned electronic consumer goods manufacturer in Britain. Here, so-called Japanese management styles have been adopted to great effect, particularly 'Just-in-

Time' (JIT) and 'Total Quality 'Control' (TQC).[52] JIT tries to match production with the marketplace, tying supply to demand inside and outside the factory, with no shortages, no stockpiles and no waste. TQC on the other hand attempts to build into production the satisfaction of consumer desires. The two always appear together as they virtually require each other.

Graham Sewell and Barry Wilkinson argue that JIT/TQC at Kay more resemble the Panopticon than the conventional bureaucratic management pyramid. They focus in particular on the heightened visibility present where JIT/TQC regimes operate. The factory is deliberately organized to facilitate seeing the products in process. Managers can more quickly pinpoint problems and assign blame under such conditions. In TQC, moreover, each operator is responsible for her or his own quality, thus becoming in Foucault's terms the 'bearer of their own surveillance'. Failure to note faults is immediately detected electronically and traced back to the operator. The UK Nissan plant runs a 'employee peer surveillance' system, in which workers watch their neighbours, again relieving management of certain supervisory tasks. This all relates back to the 'customer ethos' mentioned earlier.

Sewell and Wilkinson see this as part of a general process in which Rule's surveillance capacities can be enhanced electronically within the workplace. The physical presence pf the overseer is required less and less, the factory can be open-plan, middle-management can be dissolved, and responsibility devolved. But central management sees far better than before exactly what is going on, and has new sanctions – the self-discipline of the workers – to ensure ultimate control. The question is, what will happen when workers, with all their new responsibilities for quality, ask why management is needed at all? Holding on to the means of surveillance is the only remaining basis of power that managers have over their workers.

Post-Fordism, Disorganized Surveillance and Beyond

The peril of 'post-' prefixes lies in their suggestive power. They often imply that major social has already occurred. Especially in tandem with real enough technological transformations, the post-modern' or 'post-Fordist' or 'post-industrial' can be highly misleading. Moreover, they can generate pseudo-debates in which participants talk past each other, the one emphasizing altered circumstance, the other stressing persistence and continuity.

Such, I suggest, is the case with the debate over workplace surveillance. Zuboff's very book title emphasizes the 'machine'. She stresses discontinuity and transformation following the adoption of computer systems. But Rule and others involved in the New York study are sceptical. They see computerized Taylorism. Dandeker, too, wants to retain the connection between bureaucratic organization and surveillance. While Rule and Dandeker acknowledge enhanced surveillance capacities, such expansion is in a context characterized by continuity, not transformation.

The introduction of microelectronic technology in the workplace should not be seen on its own but against the backdrop of changing patterns of economic enterprise and management. 'Post-Fordism' represents not an entirely novel social formation but a significant departure from the old Fordist ways of mass production that simultaneously runs parallel with them. The emphasis on consumption is both enabled by and stimulates further uses of information technology. Management adopts such technologies both to pursue traditional goals of co-ordination and information exchange between divisions and the internal supervision of the workplace, and in the quest for market niches, customer service and even the 'electronic handcuffing' – also related to JIT/TQC – of companies and clients. This is 'disorganized surveillance'.

While in some companies a conventional Taylorism is 'technologized', is others worker surveillance is an unintended consequence of the constant quest for greater efficiency, productivity and, crucially, profitability. As we saw, Taylorism itself seldom appeared in a pure form; today it is a shadow of its former self. Much more significant is the anticipatory conformity noted by Zuboff in the Cedar Bluff pulp mill[53] and the self-disciplining practice exhibited in the 'Powerco' insurance company or in 'Kay,' the electronics factory. Agreed, both Zuboff and the New York researchers see a kind of perfected Taylorism in new technology surveillance, but surely the new surveillance has as many different features as similar ones?

Rule and Brantley wonder where Zuboff derived her evidence for positive attitudes among workers who welcome computer technology. They found none among their New York samples.[54] But Knights and Sturdey, who conducted the UK study, also found positive attitudes, and interpret them in terms of a greater sense of control granted workers by new technology.[55] Nonetheless, it is precisely this sense of control that paradoxically encourages workers to self-discipline and thus to comply with the norms of the organization. But this is a far cry from the overwhelmingly negative, de-skilling, coercive effects of surveillance and technical control that reading Bravereman would lead one to expect.

This kind of analysis does not deny for a moment that workplace surveillance is intensified by means of new technology. What is questioned, however, is whether the new technology alone causes the effects, and whether the new effects relate to the old causes. That is to say, new technologies are adopted, often in an *ad hoc* manner, in the context of post-Fordist practice. And that post-Fordist practice plainly differs from the old Taylorism, so that today's surveillance engenders self-discipline and anticipatory conformity rather than mere management control.

Such distancing from Braverman's capitalist conspiracies should not be interpreted as complacency, however. Real and urgent questions are raised by intensified workplace surveillance. Questions of human dignity and the addressing of genuine fears that relate to greater worker transparency were highlighted by Ellis in the case of the Puretex Knitting Company video cameras. Questions of the appropriate limits to what seems to be an ongoing process of work task scrutiny by computer; questions of alternative sytems that might be less threatening, less intrusive, less individualistic; recall David Noble's argument about computer-numerical control machine tools. Management did not have 'no choice' in that case.[56]

Indeed, it is precisely management choice that Noble stresses. One system of automated production in the machine tool shop, numerical control, was selected over another, so-called record playback. Record playback retained vestigial human skills and was thus seen as a potential source of threat, not entirely under management control. Computer numerical control won the day because it appeared to fit better with management purposes. Social choices thus informed that particular technical development, choices that, for Noble, mirror the relations of production.

Such naked desire for management control may not necessarily be as widespread in the 1990s as it apparently was in the 1970s. But the adoption of new technologies – either for direct surveillance purposes or that have indirect surveillance effects – in the capitalistic workplace is no less subject to choices. Decisions may be about actual machines, or about management styles such as JIT/TQC. Exposing such choices, how they are made and by whom, and analysing the social and personal realities consequent upon them – including the possibility that new *kinds* of power may be involved here – is a vital task for contemporary social analysis. The least we can say is that the advent of disorganized surveillance offers new opportunities for the exploration of alternatives to choices based merely on the criteria of efficiency, profitability, or doubts about workers' intelligence or reliability.

8

The Targeted Consumer

Junk Mail Marketing

A few weeks after passing a driver's test to obtain a new licence for use in Ontario, I received an invitation to join the Canadian Automobile Association (CAA). Had the Ministry of Transportation told them the news, I mused? Telephone enquiry revealed that it was in fact coincidence. CAA buys name-and-address lists from a company called Informart who in turn get them from Bell Canada. I simply showed up as a non-member in a computer matching process called 'merge-purge'. Such direct access to personal data kept by government departments is actually illegal in Canada, but these distinctions are beginning to dissolve.

Junk mail is a phenomenon that was virtually unknown before the closing decades of the twentieth century.[1] It may seem a trivial place to start, but junk mail encapsulates the kernel of consumer surveillance. Where do all those 'personalized' advertisements come from? And what do they mean, sociologically? The answer is that many companies wishing to sell goods and services have access to the electronic means of extremely precise targeting of potential customers. They know exactly where we live, with whom we live, what we earn, and how we spend it. And the sociological meaning? Junk mail is one important item of evidence that the advanced societies are in an era of 'consumer capitalism'. Self-identity and social integration are now articulated with the marketplace, not the workplace. But, paradoxically, the world of consumer freedom is also the world of social control.

Put briefly, this paradoxical argument runs thus. Coercive means of maintaining social order within capitalist nation states have shrunk to the point that they are of only marginal importance. The margin is necessary, however, because it leaves in place a reference group of people, an underclass if you will, whose non-consuming fate is worth avoiding at all costs. For the majority, though, consumption has become the all-absorbing, morally-guiding, and socially-integrating feature of contemporary life in the affluent societies. Social order – and thus a soft form of social control – is maintained through stimulating and channelling consumption, which is where consumer surveillance comes in. But this is achieved in the name of individuality, wideness of choice and consumer freedom.[2]

Returning to junk mail, however, let us look at a couple of examples. Dataman Information Services in Atlanta, Georgia, can call up instantly from a name and address a person's age, the number of children in the household, and the age of the house. In Britain, the computerized capabilities of CCN, a Nottingham-based direct mail database company, has been justly compared in scale with the Police National Computer. In two giant computers are kept details of more than 43,000,000 people, 18,000,000 households, 30,000,000 items of financial information, and over 2,500,000 personal profiles.[3] Marketing companies such as these are attempting to manage consumer demand by matching carefully the income and outlook of individuals with their proffered products. This represents one contribution to the social order of consumer society.

In fact, junk mail may be viewed as the soft end of commercial surveillance; some varieties are much more constraining. When Rudine Pettus failed to secure the lease on a Los Angeles apartment she began to get suspicious, and enquired of one landlord why she was refused. She discovered that she was listed as 'undesirable', and started to investigate how this conclusion had been reached. After considerable delay, she found that a certain 'UD Registry' kept a computer file of her details, gleaned from public information such as court reports, combined with credit ratings, obtained from yet other sources.[4] This, whether justified or not, explained her exclusion from that segment of the housing market.

What is going on here? These preliminary examples yield some clues about what lies before us. The tremendous technical resources of information technology find a vast new field in identifying, tracking, and attempting to channel the consumption activities of householders in the advanced societies. The data gleaned from available records of purchasing patterns and purchasing power are combined both to allure consumers into further specific styles of spending and also to limit the choices of those whose records indicate that at some point they have failed to conform to proper consuming norms, or have transgressed their spending abilities and accrued unacceptable debts.

In this chapter we pursue some themes already discussed in the context of surveillance by capitalist enterprises, in particular the question of how far new technologies extend practices characteristic of the workplace, that is, Taylorism. However, the issue of marketing takes electronic surveillance beyond the workplace and into the home. How far can the argument that new technologies increase surveillance capacity be applied to the domestic sphere as well? Without doubt, the household appears to be a new frontier, a new threshold, across which commercial surveillance is spreading. Even this may however be a false distinction. The monitoring of consumption intensifies surveillance generally, in all the routines of everyday life.

The important question is how far such surveillance also spells social control. It has been said that in twenty-first-century America, Big Brother will not be a political dictator so much as a 'marketing whiz'. [5] But is this analogy correct? Big Brother belongs to the political sphere of the pre-computer age. The social order of consumerism is doubly removed in that its surveillance focuses on the market and is computer-based, which means it has implications well beyond the Orwellian.

We look at the varieties of commercial surveillance, from banks and insurance companies to the proliferating purveyors of direct mail, and examine the role of the information entrepreneurs in this relatively new marketplace. The very fact that it *is* a marketplace is noteworthy; the commodification of data alters its status in some significant ways. Finally, we appraise commercial monitoring of potential consumers in terms of the criteria of surveillance capacity and ask, not only in what ways that capacity has grown, but what the implications are for surveillance theory itself. Are the concepts that were developed to account for surveillance in the modern, production-oriented context equal to the realities of today's consumer society?

Taylorism Transposed?

Commercial, or consumer, surveillance is clearly part of the strategy of capitalist enterprises. As yet, little sociological analysis of commercial surveillance exists. But what there is commonly starts by seeing it as an extension of other kinds of capitalist surveillance, conventionally associated with the workplace. This putative extension is referred to under various headings, one of which is the term 'social management'. Vincent Mosco, among others, uses this idea and he makes two important suggestions; one, that surveillance stretches more broadly and more deeply by means of electronic information services and transactions in the commercial sphere; and two, that the consequences of this go far beyond what can be grasped in terms of a 'threat to privacy'.[6] For Mosco, such commercial surveillance is intrinsically bound up with social control. I agree. But what exactly are its mechanisms? Is consumer surveillance an extension of modern management techniques, or is it part of a different social order, that in which consumerism is central? Beyond this, is surveillance only about social control?

Mosco's is not a straightforwardly Marxist account of the ways that the management motif has spilled out of the factory and into the home. Mosco hints that more than Marxism is needed here. He appeals to Foucault's stress on surveillance occurring at the 'capillary level' of the social organism.[7] Thus no fundamental social transformation takes place. Rather, by a process of accretion, 'powerful electronic systems that measure and monitor transactions for marketing, managing, and controlling groups of people ... build ... on processes of surveillance, marketing, and, control bound only by rapidly shrinking technological limits'.[8] He sees in this a subtle process that atomizes individuals, thus eroding the 'social community' and violating a 'fundamental right of self-determination'. These latter judgements, however, are Mosco's, not Foucault's.

In several extended discussions of the same issues, Kevin Robins and Frank Webster also start by seeing commercial surveillance as an outgrowth from workplace management, and trace the connections through a consideration of Taylorism. Karl Marx, they observe, expressed the classic insight that capitalist work organization deliberately separates mental from manual labour in order to increase productivity and ensure control.[9] Brainwork, in the scientific management schemes of Frederick Taylor, is concentrated in the 'planning department'. But if human skills can be expressed in machinery, then the process of subordinating labour may be streamlined further; the culmination of this is Henry Ford's assembly line.

Kevin Robins and Frank Webster take this much further, observing that the capitalist-generated gathering of knowledge, skill, and information now takes place well beyond the Fordist factory. In short, 'Social Taylorism' appears in the consumer society. The connection between workplace and household surveillance, they argue, may be found in the marketing practices of General Motors' Alfred Sloan. Back in the 1920s he pioneered the use of scientific management principles in commodity markets and consumer behaviour. He collected data on buying habits in order to build profiles of customers.[10] Market research, involving the collation of demographic and socio-economic data, placed great stress on the information-control component of such 'Sloanism'. International Business Machines (IBM) was in the 1930s one of the earliest companies to provide data services to corporations wishing to take advantage of such commercial surveillance.

Today, millions of consumers are subject of efforts aimed at directing their buying behaviour and educating them in consumer skills. New relations of power are exercised, insist Robins and Webster, within the emerging computerized Social Taylorist situation. Indeed, state power should also be seen as part of this equation; it displays Social Taylorist aspects that complement consumerism. The same authors discern many centres of power – perhaps better described by Manuel Castells as 'power flows' or by Lash and Urry as an aspect of 'disorganized capitalism'[11] – within the commercial surveillance context. The ghost of Foucault lurks not far behind this account.

Nonetheless, Robins and Webster are not exchanging Foucault for Marx. They add that 'in each of [the power relations] social knowledge and resources are appropriated and transformed into power and capital'.[12] The link with Taylorism does indeed suggest a fairly direct and coercive connection between 'capital' and 'consumer', and this raises some difficulties. Chiefly, just what kind of power is present here? My own view is that while commercial surveillance undoubtedly links the power of capital with consumer control, it does so in only indirect and uncoercive ways.

Needless to say, some other explanations of the rise of consumer surveillance appear to be rather more benign. From the point of view of the customer, new opportunities and benefits seem to abound with the advent of new technologies harnessed to spending. For instance, you can track accurately all expenditures, receive information about products apparently appropriate to your own circumstances, use convenient 24-hour automated bank machines (ABMs) to obtain cash, and even in some cases order goods and services directly from the supplier using two-way cable services that also advertise those items.

To illustrate popular enthusiasm for consumer items that actually entail fairly intensive probing of personal details, consider this. In the mid-1980s passers-by on a New York street were asked one day their opinion concerning the 'invasion of privacy' by 'modern technology'. Ninety per/cent expressed concern. But the next day, when offered a credit card with a favourable interest rate, ninety per/cent of passers-by on the same street filled in their entirety application forms requiring Social Security number, bank account numbers and information about other credit cards.[13] Consumer surveillance, in this account, is of a piece with designer goods, customized services, and other advances that take us beyond the world of standardized, uniform products and the accompanying limits on consumer choice.[14] Its enabling capacity seems unquestionably desirable.

This latter view may appear palpably naïve, but I shall argue that such a position actually accords well with the above account of social order within consumer capitalism. We have seen how Braverman's bald analysis of labour subordination by new technologies has been largely discredited. So the same kinds of questions that were raised about Taylorism and new technology should also be adduced in the consumer context. Just as a more subtle and nuanced account is called for in the sphere of production, so a careful appraisal must be made of the diverse contexts within which commercial surveillance occurs. Moreover, it is by no means clear what kind of power relations are displayed in the latter sphere. How far is consumption enabled, and how far constrained, by new modes of surveillance? In short, analyses deriving from both Marx and Foucault require careful attention and careful critique.

Three specific tasks, appropriate to such attention and critique, are to examine the 'new frontier' of the household as a site of surveillance, the course of technological innovation in consumer surveillance, and the role of what I call the 'data entrepreneurs' in the marketplace for transactional information. By looking at each of these in turn, and then considering their contribution to surveillance capacity, we shall obtain a better picture of the contemporary role and power of consumer surveillance.

The Domestic Threshold

Of course, modern surveillance already crosses the domestic threshold via numerous non-commercial conduits. Government administrative departments have for a long time been concerned with who lives where, with whom, at what economic level, and so on. However, the waves of consumer surveillance now splashing over the domestic threshold are more intensive, and flow through new channels. Moreover, while it is often a taken-for-granted fact of modern life that – to change the metaphor – the tentacles of the state now touch every home, most householders know far less about where their next commercial communication will some from and how they were singled out for attention. This section starts with a consideration of direct mail, moves next to its cognate area, credit rating, and concludes with a glance at two-way electronic services.

A striking TV documentary from Nova Films, first screened on American public television in 1991, portrayed the newest panoply of electronic devices for consumer surveillance under the title, 'We Know Where you Live'.[15] The precise targeting of households using complex computer power represents a vital tool for marketing in a very lucrative sphere; the commercial data industry itself is worth fifty billion dollars a year in the USA. The reason for its great success is that the method works for the companies actually selling products and services to the general market. In Britain, research by Direct Mail Information Services indicates that response to direct mail campaigns remains in proportion to what was sent.[16] Seven hundred and fifty million pounds worth of direct mail production and postage can generate seven billion pounds of business for companies availing themselves of data entrepreneurial services.

These companies 'know where we live' by combining socio-economic with geo-demographic data. In other words, the contents of various apparently unrelated databases are raided to pull together personal information regarding names, addresses, telephone numbers, incomes, and consumer preferences, along with the exact pinpointing and clustering of consumers in different areas but with similar tastes and purchasing powers. This classification includes differentiation by ethnicity and gender as well. A black lawyer in Dallas is pressed to contribute to Jewish causes because his name is Cohen. Women receive coupons and sample products just before their periods and just before and after babies are born.

Much data is gathered directly within computer networks, mainframe-to-mainframe (or 'CPU-to-CPU'). The big three American credit service bureaux, TRW Inc, Equifax Inc, and Trans-Union Corporation – who sell data to direct mailers – employ mainframe-based on-line systems with large database management systems. A bank requiring, say, a credit report could obtain it in five seconds. Such reports, containing names, addresses, Social Security numbers, and credit history are automatically updated each month from sources including banks, credit card companies, retailers, and car rental companies.[17]

Still in the USA, the practice of combining postal zip-codes with census and other data provides direct marketers with rich veins of information. A crude behavioural 'sociology' then clusters consumers accounding to their computer-generated 'type'. Two important things should be noted here. The first is that this profiling of consumers uses the micro-analysis of census data prepared by government agencies. Information that we must yield by law is eagerly devoured by commercial agencies for profit. At this point it is still aggregate data, but nonetheless, given the ease with which information technology facilitates the combination of this with identifiable personal data, new questions do arise. Surveillance using new technology overrides, and thus blurs, conventional distinctions between social spheres once held to be separate. It raises questions about how far governments should permit data gathered for one purpose – which may relate to equity or justice – to be used for a quite different end, namely commercial profit, without the knowledge or consent of the data subjects concerned.

The second note regarding this behavioural consumer sociology is that it depends not only upon the technological hardware and software, but upon statistical analysis. Hence it is not merely the powerful database, but also the statistical digesting of facts thus gleaned that produces the desired profile of consumers. Such statistical digesting tells stories about specific demographic groups; that they are from a particular income bracket, tend to have a similar lifestyle and educational experience, or even are from the same ethnic background. Official statistics are thus sought and used for purposes quite different from that for which they were collected in the first place. Not new technology alone, but computer power harnessed to statistical techniques, produces these effects.

Ironies abound here, however. The flip side of the coin is the plea for freedom of information, which would make all government-garnered data freely available. The liberal – and sometimes politically radical – complaint, especially in the Reagan-Thatcher years of neo-conservatism, was that governments were withholding information that should have been publicly available.[18] It is not clear to me what an appropriate response to this dilemma should be, but it does point up the increasing role of particular kinds of information as mediators of power, and the need for fresh thinking on the politics of releasing such information.[19]

Telephone numbers are also very useful to the new marketers; indeed, the telephone may become more significant than mail as a means of marketing. So-called 'smart' telephone networks are used to identify callers who use tollfree numbers to place orders or to make customer enquiries. The receiver of the call often has immediate access to the caller's purchasing power and preferences; the details appear on a screen even as the caller waits to be answered. What is new here is that the screening process occurs instantly and without the caller's knowledge.[20] But, once again, larger scale public policy is involved, in that such 'smart' telephone capabilities depend upon the establishment of Integrated Services Digital Networks that have been extensively deregulated in several countries in recent years.

In Oakbrook, Illinois, Telesphere Communications offers a service to '900' subscribers allowing the company to peg the location of incoming calls using an area code and the number's three-digit prefix. Salespersons can prepare a pitch, knowing where the calls originates. A computerized reverse directory later identifies the caller, and a database is used to identify which of forty demographic clusters, 'fit' the potential customer. Telesphere Communications hope they will soon be able to provide this service even as the customer speaks to the company.

PRIZM, a Virginia database company, supplies the demographic data to Telesphere. Different neighbourhoods are classified according to characteristics useful to the marketer. Here are the results of the behavioural sociology mentioned above. 'Furs and Station Wagons' people are big spenders with new money'. Less desirable to the companies in question are clusters like 'Emergent Minorities' who are 'almost 80% black, the remainder largely composed of Hispanics and other foreign-born minorities ... below-average levels of education and [below average] levels of white employment. The struggle for emergence from poverty is still evident in these neighbourhoods'.[21] Without their knowing it, telephone customers' residence, income, and background is revealed to salespeople, who then base their selling strategy on that information.

What this amounts to is a variation on the data-image theme discussed in Chapter Five. In this case the data, though garnered largely from official – and public – sources, is linked with sketchy personal details to form an assumed data-image. We are 'known' to those companies by means of such a data-image and, because once again this method of selling 'works', the data-image is taken to be an accurate portrayal of us. Moreover, given the relative ease with which access to such a consumer-oriented data image may be obtained, it is not inconceivable that before long government departments might take an interest in them as well.

The Lotus Household Marketplace, described earlier in this book, highlights further aspects of consumer surveillance by electronic means. Had it been marketed – and something like it may yet be marketed under a different name – it would have made available to many small and medium-sized companies demographic data on a hundred and twenty million American consumers, on highly accessible compact disks, keyed, significantly, to Social Security numbers.[22] 'We know where you live' appears to be an understatement; the files on individuals and categories of consumers are surprisingly full. Less surprising is the resistance to the spread of such systems when their existence becomes known. Written refusals to have personal data used by Household Marketplace are said to have forced its withdrawal. As we shall see in the next section, the 'caller ID' facility used by some companies is also generating opposition.

Often connected with direct mail organizations are companies concerned with credit rating. Few consumers can be unaware that their capacity to buy with credit depends heavily upon how great a risk they are deemed to be. Rating that risk is accomplished electronically. My own record is held in the files of the Credit Bureau of Greater Toronto, which monitors credit information on six million residents of Ontario.[23] Credit card users' spending activities are monitored, both in the sense that purchases are recorded and also in that on-line verification means the company knows where we are when we buy.

Similar tactics to those involved in direct mail are employed in credit rating. Indeed, the same company often performs both tasks. In Britain, for instance, CCN buys electoral rolls (voter lists) to update census records and adds to this the Post Office's Postal Address File, with its twenty-three-and-a-half million addresses sorted by one-and-a-half million postcodes.

Customer information and regional data are sold to corporate clients such as motor manufacturers and health insurance firms. Their geodemographic clustering is called the 'Mosaic'. But CCN Credit Systems also provides credit checking services. The advertised benefit is the rapidity with which clients may obtain loans. The downside, for many, is the seemingly unrestricted circulation of personal financial data which may – for those refused credit – have some very constraining effects.

Checks on creditworthiness are increasing at an accelerating pace. In Britain, for instance, the number of checks doubled between 1985 and 1986.[24] Their most palpable social benefit is that limits may more easily placed on debt, which, when overextended through multiple borrowing, is itself seen as a major social ill of the consumer society. The jaws of the debt trap yawn innocently wide for the unalert but over-enthusiastic credit card shopper. Thus it is not difficult for credit-checking companies to justify their desire for integrated systems capable of centralizing consumer borrowing information; a social sore may be healed. This was in fact the rationale given in 1987 for updating the computer system of the British United Association for the Protection of Trade and renaming it 'Infolink'.

Public disquiet regarding credit checking has focused on the practice of 'blacklisting', whereby customers are refused credit due to some alleged failure to honour debts in the past. Of course, as we have just seen, the computerized credit hurdle may help prevent the vicious spiral of helpless indebtedness. But it is often a rather blunt instrument, operating by means of record matching, which places not only individuals but categories of people under suspicion. Few today have not heard tales of how credit was refused because of some feckless previous inhabitant of the same house, some relative with the same name, or merely because the address given was 'the wrong side of the tracks'. Not only that, but even when debts are cleared, or errors identified and acknowledged by the company, the records themselves are not erased.

In one instance, in 1984 a £16 debt was referred by the British Family Album mail order company to the CCN Systems credit-checking agency. Though the debt was cleared at the time it was recorded, it was still on file in 1988, when it temporarily barred the customer form receiving instant credit in a large store. Family Album agreed, in February 1989, to delete the record when the customer complained, but the Data Protection Registrar's office found it still intact in December 1989.[25] The consumer in question was thus haunted by her data-image. But it was more than a bad dream. The system designed to prevent personally damaging indebtedness actually constrained her from activities she was fully able – financially – to perform.

In the above-mentioned examples, the household threshold is crossed by means of the letter-box and the telephone line. There has been no reason to suppose that the act of purchasing or making other financial transactions takes place anywhere but in conventional stores, banks, and shopping malls. In the 1980s, however, the advent of 'home networking' in some countries brought a novel dimension to electronic surveillance: two-way interactive systems linking external services directly with the household. Dressed as the potential realization of older visions hitherto only partially fulfilled, home networking – where it exists – also represents a further major extension of the practices involved in electronically collecting, storing, processing, and retrieving personal data; that is, in surveillance.

In one well-known early experiment, the QUBE system in Columbus, Ohio demonstrated the possibilities for homeshopping and other services using cable television. The cable system that delivers the picture to the television screen can, like telephone lines, take messages back the other way. Unlike telephone lines, though, their capacity is far greater, enabling for instance catalogue 'pages' to be called up on screen and orders taken for goods. Opinion polling and other forms of voting may also occur. The potential for garnering detailed transactional data is clearly enormous. Everything, from what sorts of films are watched on any pay-pay-movie channels to the kinds of goods purchased or opinions held, is in principle retrievable.

It must be noted that the line between technological potential and social reality is somewhat blurred in the case of home networking. In Britian, such interactive services were largely stillborn because they depended upon an anticipated adoption of cable televison, which in turn was supposed to develop through an entertainment-led consumer demand that never materialized. In France, on the other hand, the system known as 'Minitel' (actually the name of the computer terminals within homes and businesses; the system proper is called 'Télétel') was established as part of a government-sponsored scheme to create a national computer-tele-communications network. Initially, the terminals, which were distributed free to subscribers, replaced the paper telephone directory with direct access on the screen to names and numbers from the database. Of all such videotex systems, Minitel has proved the most successful. But despite government sponsorship, even Minitel has not succeeded as much as was initially hoped in the anticipated areas of home-banking and home-shopping. Personal message services have proved far more popular.[26]

In North America, some home networking has haltingly emerged, and where it has done so, has rightly attracted the attention of social analysts. In two Canadian studies, David Flaherty and Kevin Wilson[27] discuss the implications for surveillance and privacy of two-way interactive services.

Flaherty acknowledges consumer benefits of such systems but warns about the 'potentially darker – surveillance – side. He emphasizes privacy concerns and how the cable companies running them may be subject to self-regulation with regard to 'privacy'. Beyond self-regulation, Flaherty argues that individuals should have clear rights to use the courts when third-party access to personal data has been granted without consent.

Wilson on the other hand is critical of any 'balance-sheet' approach to the society/technology relationship, and is concerned rather that interactive systems are subject to 'economic pressures designed to transform human activities into marketable commodities.'[28] While not unconcerned about the 'privacy' aspects of home networking, he also invokes the notion of social management to analyse its further potential effects. Wilson suggests that the use of anonymous data, gleaned from two-way services by market researchers and forecasters, also carries dangers of social control. As he says, 'surveillance in itself does not ensure compliance, but an awareness of its presence clearly does so by subtly encouraging the individual to internalize the rules.[29]

In Wilson's view, social responses to corporate initiatives are engineered by creating and manipulating needs that have never been subject to public debate. Social management, for Wilson, threatens democratic polity by exacerbating inequities of knowledge, and making consumers more and more vulnerable to corporate power. If we add to this the issues raised above, that consumer surveillance makes extensive use of official data and that considerable weight is placed on the data-image thus gleaned, it becomes clear that ethical and political questions of some magnitude attend this crossing of the domestic threshold.

New Technologies for Surveillance?: Caller ID and Smart Cards

The example of commercial surveillance by two-way cable raises the important question of how far we should examine emerging, as opposed to already existing, surveillance practices. Perhaps comment should be held back until the real impacts of such new technologies are known? After all, technological potential is never social destiny. New artefacts and technological processes are shaped in different ways by varying cultural and historical circumstance, and unanticipated factors enter into their economic or technical success. Two-way services based on cable television simply are not at the forefront of surveillance concerns in the early 1990s. Direct mailing, which is, may be affected by consumer resistance, as in the case of The Lotus Household Marketplace, or by legislation, which may well begin to cover the sphere of private enterprise in North America.[30]

Therefore there may seem to be a good case for hesitating to comment on new innovations until their impact has become clear. With the evidence before us we may make informed judgements about the surveillance capacity involved and the actual social impacts. The problem with this approach, of course, is that once new systems are firmly established, they become very hard to alter, if that strategy seems to be called for.[31] Moreover, their use may generate related technological innovations which quickly multiply the social consequences, as in the case of Automated Bank Machines (ABMs). Also the pace of technological advance is often very rapid, and the argument is frequently made that social safeguards should be built in to new technologies.

ABMs, to take up the example, rapidly have become a feature of late twentieth-century life. The banks which use them clearly benefit; the costs entailed are less than half of those for a human teller. The chief consumer benefit is probably convenience; ABMs permitted the 24-hour customer, seeking one-stop financial services. But once again, from a surveillance perspective, ABMs enable banks to pinpoint personal preferences and even physical movements and to add these to the profile built from transaction patterns. Now cardholders can obtain services from other banks than their own, especially where one bank-holding company such as Citicorp own many smaller ABM nets.[32]

Newer developments, sold as enhanced consumer advantages, each also hold in store an enhanced surveillance capacity. The American telecommunications gaint, AT&T, for instance, recently introduced a 'Universal Card' that combines several functions. It is at once a bank card, a credit card and a telephone card. Convenient for the customer, to be sure, but the Universal Card also unites otherwise discrete data to which corporations such as AT&T are glad to have easier access. Its loss might also make the bearer somewhat vulnerable.

Another example of new surveillance technologies that promise to contribute to the ever-growing traffic in personal data is the 'Caller ID'. This telephone service lets the person being called see the calling party's number before they answer the phone. The device, available on certain computerized telephone switching systems, uses a modem that, triggered by the first ring, calls up the temporarily stored datum of the caller's number, and displays it on a screen attached to the handset.

In Australia, where Caller ID is also known as Client Line Identification, the challenge of Optus to the previous monopoly of Telecom involved interconnection between rival systems to make caller ID possible. An inquiry was initiated in 1992 to determine what regulation may be required, following reports that caller ID has sparked tremendous controversy in North America.[33] In Canada, caller ID was first made available in selected cities – Montreal, Ottawa, Toronto – and provinces during 1991. Police have reported dramatic drops in obscene calls in Ottawa and Quebec City. In Montreal, however, complaints have been lodged regarding the new ease with which abusive husbands could discover the whereabouts of their wives.[34]

Caller ID was first introduced in the USA as part of a 'Custom Local Area Signalling Service' (CLASS) in New Jersey during 1987. Since then, the issue has become something of a *cause célèbre* among civil libertarians and consumer groups. As Oscar Gandy suggests, caller ID is a two-edged sword.[35] Recall the question of what is known about customers and clients by salespeople called on toll-free numbers. Consumers object that their privacy may be violated or their choices limited if salespeople know in advance – or worse, think they know – their caller's socio-economic position and geographical location. On the other hand, caller ID facilities are advocated by those wishing to stop obscene phone calls, avoid bogus pizza orders or track down burglars. There is, of course, more to the debate than this, but clearly the dilemmas lie deep.[36]

The debate over caller ID and related services is likely to intensify during the 1990s as ISDN systems replace older telephone switching systems. The so-called 'intelligent network' will not appear overnight, however. Rather, the development is piecemeal, fragmented, and sometimes staggered or meandering.[37] But the issues uncovered by it go well beyond the current experience, and sometimes abilities, of policy-makers. What happens early on tends to be determinative for later developments.

For instance, the capacity to stop one's number being revealed to the person called can be achieved either by a free 'per call' facility or by charging the client for each occasion a caller identification is blocked. Telephone companies, for course, would prefer charges to be made for every service, whereas regulatory bodies may recognize that this produces unacceptable inequity.[38] At present little consensus exists, but with the trend towards more national and international agreements in technology policy, compatible policies are likely to emerge. It presents a huge challenge to policy-makers to permit developments of a sufficiently flexible kind that issues of justice and freedom are not excluded during preliminary experiments.[39]

It is entirely appropriate, then, for novel uses of information technology for surveillance themselves to be monitored by critical social analysts. While some new gadgets may fail to gain a foothold, genuine innovations may also occur that have far-reaching implications. Smart cards, like caller ID, appear at present to hold the potential to make just such a difference.[40] Smart Cards have embedded within them tiny chips of integrated circuitry, enabling the storage of data in the card. Numerous uses have already been found for these, especially in Europe, where phonecards are commonplace; banks and health services also use them, and many companies employ them for internal security purposes.

In Canada and the USA various smart card experiments have been tried or are under way, on both large and small scales. A Vancouver restaurant owner, for instance, uses a smart card system to build profiles on regular customers, using a system that is not traceable back to the individual cardholder.[41] On a much larger scale are pilot schemes that store detailed data in relation to a number of different agencies. A commercial card system was launched in Québec in 1990, and in Ontario a card that holds medical, insurance, pharmaceutical and other data is being tried.[42]

One reason why such smart card development interests surveillance analysts is that, as well as increasing storage capacity and integration, such schemes may also involve merging databases of public – government administration – and private – commercial – agencies.[43] At the same time, it is argued that new protections and limitations on abuse are also available using smart cards. For instance, because they possess them, cardholders are said to have greater control over their personal data.

New services, based on extensions of existing technology, appear constantly. Consumer capitalism continually innovates in the quest for new markets and maintained profit shares. In the present climate of telecommunications deregulation and the establishment of large scale ISDN systems, it is hard to follow, let alone soberly analyse, the social consequences of such innovation.

Yet as the examples chosen here suggest, the tendency is for the asymmetrical relationship between corporate organization and individual consumer to be exaggerated by every new gadget and service. Claims regarding consumer benefit – some of which may be perfectly legitimate – hardly have time to be tested before the next innovation appears. And issues of social division, reflected accurately in the consumer surveillance described here, and human dignity are seldom even considered. It is imperative that such trends be subjected to responsible social and political analysis, even if they continue to lag behind the perpetual renewal of technology.

Data Entrepreneurs and Strategic Information

Already it is quite clear that the big actors in this drama of commercial surveillance are the major corporations. They have the capital to invest in huge electronic systems and the incentive of market shares and profit; they are also goaded on by increasingly tough competition within the global capitalist system. This section is about those corporations and has two main foci. The first is the significance of the 'information commodity' to these companies and to their increasingly voracious appetite for personal data, and the second is the role of military analogies in the description and justification of what they do. This is the world of 'strategic information systems' in which customers are 'targets' on which companies require 'intelligence'.[44]

As we noted elsewhere, to refer to the emerging social formations of the advanced societies in the late twentieth century as 'information societies' is misleading. There is a sense in which societies have always been information-based.[45] The exchange of information, otherwise known as communication, is a constitutive aspect of all human sociality. There is a further sense in which all modern societies are information societies, regardless of their knowledge or use of electronic technologies; personal data is routinely garnered on subject populations in the nation-state and workplace.

So what if anything distinguishes today's electronic technology-oriented 'information societies'? Working within the perspective of Harold Innis, William Melody suggests that a crucial difference lies in the relation of information to the market. The technology-led capacity to supply huge amounts of information in digital form has coincided with the discovery that such information often has a high market value. In other words, data can command a price as a commodity.[46] As Melody observes, 'Information that was previously outside the market and not included as economic activity has now been drawn into the market'.

Now, much of this information, such as that sought for industrial, professional and commercial uses, has its greatest economic value in scarcity rather than widespread distribution. For such uses, the aim is to tap specialized 'inside' or superior knowledge of competitors, suppliers, government descision-makers and, of course, consumers. Whoever can monopolize this data can maintain the upper hand. And because it is relatively expensive to establish large databases but relatively cheap to extend the market for services already created, the tendency is towards centralization and monopoly on an international basis.[47] The same factors also stimulate intense competition between corporate rivals.

Hardly surprising, then, that the data entrepreneurs freely use military analogies. (Of course, their technological apparatus frequently orginates in military domains). Business strategy – especially that using the geodemographic data discussed earlier – may be compared with the map-room scenes of war movies. As one article on desktop mapping software puts it, 'If you're on the front lines of the business battle . . . Understanding the spatial relationships contained in business data is the critical success factor in decisions about such matters as situating new stores, expanding into new territories, and developing new products'.[48] Not surprisingly, the software packages include programs such as 'Tactician', the wrapper for which shows a helmeted soldier in front of computer screens with a data-encircled globe above his head.

As far as theory is concerned, some analysts argue that a whole new paradigm for information management has emerged. Charles Wiseman calls this 'Strategic Information Systems' or SIS.[49] This includes, but takes us beyond, the 'intelligence gathering' function to the more generalized use of information systems to enhance competitiveness. It may occur by various means such as extending markets, improving efficiency, or linking with suppliers.

One of the many companies which Wiseman claims have 'SIS vision' is the American Dun and Bradstreet. In 1841 Louis Tappan founded the Mercantile Agency, the first credit-reporting company in the USA. Soon it was run by R. G. Dun. A few years later, the Bradstreet Agency was formed, and they eventually merged in 1930. By 1978 D&B had become a 763-million dollar diversified information services company including business information, publishing, marketing, and broadcasting divisions. In 1979 it bought National CSS, a leading computer services company, along with another television station and several cable systems. By 1983 D&B was a 1.5-billion dollars organization with 45% of its revenue coming from business information services. In 1984 D&B bought A. C. Neilson, the leading consumer research concern . . . and so the story continues.

The point of this excursion is to demonstrate why consumer surveillance has become such a major feature of contemporary societies. The so-called 'SIS vision' of D&B is summed up in their corporate commitment to the co-ordinated development of information gathering, technology application, and management. Similar visions are shared by the other super-corporations in the business information field, including those already mentioned: PRIZM, Equifax, Infomart, Infolink, CCN and others.

The strategies of such companies takes various forms, and from the surveillance point of view it is important to distinguish between them. At this point, perhaps the most general distinction might be between market research, which relies upon statistical data not necessarily tied to individual identities, and actual marketing to identified individuals. The former is bused in the attempt to manage the behaviour of collectivities, large or small, such as the 'pools and patios' or 'emergent minorities' grouping noted above. This is where misgivings about social management arise, with their attendant fears about social control.

Marketing is used to try to persuade individuals to buy products or services. While this may well have disciplinary elements, it is more often privacy concerns that are expressed here rather than a sense of threatened autonomy. Further reflection on why military-style 'tacticians' are targeting the predominantly female market concerned with grocery coupons and personal hygiene advertisements should reveal the gendered dimension of this. But it is important to note that social management, along whatever social trajectory, may occur even where privacy legislation or regulation exists. Indeed, the existence of privacy legislation may serve to legitimate the soft social control function, by reducing public reticence about using electronic information and communication systems.[50]

Commercial Surveillance Capacities

With this vast industry gathering personal data, whether anonymous or not, what are the implications for surveillance capacity? Without doubt, surveillance capacity is augmented by several of the systems we have examined in this chapter. The elements of surveillance capacity, you will recall, are the size of files, the comprehensivity of reach, the speed of data-flow and the degree of subject-transparency.[51] Electronic Funds Transfer (EFT) systems illustrate well the growth in surveillance capacity.

One of the most important information technology developments over the past decade has been the growth of EFTs, which increasingly use Point of Sale (POS) facilities (generating the acronym EFTPOS). The Sainsbury's retail food store chain in Britain, for example has been using these for some time. Any company using EFT systems can increase its effectiveness by exerting more control over clients who deviate from preferred practices. Using a POS terminal linked to a banking network can ensure that customers are able to pay when services are rendered. Current credit card checks, observes Rob Kling, 'only attest that a customer is a good credit risk in general, not that he is creditworthy at the time of a particular transaction. Thus, increases in the speed of information flow may help, businesses decrease their losses through poor credit decisions'.[52] The files are larger, the reach is greater, transactions are faster and subjects are more transparent.

For most of the time, however, consumers do not fall foul of such surveillance systems. Indeed, as we noted above, the services or convenience the systems represent are regarded as benefits. They permit easy access to desirable resources. Consuming is paraded as a matter of personal choice. Freedom to select between alternatives is touted as the acme of the unconstrained life. Only when the customer runs into debt or when inaccurate records are used[53] does the weight of much more coercive action descend. Those who do not deviate from desirable levels of consumption regard most forms of commercial surveillance as aspects of convenience and comfort in the consumer society. Temporary scares over privacy may surface from time to time, but these are mere blips in a smoothly running megamachine that constantly gathers, stores, matches, processes, and sells personal data.

Examining in detail the commercial surveillance aspects of banking, insurance, credit card and other agencies does reveal considerable increases in surveillance capacity, as our earlier example illustrate. In general terms, more personal data circulate, usually without the knowledge or consent of the data-subjects. There data may be used to persuade or manipulate consumers both as members of groups (social management) or as individuals (*via* direct mail, telephone selling, and so on), sorting them through pseudo-sociological statistics and crude classifications. The massive sales that can be traced to direct mail drives attests clearly to the effectiveness of such practices.

By the same mechanisms the consumer society simultaneously help to exclude its undesirables, the underclass of non-consumers, would-be consumers or flawed consumers. For them is reserved the older, fuller panoptic surveillance, which not only sorts into categories, but closes in automatically on deviants to constrain their options. While consumer surveillance surely does exhibit panoptic traits – unverifiable observation, behavioural classification and so on – the actual mechanism of social integration and criterion for social participation relates to 'free choices' made in the marketplace.[54] Discipline is present, but not the carceral, coercive discipline of the panopticon. Rather, consumers are seduced into conformity by the pleasures of consuming what corporate power has on offer.[55] This is the indirect means of soft social control described at the start of this chapter.

Much hangs, of course, on the notion of 'free choice' within the consumer marketplace. Discussion of 'surveillance capacities', with its negative connotations, might seem quite inappropriate in a sphere dominated by the discourse of 'free choice'. The illusory aspects of this have to be exposed, however. Under the guise of greater choice the cost of basic services – such as cable TV – is frequently driven up by artifically constructed 'choices'. Caller ID offers another illustration. Customers within CLASS service areas may be offered both caller ID facilities and the opportunity for their number not to be displayed to those they call, and each of these carries a price-tag. Cellular phones may be the next phase, in which each member of a household has to have their own receiver in order to have a communications ID. We return to this in the next section.

Consumerism and Surveillance Theory

Consumer surveillance, well beyond that practised in the capitalist workplace or the nation state clearly represents a major field in its own right. This is what makes it especially significant for the sociology of surveillance. Orwell never dreamed that such powers of surveillance and control would be possessed except by the nation state. It is noteworthy, though, that consumer surveillance utilizes data garnered by government departments, especially from censuses, and that it relies upon new information-technology systems such as ISDN that are permitted or regulated by the state.

As far as the links with workplace surveillance goes, the concept of 'Social Taylorism' may yield some clues about management strategy in attempting to supervise consumption, but it throws little light on the experience of surveillance in consumer society or on the kind of social order achieved by its means. Consumer surveillance is generally not direct or coercive, but it does succeed spectacularly in teaching consumer skills and encouraging consumers to internalize marketplace rules of behaviour, despite the reported scepticism of many consumers about direct mail advertising.

The rapidly growing role of the so-called information commodity is central to understanding consumer surveillance, and has two facets. Large corporations – the data entrepreneurs – are involved in huge operations that easily match the scope of some government databases. Such corporations have frequent recourse to military analogies for their strategies, and constantly seek for technological innovations that will support and upgrade these strategies. The power of the data entrepreneurs is highly asymmetrical with respect to individual consumers, who often lack the knowledge, will or organization to effect any resistance or change. The rejection of the Lotus Household Marketplace software may represent the glimmerings of raised consciousness here, but to claim more for it would be unrealistic. Whether disputes over Caller ID will do any more for such raised consciousness remains to be seen.

The other facet of the information commodity is that in consumer surveillance terms it is constituted by a particular kind of data image. Statistical digestion of data digitally culled from diverse sources provides data entrepreneurs with profiles of consumers as members of certain crudely defined social groupings. Others, based on individual identification, depend on data such as the all-important credit rating, not merely to distinguish between different types of consumer – gender and ethnic background loom large – but to form judgements as to who is credit-worthy and who is not. These sorting mechanisms may clearly be understood in panoptic terms, but not only in panoptic terms. Consumer surveillance mirrors and reinforces social divisions based on levels of ability to consume, but it also enhances the general transparency of contemporary consumers.

Consumer surveillance entails a massive intensification of surveillance throughout society, and technological innovation is constantly enhancing its capacity. Subject transparency is especially augmented. Connections with the nation state and with the capitalist workplace – Social Taylorism – should be pursued, but consumer surveillance must also be viewed as part of an emerging set of social arrangements, articulated with consumption, that is also a departure from what we already know about surveillance. Similarly, the Orwellian and panoptic metaphors still offer insights but cannot be expected to tell the whole story.

Comments made about rapidly changing technologies must be borne in mind here; the need for fresh thinking and flexible policy-making is paramount. Right now some evidence suggests a shift away from direct mailing to the use of the telephone in conjunction with television advertising, in which the interactive potential of ISDN systems will be exploited to the full.[56] Electronic scanners in supermarkets which automatically discount loyal customers and monitor shoppers' ongoing purchases and savings already threaten the usefulness of paper coupons. The connections between these shifts and a theory of the social order of consumption have yet to be made.

Indeed, the systematic monitoring and intervention in personal tastes, fashions and symbols by means of the kinds of processes indicated here calls for a general recalibration of social theories of surveillance.[57] While Zygmunt Bauman's work on consumerism as a central feature of a putative postmodernity is singularly important, even he has little to say about how sophisticated surveillance of consumers is articulated with it. Nonetheless, in our quest for a critical perspective, his comments on the duplicity of consumerism are worth heeding. One face of this is the (false) promise of universal happiness following from freedom of choice, while the other is that the problem of freedom (supposedly) is resolved once consumer freedom is offered.[58] These hidden assumptions on which the social order of consumerism operates cannot be ignored within any responsible theory of consumer surveillance.

Surveillance theory must take into account, therefore, both how data-subjects are constituted as consumers and how their patterns of consumption are channelled through commercial surveillance. With regard to the former, vital questions of human identity and dignity are raised, alongside issues of freedom. And touching the latter, questions of social division, both between consumers and non-consumers and along the fault lines of gender and ethnicity, provoke critical analysis in terms of justice and social participation.

Though we cannot predict the long-term consequences of structuring social participation around consumption, or of limiting personal or collective responsibility by means of the disciplines of consumer surveillance, it seems clear that they add up to some social circumstances not entirely precedented in previous modern experience. However much consumer surveillance practices may resonate with Taylorist or panoptic methods, it must be recognized that the leading principle of the consumer order is pleasure, not pain or coercion. What remains to be socially analysed and politically challenged is the peculiar threat of consumer surveillance to exacerbate social division and undermine human dignity.

Part III

Counter-Surveillance

In the remaining four chapters we shall assess just how adequate are the analytical approaches and political responses to the rise of surveillance society. In Chapter Nine I ask what exactly is the challenge of surveillance and also what challenges have been made to surveillance in the later twentieth century. The latter take the form of technical challenges on the one hand, expressed through privacy laws in particular, and so-called mobilization challenges on the other. Mobilization challenges have to do with the role played by social movements in attempting to bring about broader-based change than mere legislation. While progress has been made on both fronts, I conclude that issues raised by contemporary surveillance have yet to be met by truly appropriate responses. That is, ones that take seriously both human dignity and identity, and justice and social participation.

In Chapter Ten I explore in greater depth than hitherto the question of privacy. This is not because I hold out great hope in the coherence, salience or effectiveness-in-opposition of this concept. To the contrary, I argue that the concept of privacy, though of limited use in carefully defined contexts, is fundamentally flawed as a means of coping with the challenges thrown up by surveillance today. The concept has a long history, and prompts important questions, but in the end is hopelessly bound up with property, patriarchy and privilege. Privacy actually grows from the same modern soil as surveillance, which is another reason for doubting its efficacy as a tool of 'counter-surveillance.'

Chapter Eleven broadens the question by returning to the images of Big Brother and the Panopticon. While they have contributed to social theory, they are also dystopias, visions of undesirable society. As such they both blinker social analysis by refusing to see the dualities and ambiguities of surveillance, and as political outlooks they tend to sink us in the sands of pessimism and paranoia. Alternatives exists, however. The notion of 'undistorted communication' points us in the right direction, towards an ungrounded critical theory. Augustine's 'other city' also provides vital clues. Key concepts informing constructive alternatives include personhood, participation and purposes.

These ideas are pushed just a little further in the final chapter. While the realities of today's surveillance, particularly its computer and consumer aspect, suggest strongly that modernity is in process of fairly fundamental change, postmodern discourse has yet to move us beyond paranoia. The concepts of participation, personhood and purposes are offered as a contribution towards shaping surveillance for a different and more desirable future.

9

Challenging Surveillance

[Given] the current depth of the true problems raised by technological development, no political action in the normal, strict sense of the term is adequate today.

Jacques Ellul[1]

The Challenge of and the Challenge to

The chapter title is a deliberate *double entendre*. This book attempts to explore the meaning of surveillance in the late twentieth century, especially in the light of the rapid development and deployment for surveillance of new technologies. Now I want to shift the focus somewhat. On the one hand it is appropriate to pause and assess the nature of the challenges thrown up by contemporary surveillance systems, challenges both to sociological analysis and to democratic polity. On the other hand, we must ask what sorts of challenge have been posed to surveillance itself. What sorts of resistance are placed in the path of the machine, for what reasons and with what effects? This chapter, then, represents a watershed, as it examines the challenges *of* and *to* surveillance.

The word 'challenge' is also used intentionally. Much discussion of surveillance quickly relapses into the paranoid, where surveillance is viewed overwhelmingly and monolithically as a threat. This is especially true of those forms of analysis whose starting point is the omnipresent power of the Panopticon, but it also echoes in the idea of 'Big Brother'. Good reasons exist for resisting the paranoid, however. For one thing, surveillance systems emerged historically in a symbiotic relation with democratic government and the extension of citizenship rights. For another, in no case discussed here does surveillance appear as an unambiguous or unmitigated evil. A more or less obvious social benefit accompanies its spread in virtually every case. Whether or not this is conceived as a dialectic of control, as discussed in Chapter Four, surveillance does seem invariably to exhibit two faces. Under these circumstances it is hard to insist that surveillance is necessarily or inevitably negative or constraining in its consequences for human social life.

Nevertheless, the question persistently raised within this book is, how far does new technology make a difference? Are novel features appearing on the surveillance landscape that might alter the perception of change from challenge to threat? If we review the various factors analysed earlier we are reminded that electronic technologies facilitate the expansion of indirect, impersonal, control, of more knowledgeable organizations on which modern populations are increasingly dependent. Electronic technologies have augmented and amplified surveillance capacities in several significant ways, so that whatever else is said about it, surveillance is clearly intensified in contemporary advanced societies. In what ways does the quality or magnitude of this intensification present new challenges for human personhood or democratic polity today?

Two kinds of answers to this question may be offered. We may consider the actual responses to intensified surveillance that have emerged over the past two decades or so. These in turn may be divided into technical responses, those that seek legal or technological means of restricting or adding security features to surveillance systems, and mobilization responses, that seek to organize opinion or opposition to surveillance. Examples of the former would include the passing of laws regarding data protection and privacy, while examples of the latter would be the activities of civil rights or consumer groups that attempt by legal, lobbying or other means to protest or limit the spread of surveillance. Of course, their activities and ambit overlap, and the one – mobilizing opinion – may lead to the other – changes in law. So they may also be viewed as two ends of a continuum, with resigned acceptance is at one end, fundamental opposition at the other.

Modern societies are almost by definition preoccupied with problem-solving. That is to say, it is a condition of modernity that societies become increasingly aware of themselves through the processes of management, planning, and so on. The logic of technological and bureaucratic development frequently proceeds on the assumption that problems created by them are in principle solvable by a similar logic. Surveillance is no exception. If technological advancement produces perceived problems, then some technological fix – encryption? enhanced security? – or legal remedy – data protection or privacy law – can be applied to overcome it. This kind of solution basically accepts the *status quo* while acknowledging that improvements are always desirable. Another kind of approach is much more doubtful about the *status quo*, and is visible through an analysis of social movements.

An understanding of the dynamics of social institutions in the modern world – capitalism, industrialism, the nation-state, militarism – has led some sociologists to expect to see social movements generated in opposition to those institutions. Indeed, over the past two decades sociologists have argued strongly that the more conventional politics of modern societies is being challenged by social movements, whose concerns transcend traditional debates resting on class, nation and so on.[2] But while the opposition of Green movements to industrialism or peace movements to militarism may appear to echo the more venerable and historically longer-term labour movements' resistance to capitalism, it is far from clear that surveillance has generated much by way of systematic opposition in terms of identifiable social movements, though there are signs that this may be changing. Later in this chapter we shall examine both the status and achievements of such groups and movements, and also possible reasons for their relative absence or weakness.

Secondly, the sociological analysis of electronic surveillance prompts questions about which sorts of social and political response might be more appropriate, and which less. This partly depends on the framework for analysis that is chosen. Obvious candidates would include the discourse on privacy arising from a 'post-industrial society' theoretical approach, discourses of control from within Marxian – capitalist society – or Weberian – 'bureaucratic society' – approaches, or discourses of power arising from Foucaldian or 'postmodern' approaches.

In each case, however, the sorts of response available relate to two further questions. Indeed, all social theory relies implicitly or explicitly upon views of two matters: what constitutes human personhood, and what constitutes the 'good society'.[3] In the chapters that follow I shall address these two questions insofar as they apply to the sociological analysis of surveillance. On one side of the watershed is the investigation undertaken in this book into the origins, development and consequences of surveillance in modern societies, with special reference to the role of new technologies. On the other side is an analysis of actual and potential responses to surveillance. Both are similarly sociological in style. But while the first is more descriptive and analytical, in the second I try to make more explicit the underlying normative stance and its implications for a critical theory of surveillance.

It is not that the cluster of concerns often alluded to under the 'privacy' rubric has particular relevance to questions of personhood or philosophical anthropology, while those that draw on the language of 'control' have more to do with political philosophy. Each is bound up with the other in complex ways so that one may not be considered in isolation from the other. They are both practically linked and also demand an integrated normative basis for the social theory of surveillance.

The Challenge of Surveillance

While surveillance is by no means a novel feature of human society, in the modern world surveillance has become both more intensive and more extensive. Surveillance which would today, in modern societies, be thought fairly invasive occurs in traditional village communities. The routine and mundane activities of everyday life are open to the scrutiny of others, though it may not be particularly systematic. Villagers are known to each other as fellow-workers, kin, and as members of worshipping and governing communities. Much of this kind of surveillance has declined and diminished in modern societies. For many, if it exists at all, it is now a mere memory of times or places where face-to-face relationships and limited geographical mobility meant that everyone knew everyone else's business. Vestigial traces still remain, but little more.

Of course, in particular contexts, systematic surveillance was present in ancient times, whenever the state wished to keep records on populations for military reasons or to control a labour force for public works. We saw how in Old Testament times censuses were taken, apparently to make the Israelites' wandering in the wilderness more orderly or to support the institution of the monarchy.[4] But in this case numbering and classification was a rather remote affair and only touched lives of specific groups and at a limited number of points. One might say that surveillance in non-modern contexts is either intense but unsystematic or systematic but remote. By contrast, most surveillance today is both systematic and intense.

·Even in colonial times in New England, which David Flaherty has researched in relation to 'privacy', it is clear that surveillance simply did not occur with anything like the pervasiveness or systematic comprehensiveness experienced today. True, the seventeenth-century Puritan colonists instituted a fairly strict regime of mutual oversight. As Flaherty says, 'Puritans were encouraged to subordinate privacy to the more pressing purpose of collaborating in the creation of a City set upon a Hill for the edification of the rest of humanity.'[5] But as the power of the Puritans waned, so 'its dominance over routine activities receded . . .'[6] Two centuries were to pass before surveillance of everyday life by large organizations would really start to expand at an accelerating pace.

In Chapter Two we examined the argument that surveillance in modern societies accompanied the development of democracy, and citizenship rights in particular.[7] This argument is important for a number of reasons, not least because it focuses on the relation between surveillance and the opportunities for social participation. Now that surveillance reaches well beyond the requirements of the nation-state and the capitalist workplace to the realm of consumption and the household, it is worth asking again how surveillance relates to social participation. To what extent is surveillance enabling in this regard, and to what extent constraining?

Another big question addressed here, however, is whether or not the development of new surveillance technologies makes a decisive difference to surveillance trends. Does this 'new surveillance' help to steer modern societies towards an Orwellian *Nineteen Eighty-Four* situation, towards what Gary T. Marx calls the 'maximum security society', or even to something else as yet only fuzzily apparent?[8] The prison imagery is echoed in several recent studies that draw upon the concept of the Panopticon as a means of understanding the significance and mode of operation of electronic surveillance. But Gary Marx's primary focus is on the new, mainly electronic, technologies themselves.

Gary T. Marx constructs a good case for the cumulative difference made by specific surveillance technologies, in that they transcend darkness and distance, are more intensive, invisible, involuntary and so on. But he also observes that 'organizational memories are extended over time and across space,[9] which may signal even more profound ways in which new technologies do indeed portend a new surveillance. As I argued in Chapter Three,[10] it is above all the power of information technology which is in view here; that is, computers linked by telecommunications.

The history of modern societies is marked by moments at which new techniques – themselves the product of specific social circumstances – do make a decisive difference to the ways that social life is ordered.[11] During the nineteenth and early twentieth century the clock, in conjunction with the timetable, became a centrally significant device for co-ordinating human activities in time and space. It seems quite plausible to suggest that an analogous shift is taking place in the later twentieth century. Now the computer, merged with telecommunications, serves to articulate and co-ordinate human activities, but on a massively amplified scale compared with what clocks and timetables could achieve.

To concentrate thus on the consequences of technological development certainly does not constitute technological determinism. After all, as I indicated a moment ago, it was precisely the growth of democratic polity, plus the felt need for greater military and economic co-ordination, that give the new technologies their chance. Rational, instrumental calculation existed long before the advent of computers, even though they now embody, express and indeed reinforce just such processes. But it is precisely that remarkable capacity of computers to contribute to the processes of co-ordination and control that make them so significant in the surveillance context.[12]

As we have seen, computer-power is now central to the apparatus of surveillance within the nation-state (and beyond, as a globalized phenomenon), and to monitoring and supervision in the workplace – and again, beyond; 'place' is actually less important to the computerized enterprise. Computer-power is also central to commercial surveillance, seen by some as 'social management'. Both in specific ways, then, and also in terms of the general impact of computerization, new technology may be crucial to a 'new surveillance'. However, it remains an open question how far the use of information technology increases the power of organizations over the populations under surveillance. How far is social order constructed and maintained through consumer seduction and classificatory constraint by computer?

At this point our earlier discussion of the Panopticon comes into its own. An increasingly commonplace argument is that what Bentham's Panopticon lacked by way of technological sophistication has now been realized courtesy of information technology. Making visibility a trap,[13] subordination *via* uncertainty, rule by classification; all these may be accomplished routinely, remotely, and efficiently using computer databases. Data subjects collude with their own surveillance, whether by using credit cards, quoting driving licence numbers, or making telephone calls. The Panopticon metaphor has been effectively linked with surveillance at the state administration and policing levels, and within capitalist surveillance in both workplace and consumer contexts. Some have also more than hinted at the emergence of a kind of societal Panopticon.

As we have seen, in fact different kinds of argument operate here. The Panopticon metaphor is pressed into service within quite widely varying accounts. These range from the highly specific and particular – Zuboff on management practices or Gordon on criminal investigation[14] – to the generalized. Among the former, specific situations must be analysed. It clearly will not do simply to see the quintessentially modern Panopticon reproduced and amplified electronically, as if this form of social control necessarily persists once it is established. Among the latter, Poster's analysis of what he calls the 'Superpanopticon' stands out. He discusses the ways that the Panopticon as a technology of power, in Foucault's sense, has been electronically extended in the later twentieth century. Not only does this mean that the population is monitored 'silently, continuously and automatically along with the transactions of everyday life'[15] but, according to Poster, that the public/private distinction is eroded and another self is constituted for the individual, which may be 'as socially effective as the self that walks in the street.[16]

The difference between Poster's position and those of others who have discussed the Panopticon in an electronic context lies in his stress on the linguistic experience entailed within it. It is the electronic nature of the communication that distinguishes this surveillance from others. Poster insists that social analysis be concerned to explore these 'new modes of linguistic experience in a manner that reveals the extent to which they constitute new modes of domination'.[17] This of course is precisely the point of our analysis in this book, in particular the empirical examination of the four surveillance spheres; administration, policing, workplace and marketplace.

Nonetheless, we did note certain potential pitfalls associated with the Foucaldian account of the Panopticon. Poster is sensitive to some of these, particularly the requirement to avoid Foucault's apparent tendency, despite himself, to 'totalize' his explanation. This produces an account in which everything is explained in terms of ubiquitous power, and which sometimes implies that quite different social situations – prisons, factories, domestic living rooms – are really essentially subject to the same kinds of power. Foucault also carefully eschews the 'metaphysical',[18] but in so doing indulges in moral outrage without either acknowledging it or elaborating on its basis.

Accepting the force of Poster's challenge to analyse the dominative power of electronic surveillance involves several related tasks, as I see it. One is to explore how the 'Superpanopticon' can work at all if people are unaware of its operation. A second is to avoid totalizing by acknowledging differences between social situations under analysis. This is where the empirical analysis comes in. A third is to lay bare the basis of critique, to which the two subsequent chapters are devoted.

As far as the empirical study[19] is concerned, the main conclusions of this book may be summarized as follows. Firstly, the range of setting within which the investigation of electronic surveillance may be undertaken is enormous. Among other things, we have looked at the Operational Strategy in the British Department of Social Security, the Ontario Health Card, The US Internal Revenue Service, Project Metropolit in Sweden, electronic ID cards in various countries, the electronic tagging of offenders and undercover police operations in the USA. In the domain of private enterprise one might mention computer matching in various contexts; employee screening, remote monitoring of employees, the surveillance side-effects of information management using computer databases, direct mail, telephone called ID services, geodemographic market clustering, and videotex. These systems are constantly multiplying and expanding, frequently 'feeding on themselves' as James Rule says.[20]

It is important to be aware of this vast range of applications of computer-based technology, simply because the computer does make such a difference. Above all, information technology enables many other processes to work and tasks to be performed. Even without going so far as to specify qualitative changes following in the wake of computers, it is essential to get a grasp of the magnitude of the alternations that these new technologies have engendered. As Jacques Ellul, whose work on the 'technological society' antedated current sociological concern with technology, says, 'I must now rethink a good portion of my theory on the technological world because the computer is having ubiquitous consequences *unlike any other technology*'[21] (my italics).

Secondly, in all these contexts, though more pronouncedly in some than in others, surveillance capacities are expanded using information technology. In terms of the ability to store files, the comprehensivity of reach, the speed of data flow within and between systems, and the degree of subject transparency, surveillance is intensified. For James Rule, with whom the concept of surveillance capabilities originated, limitations on these capacities is all that stands between us and the 'total surveillance society'. Today, the expansion of surveillance capacities becomes more generalized as increasing contacts are established between hitherto separate surveillance realms, making it more and more difficult to maintain earlier sociological distinctions between those realms.

Thirdly, new categories of social relationship do seem to be emerging, based upon the 'data-image'. This, by the way, is a significant aspect of the 'electronic text' noted by Poster. As computer-telecommunications systems facilitate the co-ordination and articulation of social activities in time and space, thus reducing those kinds of distance between people, other sorts of distancing may paradoxically be ocurring. As far as data-subjects are concerned, some trust must be vested in the abstract systems on which we all rely from day to day. But this is a different kind of trust from that obtaining, typically, between people.[22]

Questions of trust and identity relate closely with conceptions of human dignity. But surveillance systems do not operate on such criteria, and it is not clear how anything different could be case. It would not be surprising if trust turned rather easily to suspicion on the part of data-subjects as the full significance of new surveillance systems becomes clearer. And not only on the past of data-subjects, either. The phenomena of computer fraud, hacking and so on demonstrates that new technologies also present new opportunities for revenge on the 'system', not to mention others, such as refusing to hold credit cards, for avoiding it. Neither is a paranoid fear of the instrumental gaze without moral discernment[23] the whole story of 'distancing'. Distancing can also be seen as a boon to those used to discrimination on the basis of skin colour, gender, or disability. Software can be structured precisely to minimize prejudice.[24] The dialectic of control, it seems, is only thinly or temporarily veiled.

Fourthly, the evidence from different social spheres in succeeding chapters of this book has made it increasingly clear that, whether or not new surveillance technologies have consequences of their own, they help to reproduce and reinforce existing social divisions. Whether in social welfare administration, policing, the workplace or the marketplace, cleavages between labour and capital or, perhaps even more significantly, between consumers and non-consumers, do not appear to be healed by virtue of new surveillance processes. To the contrary, panoptic classification devices, along with the categorization of populations for inclusionary order or exclusionary control, are encouraged and facilitated by information technology.

To speak of a 'new surveillance' or to discuss the dimensions of the emerging 'surveillance society' is not hyperbole. The range and depth of quantitative changes alone would be sufficient to warrant the use of such language, without ever relapsing into technological determinism. However, much of the evidence presented here also hints strongly that the possibility of qualitative changes should not easily be discounted. The rise of surveillance networks that are integrated across the conventional boundaries of polity and economy, the idea that a new disorganized – that is, less hierarchically systematic – surveillance is visible in the workplace, the novel ways that consumer surveillance crosses the domestic threshold and the pervasive importance of electronic language, seen above all in the data-image, all testify to the emergence of apparently unprecedented social arrangements within the surveillance rubric.

So much for the social analysis of the new technologies, their origins and their consequences. What of the actual experience of this new surveillance by its subjects? If we concentrate for a moment on the negative aspects of surveillance society, certain motifs tend to recur. Fears about 'Big Brother', concerns about democracy, and worries about personal dignity have given rise to resistance, albeit of a limited and muted kind. Such unease, suspicion or hostility has been expressed in a number of ways during the past two decades of electronic surveillance expansion. Some of it finds voice in legal limits on modes of data collection, storage, or use, while some goes well beyond such regulation to more radical opposition. To this we now turn.

The Challenge to Surveillance: I   Privacy Law

In 1973 Sweden passed the first national data protection law in the world. Sweden could also be seen as one of the most bureaucratically organized welfare state societies in the world, so this achievement might be thought quite fitting. For instance, Sweden had a system of national identification numbers for citizens from 1947, at just the time when pressure was mounting in Britain for the dismantling of a similar scheme set up as a war-time contingency. On the other hand, as its detractors are quick to point out, the kind of data protection installed in Sweden itself depends on highly bureaucratic regulation.

Sweden, like several other countries that have developed forms of data protection legislation, looks to an 'event' which stimulated such law. In this case it was public concern about the Swedish population census of 1970.[25] In the USA the Watergate crisis would supply massive impetus for legal measures concerning privacy, while in Britain pressure from European trading partners finally gave the necessary fillip to the legislative process.

Actually, the early 1970s were the crucial seedbed for early data protection measures. In Germany the State of Hesse passed a Data Protection Act in 1970. In 1972 The Swedish Parliamentary Commission of Publicity and Secrecy of Official Documents issued a report on *Computers and Privacy*. A Canadian Task Force on Privacy and Computers released its report in the same year. In 1973 The American Department of Health, Education and Welfare issued its report on *Records, Computers and the Rights of Citizens*. In 1974 The French Ministry of Justice appointed a Commission on Informatics and Liberties.[26]

Consideration of the consequences of computerization of personal files usually preceded legislation by several years. It is no accident, as far as data protection legislation is concerned, that government departments began their serious computerizing programmes at a time when fears of the Orwellian society were fuelled by cold war depictions of totalitarian regimes in Eastern Europe. By the early 1970s it had become clear to policy-makers that the question was not how to prevent the computerized storage of personal data, but how to mitigate its perceived negative effects. And that is how the debate has been conducted since.[27]

Mention the word 'surveillance' to people and the chances are that the discussion will soon turn to 'privacy'. The latter is seen to correspond to the former is its opposite, or perhaps its antidote. Socially, there are good reasons for this; the so-called private sphere has become a prized component of liberal capitalist societies with a stress on individualism. In state socialist societies, 'privacy' may well not be the first alternative term that springs to mind at the mention of surveillance. Legally, over the past two decades citizens of the advanced societies have sought recourse to privacy or data protection legislation to try to counter what are perceived to be the invasive aspects of new surveillance. As we shall see, some have followed the Swedish example, others have devised alternatives to it.

Sociologically, this kind of response may be located within what might be called 'postindustrial society theory'. In this perspective, technological change is vitally bound up with the future progress of the advanced societies. Difficulties this change presents may be countered, not by structural modifications, but by piecemeal improvements. Does data collection threaten privacy? Technical and legal solutions may be sought with which to neutralize such threats. Indeed, the very appearance of political strife becomes less likely as technical decisions become predominant.

This is not intended as a cynical introduction to privacy legislation. It is easy to scoff at so-called 'bourgeois rights'. I would insist that privacy law is tremendously important, not least because it institutionalizes in law the idea that surveillance should not be permitted to grow unimpeded. But it would be dishonest to conceal my view that what can be achieved by means of legal measures is chronically limited, not only in the sense that such measures may be 'too little, too late' but also in the sense that law itself is inadequate to the task of regulating electronic surveillance. Social, cultural and political approaches, though less tangible, may be more appropriate.[28]

Having said that, let me turn to the question of what data protection and privacy law actually sets out to do. While differences indeed exist between the various countries that have adopted some form of data protection legislation, several common features appear in each case. For a start, it is the use of computers to store personal files that led to the initiation of all data protection law. The chief reason for this would seem to lie with the computer's capacity to store, process and manipulate information, and not just data. That is, the computer's ability to *concatenate* data is of crucial importance.[29] A datum, such as a name, on its own means little. With an address, phone number and bank number it is sensitive information. The reason that the Swedes and the British chose to speak of 'data protection' arises from this. Law may not regulate machines, data, or users, but only the kinds of tasks – the 'applications' or 'processing' – performed by computers.

Similarly, the kinds of principles enshrined in the British 'Lindop' Committee's recommendations of 1978 lie behind most legislation. The object is that 'the right people (and only the right people) are able to use the right personal information (and only the right personal information) for the right purposes (and only the right purposes)'.[30] This second feature relates to the degree of ease with which personal information may circulate beyond the data subject's control.

Principles arising from the Lindop Committee's work are now enshrined in the Council of Europe Convention, with which all European Community countries must comply and which in turn affects their North American trading partners. The principles refer to the lawful and fair obtaining of information, its being held for specified and legitimate purposes and not disclosed in ways incompatible with those purposes, its adequacy, relevance and limited nature in relation to those purposes, its accuracy and up-to-date character, and its being kept in name-linked form for no longer than necessary for the purposes stated. In addition, the principles state that subjects have a right of access and entitlement to correct or erase wrong data, and that security measures be taken against unauthorized access, alternation, dissemination, loss or destruction of data.

A third feature of data protection legislation is that it is generally viewed as the quest for a 'balance of interests'. That is, if privacy is the goal, it cannot be seen as an absolute value, but rather as one that may only be asserted in relation to others, such as the duty of the state of treat all citizens equally, say by insisting that births, marriages and deaths be registered. The ghost of John Stuart Mill may be discerned not far behind this third feature. The balance of interests frequently sets privacy against 'subject friendly' interests such as accuracy of bank records, promptness of welfare payments and effective diagnosis and treatment of patients.

A fourth characteristic of data protection law – in some countries, not, notably, the USA[31] – is that it gives power to independent bodies to adjudicate in situations of conflicting interests. Such conflict would occur where errors or abuse were detected within subject-friendly systems (leading to, say, wrongful dismissal or files actually getting into the wrong hands). Or conflict would occur when subject-hostile systems are operated. These include credit-reporting, pre-employment screening and systems run by security services, police intelligence, or immigration control. Given the situation where government is one of the biggest users of computerized surveillance systems, it would hardly be appropriate for data protection agencies to be *within* government. Ironically, in the British case, the Home Office, which uses some of the most subject-hostile systems, was charged with the task of setting up the Data Protection Registry. No wonder, suggests Paul Sieghart, Britain was so slow to install such legislation![32]

Some significant differences in data protection practice also exist. One relates to the kinds of databanks covered. In Britain, for instance, private companies as well as government departments must comply with the Act, whereas Canadian law covers only the latter – for example, credit card companies are largely exempt in Canada. Another difference is that some laws cover only computer files (as in Britain) while others (in the USA or Canada) cover manual files as well. Agencies wishing to evade the force of data protection law would, in the former case, merely have to transfer files to a manual system to achieve examption. A third difference, already alluded to, is that some countries such as France and Sweden have chosen a fairly bureaucratic method of registering all databanks, whereas others have taken the route of reliance on the courts (as in the USA) or a commissioner (in Canada). David Flaherty, for one, regards the American model as quite inadequate to the magnitude of the task of resisting surveillance, although he is also fearful that the heavily bureaucratic models, such as the French, may become little more than legitimators of new technology. Moreover, a bureaucratic cure for bureaucracy could well turn out to be iatrogenic, that is, an antidote that causes further problems.

Needless to say, even bigger differences would emerge if one looked at surveillance and data protection in a broader context than Western Europe and North America. Even within Europe, it is as yet unclear how the West German Data Protection Commissioner will relate to surveillance issues raised by the union with East Germany. Countries such as Japan and others on the 'Pacific rim' may encounter difficulties in formulating law appropriate to the their own legal and cultural traditions. Indeed, data protection provides an interesting case study in the globalizing of law. Eddy Kuo, of the Singapore National University, warned recently about the dangerous lag between the development of surveillance systems on the 'intelligent island' of Singapore, and legal protection for citizens.[33] And in countries like Thailand, Indonesia, and the Philippines, which are rapidly adopting sophisticated surveillance technologies, sometimes of kinds proscribed by Western governments, there is as yet no legal protection.[34]

Critics of data protection legislation express their concern at different levels. Some argue that Acts passed require modification and strengthening, sometimes in terms of definition or coverage, sometimes with relation to the sharpness of the 'teeth' granted to the regulatory body. John Shattuck, for instance, criticizes the US 1974 Privacy Act for its tautologous definitions of items like 'records' or 'systems of records'.[35] Flaherty cautions that in their efforts to cope with actual day-to-day demands, data protection agencies can quickly fall behind the accelerating technological changes occurring in the surveillance field, changes which they are in any case often incompetent to comprehend, let alone adjudicate.[36]

Few argue that data protection law represents a fundamental mistake. This applies even to sceptics such as Britain's Duncan Campbell and Steve Connor, who see the Data Protection Act of 1984 as a cynical exercise orchestrated by bureaucrats whose sole concern was to obtain the minimum necessary to appease European trading partners, and which consequently is riddle with loopholes.[37] Nevertheless, as Geoffrey Brown observes, deep difficulties do still attach to data protection legislation, not least of which is the stress put on self-protection.[38] As he remarks, this in turn presupposes a citizenry sufficiently well-informed and motivated to use the available protective machinery. As it is the case that, even in the countries we have been primarily concerned with, a large proportion of citizens cannot even name the prime minister or president, this is not a reasonable presupposition.

In the light of the challenge of surveillance revealed in the sociological analysis of contemporary societies, it hardly seems that data protection law is an adequate safeguard. What Western societies have produced may be more or less workable, and may afford some much needed basic protections against ill-defined dangers. But the pace of technological change, facilitating for instance *de facto* national data systems, and the spread of interrelated surveillance over vast tracts of social life often barely touched by law, such as the sphere of consumption, are two major factors illustrating the impotence of law on its own.[39] A third is uncertainty about how exactly contemporary computer surveillance works and what its long-term social and cultural consequences will be. It is Hardly surprising, then, that some groups either supplement or substitute their concern for legal remedies by turning to more radical modes of critique.

The Challenge to Surveillance: II Social Movements

In 1985, when the Australian government proposed to establish a national electronic identity card scheme, a number of groups and individuals, encouraged by public opinion, successfully blocked the plan.[40] Computer scientists attacked the idea in its technical detail,[41] the New South Wales Privacy Committee and others questioned its efficacy in reducing tax and welfare fraud.[42] The matter was debated fiercely in the national newspapers and eventually quashed in parliament when civil libertarian Ewart Smith showed Senator John Stone a legal loophole which gave the opposition its chance to prevent the bill from ever becoming law.[43]

This might be called a 'mobilization response' to the challenge of surveillance, and it links the rise of surveillance society to the growth of social movements. Another perhaps more telling example would be what Langdon Winner calls the 'computer populism' that rose in protest against the 'Household Marketplace' software advertized by Lotus in 1991.[44] In this case, the organization known as Computer Professionals for Social

Responsibility (CPSR) galvanized action through national and international networking. Consumer and professional groups were concerned about the lack of protection for personal identities offered by this marketing tool and about the fact that Social Security numbers were being used as universal identifiers. Although Equifax – who supply data to Lotus – assured the public that their product had been 'misunderstood', it seems that in fact it had been understood all too well.

One approach to the emergence of so-called 'new social movements' is to connect them to the institutional dimensions of modernity, after the style of Giddens, for example. This would stimulate a search for identifiable organizations and groups whose activities run counter to central institutions of modernity. While this provides a useful springboard, it also raises several difficulties. One such is the problem of identifying the institutional spheres – where, for instance, does patriarchy feature in this scheme? Contemporary feminism clearly finds expression in 'movements' today.

Another difficulty we encounter directly in relation to our theme is that while someone like Giddens writes illuminatingly on surveillance, the only movements he offers in relation to it are the rather vaguely defined 'free speech', 'democratic' or 'human rights' movements.[45] However, this apparently disappointing vagueness may turn out to be a virtue. Perhaps we should not expect there to be social movements of similar kinds, generated by specific institutional dimensions of modernity.

Now, in saying this I do not wish to imply that social movements have somehow been ironed out, flattened by the pressure of dominant political and cultural forces. Far from it. Indeed, as Alain Touraine notes, it is precisely this kind of dismissal of social movements that one hears from the pessimistic disciples of Foucault.[46] Granted, I have tried to indicate how the mechanisms of political and cultural control are being reinforced steadily by electronic technologies. But such a conclusion manifestly does not exclude the possibility of countervailing forces gaining a significant voice.[47] Indeed, the theorem of the dialectic of control would lead one to expect just such possibilities to emerge.

If technical responses to the challenge of surveillance may be thought of in terms of postindustrial society theory, then mobilization responses relate to some kind of critical theory of postmodernity. In Chapter Eleven I shall comment on this in more detail, in the context of discussing social participation and the 'good society'. For the present, let me merely suggest how 'counter-surveillance' movements may be understood sociologically. I propose that on the one hand we should expect to witness the spread of such movements, directed towards curbing new forms of surveillance, but on the other, that they will not necessarily be highly visible, organizationally strong, or long-lasting.

Alberto Melucci's analysis of social movements argues that the symbolic challenge they present is of utmost importance.[48] He comments on what he calls peace 'mobilizations' – even they do not qualify as 'movements' – as displaying no analytical unity. Rather, he suggests they be understood as expressing the conflicts of complex societies, not just as responses to the threat of nuclear annihiliation. Which begs the question; what, then, are these 'conflicts'? His answer, interestingly enough, focuses precisely upon the issues that are the burden of this book.

Contemporary societies are increasingly 'informational', he says, and as such constantly expand the realm of the artificial, the (electronically) 'built' environment. Time and space are redefined in important ways so that, for instance, little room is left for 'unifying the fragments of personal identity'.[49] Moreover, with operational logic, information is not a shared and widely available resource, but rather is controlled by the few. Access to knowledge and information becomes a field of power and conflict. That he sees nuclear war as an ultimate social intervention in an artificial world, important though it is, need not concern us here. The point is that the 'social' realm becomes one of power, risk and responsibility.

Melucci concludes that the analysis of social movements amounts to an analysis of ways that power is made 'visible' under the conditions of 'informational' societies. He warns against seeing such movements in overly-institutional terms. Rather, they are likely to work through temporary organizations, public campaigns and 'submerged networks'.[50] He proposes that a key task for postindustrial democracy is to expand the arena of 'public space; not for movements to becomes parties, but for their message to be heard and translated into political decision-making, without loss of autonomy.

This analysis provides a plausible framework for understanding the 'Australia Card' example with which I started this section. And other cases, such as the Lotus Marketplace, make sense within the same framework. This highlights ways in which so-called submerged networks become temporarily visible and mobilized around a key issue, indicating that indeed the countervailing forces against surveillance do exist, though not necessarily or always in the form of conventional pressure groups, lobby groups or political parties.

Some such relatively formal organizations do exist, of course, and play a crucial role, especially in providing background research, when 'significant events' occur. The American Civil Liberties Union or the British group Liberty (formally the National Council for Civil Liberties) are prominent examples. Other organizations, such as the Green Party in Germany, have made valuable contributions to surveillance and civil-liberties debates, even though their main mandate lies elsewhere. (It should be noted that the German coalition groups against electronic identity cards failed to prevent their adoption in 1987!). In Britain and elsewhere, consumer groups have also joined forces with those questioning the assumed benefits of electronic surveillance, notably in relation to debt blacklisting and direct mail.[51]

Another illustration of the dialectic of control, I think, is the proliferation of movements which themselves are computer networks to share their concerns. These include the new 'Privacy International' with its links to 'Computer Professionals for Social Responsibility' in the USA, the 'Electronic Frontier Foundation', and 'American Liberties and Informatics'. Such networking is likely to become increasingly important as a means of mobilizing appropriate assessments of surveillance by electronic media.[52]

Though it has not been mentioned before, the role of the mass media in providing analysis of surveillance is also significant. In the context of 'informational societies', social cleavage occur along non-traditional lines, and journalism can become a source of alternative viewpoints. With regard specifically to surveillance, in Britain a highly controversial series called 'Secret Society' was screened by the BBC in 1987, including on episode on the 'Zircon' spy satellite that was impounded by MI5 from the BBC's Glasgow studios. And in the USA and Canada viewers have been exposed to detailed documentaries such as the 'We Know Where You Live' programme on direct mail.

Beyond the Watershed

The growth of contemporary surveillance may justly be seen as a 'new surveillance' or in terms of a 'surveillance society'. The range of surveillance settings has increased dramatically, and surveillance capacities are expanding in each dimension. New categories of social relationship are emerging in relation to the data image, and social divisions, especially those articulated with consumption, are reinforced.

We have looked at technical responses to this growth of surveillance capacities, especially in the form of legal limits. While they contain some vital principles, and serve to provide some buffer against abuses, they also tend to be minimalist, ambiguous, and geared to permitting citizens to protect themselves. When are called mobilization responses differ from technical responses in that they attempt more radical questioning and opposition to perceived negative consequences of surveillance practices, although their key aims often include pressure for adoption of legal limits. They relate to social movements, and the number committed to what might be called 'counter-surveillance' is growing, often spurred by technological developments such as Caller ID, smart cards and national identification systems. Some may turn out to be short-lived, specific mobilizations to counter some blatant offence against public opinion, others more permanent manifestations of resistance.

So what else can be done? It seems to me, as Ellul says in the epigraph to this chapter, that conventional political responses are inadequate, given the profundity of the problems we have uncovered. A more immediate task, then, is to explore further just what those issues are. So in succeeding chapters, while I continue to pursue the sociological analysis of the surveillance society, I make more explicit what I see as an appropriate normative framework for that analysis, in terms that first go beyond privacy to personhood and human dignity, and secondly go beyond dystopia to social participation and the 'good society'. As I hinted before, overturning Bentham's secular parody of divine omniscience, and allowing the theme of surveillance as care-and-control to inform social analysis, provides essential elements for a constructive critique.

10

Privacy, Power, Persons

But he that filches from me my good name
Robs me of that which not enriches him
And makes me poor indeed.

Iago, in *Othello*

Mirages of Modernity?

At the end of the twentieth century, names are worth a lot. A good name, said Iago, is the jewel of the soul; little did he guess that names could become more valuable in money terms. But consumer surveillance has changed all that. Name lists, once merely valued administratively by the nation-state, are now bought and sold as well. Personal identification becomes a commodity. Direct marketing demands name-lists, which can be culled electronically from diverse and remote databases and sold at great profit. Our names thus circulate far beyond our control among others who do indeed make a gain.[1] But do we citizens and consumers really lose out in this transaction?

Answers to this question vary. Some dismiss the whole matter as a trivial aspect of progress towards a consumer-oriented economy. Others fear that some invasion of privacy is involved; why should others – governments or corporations – have access to personal details connected with my name? Yet others see here an extension of capitalist social relations into the marketplace. Where once workers were diminished, now consumers are de-skilled and lose personal autonomy. A fourth response suggests that in fact notions such as 'individual' and 'autonomy' are mirages of modernity;

what electronic surveillance does is to show more clearly how 'selves' are constituted and controlled.

In this chapter we survey these responses, and their interconnections, and in particular probe the most widespread response, that of the 'privacy' debate. This is not because it is the most cogent or apt response however. Where privacy was already of doubtful value in responding to surveillance by the nation-state, it is even less use in an era of consumer surveillance. Indeed, I argue that we must understand, but go beyond, privacy and power to some more adequate concept of personhood if the challenge of the surveillance society is properly to be met. In a strong sense the apparently trivial 'name', bundled together with a million others within a computer database, may not be uncoupled from the 'good name' with which none of us is willing to part.

Privacy Invaded

Talk to anyone about electronic surveillance and they very quickly tell you what's wrong with it. Their privacy is invaded. Government departments are accused of snooping, prying, and spying on hapless citizens. 'Big Brother', it appears, has now extended his operations to the workplace computer; employees' activities are scrutinized with increasing intensity. Even the once-sacrosanct home is now penetrated by the relentless gaze of marketers who ceaselessly sift through our personal details in order to tempt us with yet new commodities. It seems there is nowhere to hide; everything is public, transparent, visible to invisible others. The sheltering walls of privacy have been digitally dissolved.

However privacy may have been conceived in times past, today it is tightly tied to avoiding surveillance. As surveillance intensifies in all spheres of social life, so more and more appeal is made to privacy as a reason for withholding personal information, or trying to control its unrestricted circulation.[2] If public opinion polls are anything to go by, concern for privacy, especially that relating to new technology, is on the rise.

Canadians surveyed in London, Ontario, in the mid-1980s claimed that privacy is diminishing in the later decades of the twentieth century, and are particularly bothered about increased transparency of data on personal bank balances, credit ratings, income and health records. Although about half those questioned reported worries about whether federal and provincial governments used information properly, a larger proportion feared that private business could not be trusted in this respect. Indeed, despite their reservations, respondents thought governments should regulate private companies' use of personal data.[3] And by 1993, according to a much larger study, Canadians were still very concerned about their 'privacy'. In a survey of 3,000 Canadians, sixth per cent claimed to have less personal privacy than a decade ago. At about the same time, Quebec introduced Bill 68, the first proposed extension of data protection to the private sector in North America, and the Canadian Direct Marketing Association produced its own 'Privacy Code'. Public anxiety about privacy shows little sign of abating in Canada at least, and measures are being taken to allay fears.[4]

In the USA too, reported concern over privacy is rising. After the Watergate affair subsided in the mid-1970s, so did expressions of concern about privacy. But from the mid-1980s indicators started to quiver and climb again, this time more in relation to the diffusion of computer technologies and a growing realization of their potential.[5] By the early 1990s, when particular technologies – such as caller ID – and processes – direct mail – were singled out for attention, interest in privacy protection was again high.

A 1991 survey in *Time* magazine showed that 76% of those polled were 'somewhat' or 'very' concerned about the amount of personal data collected by government and commercial agencies.[6] An Equifax study found 70% of respondents indicating that it was a 'bad thing' that businesses could buy data about their characteristics as consumers.[7] Many Americans, it seems, would prefer to be asked for permission before personal data is passed from one company to another.[8]

Consumer surveillance strikes an especially negative chord precisely because consumption is supposed to be the realm of freedom. Unfettered choice is the epitome of the modern marketplace, so the discovery that choice is subtly, and not-so-subtly, guided is somewhat galling. The same space that seems to offer unlimited liberty reveals itself as a site of intense scrutiny, of would-be consumer constraint if not of social control. The plea for privacy in the consumer sphere is thus the indignant demand of those who, paradoxically, are committed to consumer conformity. To be socially integrated is to prove one's personal standing by purchasing appropriate goods. Symbolic consumption is central; but knowing what is appropriate depends on targeted marketing, which in turn depends on the circulation of personal data.

To see privacy in relation to consumption patterns is not just paradoxical, an isolated blip on an otherwise linear graph.[9] It is also symptomatic of privacy that it alters with social and cultural currents, and that it differs in meaning from society to society. Such cultural variation must be the starting point for any adequate understanding of privacy today. So we begin with a brief look at the recent history of privacy in the modern world, noting ways in which private space is felt to be contracting.

The Public and the Private

Commonsense distinctions have always been made between the public world, open to the community, subject to magistrates, and the private. In the worlds of French social historian Georges Duby,

> a clearly defined realm is set aside for that part of existence for which every language has a word equivalent to 'private', a zone of immunity to which we may fall back or retreat, a place where we may set aside arms or armour needed in the public place, relax, take our ease, and lie about unshielded by the ostentatious carapace worn for protection in the outside world.[10]

Historically, the private has usually been associated with the domestic; thus privacy is not the same as solitude. For the domestic sphere contains those of different age, men and women, and, in ancient and some more modern times, masters or mistresses and servants. Thus the private, though possibly insulated from prying or encroachment from without, is not necessarily tranquil within. As the recent history and sociology of the domestic shows, all too often it may be an arena of tension and conflict, both between men and women and between parents and children.

In ancient times privacy was not regarded as an important site for self-development at all. Rather, privacy resonated with privation, a denial of the genuine social relations to be found outside it; for the Greeks at least, freedom and equality were to be found in the public sphere.[11] This of course glosses over the sexual inequality of the domestic sphere and the dependence of the public sphere on both that private inequality and on slavery. But the point is well taken that privacy was not always a valued moral condition.

In Roman times, and indeed into the present, the architecture of a house gave strong clues as to what was public and what private. From the gate, which protected both property and morality, to the layout of semi-public rooms into which visitors could be admitted, walls and closeable openings spoke of distinct spaces. The porch over the entry into a Roman home was particularly significant as 'ambiguous space',[12] projecting into the street but not part of the home's interior. The dividing line between the public and the private remains ambiguous, and thus also, from time to time, contested terrain.

Since the Middle Ages, as we have seen, the state has taken more and more interest in the everyday lives of citizns. At the same time, the growth of new forms of economic life associated with capitalism, declining involvement in collective ritual, and the internalizing of religious life promoted the individual and made private life more diverse. Thus domesticity came to be a female preserve – though patriarchy prevailed, of course – private businesses were set up in workshops and offices, and private gathering places emerged such as the café or club. As the modern nation-state emerged, however, even these private spaces became vulnerable to administration, intrusion or regulation.

Even in these examples, ambiguity abounds. Take the *salon* at the time of the French Revolution. This was a meeting place in a private home where dissidents could convene without fear of police spies, but would still have to observe conventions of conviviality and good taste as defined by the hostess. Yet the discussion concerned 'public' matters; indeed 'the public' in its modern sense was born in places like these.[13] Even when the 'public' café democratized the *salon* as a yet 'private' space for meeting, it was still mainly men, with their leisure and freedom from domestic obligation, who could indulge. As Alvin Gouldner observed, in the emerging modern public sphere people were accountable – they had to disclose matters, give an account – but this sphere rested on another, private, sphere in which dominant men gave very little account at all. Private interests, which might clash with those of others, led to a restricting of the flow of information there. For Gouldner, a 'possessive, self-protecting individualism' lay under the growth of privacy.[14] The 'information age' has done little to erase this.

Another ambiguity relates to the gender composition of public and private space, and attitudes towards external intervention within the domestic sphere. Abused women frequently welcome such attention and, indeed, deplore the lack of seriousness with which issues such as domestic violence and rape are treated by public authorities such as the police. This extends to the era of information technology, where surveillance methods such as the caller ID may be used to the benefit of just such women. Similar ambiguities attend the case of ethnic minorities, who find themselves, typically, receiving disproportionate surveillance attention, and are simultaneously glad of surveillance schemes that shelter them from racial attacks.

Public and private realms never develop independently of each other. As they were re-ordered with the advent of modernity, the distinction sharpened. The state, that governed by law the public domain, also legally defined the private as a place where the encroachments of the state could legitimately be resisted. In another, but related sense, however, what was 'private' was what could be concealed from others. The more that anonymous, impersonal relations developed in the growing cities of the modern era, the more differentiated the 'private' relations became. As Giddens puts it, 'the public only becomes fully distinguished from the private when a society of strangers is established in the full sense, that is, when the notion of 'stranger' loses its meaning'.[15] The upshot of this is, in Gouldner's words, that 'the fate of both the private and the public spheres is thus inextricable. There can be no transformation of the public sphere that is not, at the same time, a transformation of the private.[16]

Diminishing Private Space?

Only in modern societies does privacy rise to an elevated position as a desirable state, a realm of freedom from the remorseless 'colonization of the life-world', to use Habermas' telling phrase.[17] The process of colonization may be observed taking place at different rates in different places. In the USA in the 1930s, listeners levelled bitter accusations at radio stations and networks for the intrusion of commerce into the home by advertising. Wherever modern welfare states have developed, colonization has accelerated, and in the later twentieth century this has been tremendously augmented by the growth of consumer surveillance. Nonetheless, it is also important to remember that from the earliest phases of capitalism the quest of predictable control has created highly disciplinary situations, 'free enterprise' entrepreneurs notwithstanding.[18]

Privacy connects closely with freedom; at least, it does in accounts given by men. Women, as we have seen, have reason to be less sure of this. However, in popular parlance it is often conceived by both men and women as, on the one hand, freedom from the encroachments of the state and economy and, on the other, as freedom to reveal only what, and to whom, one wishes. But a now-familiar paradox lurks here. As Edward Shils and others have pointed out, the extension of surveillance, which appears to threaten privacy in both senses, actually emerges in response to processes set in train precisely to protect such freedom.[19] Citizenship rights defend individuals from arbitrary state power, granting legal recourse to privileges such as 'free speech'. Moreover, modern capitalism has created unprecedented tracts of 'private space' for familial relations and self-expression.[20] And contemporary consumer capitalism defines itself and organizes its control mechanisms in a context of personal freedom. So why is surveillance seen today as malign, threatening, and negative?

The answer, sociologically speaking, lies in the complex web of social relations within which self-identity is formed and maintained in the modern world. Like 'freedom' or even 'technology', privacy is a *social* relation.[21] It is mistaken to reduce it to the merely technical or legal.[22] As we noted above, public and private realms are not fully distinguished in modern times until Simmel's 'society of strangers' is established.[23]

Whereas in pre-modern times surveillance was generally a matter of personal, if not face-to-face, knowledge of others, now impersonal and increasingly abstract systems monitor and process our personal data. Self-identity, once felt to be given by God, family, clan, community and perhaps nation, is now a matter of negotiation.

Self-identity today still rests in part on personal knowledge, but also relies on the production of documents that include not only the passport and birth certificate but the driver's licence, social insurance number and credit card. What still remains of self-identity, to be negotiated on the basis of personal knowledge, is highly valued. Erving Goffman has written much about the 'back regions' of life, those 'offstage' areas where the public production, the performance, can be relaxed.[24] The relief of not having to 'give account' is central to the desirability of those back regions, the private. The tension of heightened pressure to perform, in situations such as Goffman's 'total institutions' – the prison or asylum – is just what people hope to avoid. Homes especially thus come to be valued for the respite offered from the demands of public accountability.

This notion of the private remains ambiguous, however. Any gender-sensitive approach will rightly be concerned about the apparent lack of accountability in the 'private' sphere. It is precisely this sphere that may conceal abusive relations. Patriarchy is buttressed by such concepts of privacy. Injustice in the domestic sphere is in fact a matter of public concern.

But privacy as withdrawal from accountability has other dimensions as well. The phenomenon of 'privatism' has exercised social analysts, particularly since the Western consumer boom following the Second World War.[25] The focus on the private sphere as the locus of real life, the leisure world apart from the demands of 'society', deflects into domesticity any energies that might be directed to the common good. In the 1990s this phenomenon is if anything more marked, and is popularly labelled 'cocooning'.

Liberalism, the predominant political outlook of modernity, has reinforced this conception of privacy. The sphere of thought and action regarded by John Stuart Mill as 'private' essentially relates to liberty from public interference. 'Over himself (*sic*)', asserts Mill, 'over his own body and mind, the individual is sovereign.'[26] The preserving of privacy, in this view, is seen either – at one extreme – as a value in itself or – more frequently – as a value to be balanced with others or – on occasion – as a means to realizing other values.

The alternative to preserving privacy is often starkly stated in totalitarian terms. The point is best made by quoting its opponents; Lenin, in 1920, announced that 'we recognize nothing private. Our morality is entirely subordinate to the interests of the class struggle of the proletariat'.[27] The Nazis in the 1930s commented that 'the only person who is still a private individual in Germany is somebody who is asleep'.[28] Or Mao Zedong in the Chinese Cultural Revolution of the 1960s, explaining what makes good communists, said they will be 'more concerned about the Party and masses than any private person . . . '[29]

This conception of privacy connects neatly with private property. Mill's sovereign individuals were characterized by freedom to pursue their own interests without interference, by rational, calculating and self-motivated action in transforming nature to their own ends.[30] This presupposes a highly competitive environment, in which one person's freedom would impinge on another's, hence the need to balance values like 'privacy' with others. In this tradition, laws relating to privacy attempt to weigh the interests of the private individual with that of the sate's 'need to know' about him or her for the purposes of assuring voter rights or meeting claims to welfare benefits.

The liberal view of privacy finds contemporary expression in studies and in legislation that relates to the work of Alan Westin. One of the earliest to make systematic analysis of surveillance by computer, Westin's liberal approach is taken by many to be seminal and classic. In the 1960s Westin warned that new technologies were presenting unprecedented opportunities for undesirable curiosity on the part of recorders of private data. However, as 'society' must protect itself from anti-social behaviour, limited surveillance may be justified on those grounds.[31]

Westin's views have become very influential in the field of computer surveillance and privacy. Although, as we shall see, his liberal approach leads him to turn contemporary consumer privacy into a matter for the marketplace to resolve, the virtue of his work was to suggest that privacy should have a new meaning in relation to computer data. John Stuart Mill, aftr all, lived at a time when the administrative surveillance by the modern state was still at a rather rudimentary stage. 'Dataveillance' would have meant nothing to him; Mill's private sphere was not what ours is today. In particular, today's privacy refers less to sexual activity, excretion, or sleeping, so much as to knowledge and information. These latter refer to something else than themselves, suggesting that data privacy is actually different from other kinds of privacy.[32]

The liberal approach, which has totalitarianism as its dramatic antithesis, tends to conflate privacy as resisting intrusion, and interference with privacy as controlling what we reveal about ourselves. It sometimes fails to note that the totalitarianism seen 'abroad' or in other historical periods may be present as a tendency within supposedly democratic societies. But the idea of a balance of interests sits uneasily with today's realities of large scale surveillance not merely by government but also by megacorporations. As we turn our attention to the peculiar problems of privacy associated with information, we shall see that the liberal approach, though still popular offers less and less help.

Privacy and Property

Privacy sought in relation to information, and particularly computer data, is different from other kinds of privacy. This entails a fresh approach from those traditionally followed, both in sociology and in law. In the 1960s an American jurist, Dean Prosser, unwittingly clarified one difference. He suggested that the essence of privacy could be seen when a public figure tries to protect his or her personal life from intrusion by nosy reporters. But in fact this is inverted and extended in current discussions of privacy, where ordinary people try to defend themselves against intrusions by curious public agencies, the police, government department or credit card company.[33] Prosser's suggestion belongs in a bygone era.

Realizing that things have indeed changed, the British Government's Lindop Committee on data protection (reporting in 1978)[34] argued that data privacy should refer to an 'individual's claim to control the circulation of data about himself'. This immediately shifts attention away from the sociologically ambiguous 'private sphere' and from what might be seen as equally dubious categories of 'secrecy' or 'anonymity.[35] Even so, as Geoffrey Brown rightly objects, this definition is somewhat sweeping![36] Lots of personal information about me circulates pretty freely among friends, colleagues and kin, without malice, and I have no objections to this.

The real problem, Brown goes on, is 'the possibility of the wrong bits of information getting into the wrong hands, or getting there by the wrong means or through the wrong channels'. With this in focus, not only questions of injustice or social control but also issues of power and of personhood come to the fore. This approach also shifts attention away from one centred on property, on which Prosser's case rested, and which is also tied up with the demarcation of private space.

Unfortunately, Brown's proposals are likely to remain unheard in the present consumer climate, where the discussion of privacy as *property* returns to haunt us. People may rightly be disturbed at the discovery that personal data about them circulates well beyond their reach within some government department or consumer corporation; rightly, if it is agreed that personhood and self-identity are violated by involuntary disclosure, and that relations of trust are made more fragile thereby. But an increasingly common response is to claim not just certain rights to oversee or control the circulation of personal data, but actually to own them. In societies that rapidly have commodified information as a means of perpetuating social contnrol through consumerism, it comes as no surprise that people believe they possess their data-image.

In the USA a group of householders, feeling themselves beleagured by junk mail, have formed an organization called 'Citizens Inc'. They turn the tables on telemarketers by attempting to bill their companies for the use of their domestic telephone, time and personal details.[37] Others have proposed that property rights be established over the commercial use of personal data. Brokering firms would handle such rights on behalf of their clients, operating the enterprise on similar computer networks as those used by the direct marketers. The quantity of unsolicited mail would diminish while its quality would rise.[38]

This kind of approach is also advocated by Alan Westin. In testimony given before an American House of Representatives Subcommittee on Government Information, he interpreted results of the 1990 Equifax Survey on Privacy[39]. Between what he calls 'privacy fundamentalists' and 'greatly concerned', is a group of 'unconcerned' people whose views could swing either way, depending on a number of factors. Because he cannot explain why individuals might trade privacy for consumer benefits, Westin proposed that the market should decide. Corporations should make special offers to those willing to cede control over personal information, thus making so-called privacy fundamentalists pay higher prices. *Et voila!* '. . . a highly responsive and democratic way of institutionalizing consumer choice' declares Westin.[40]

This debate will no doubt continue and intensify as the value of personal data rises along with public awareness about what is happening. The completely free market alternative seems to me to invite abuse, analogous to the case of the poorest selling their blood in countries where this is permitted. True, we already inhabit societies where personal data are commodities, and where some people – but not, it is noteworthy data-subjects – are profiting from their sale. But can this unfairness be redressed, and some measure of control over personal data be regained by data-subjects, only by instituting a system of 'royalties'? In my view, such a quest would simply disadvantage the less well-off.[41]

Disentangling the threads of debate over privacy is a daunting task. Distinguishing between privacy as control of personal data circulation and older ideas of privacy as defending space may be viewed positively as contributing to a contemporarily relevant concern. But the trend, at least in North America,[42] is not to explore the deeper meaning of privacy in relation to communication, self-identity and thus human dignity, but to relocate it in the economic sphere. This is the danger of the personal data royalty scheme. Privacy is property, again.

Privacy or Autonomy?

Though many use 'privacy' as the way into a critique of surveillance or as a means of countering its unlimited spread, others are understandably sceptical about the whole approach. Thus it could be said that today's surveillance society – and especially its consumer aspect – presents us with such pressing and/or unprecedented challenges that to fall back on 'privacy' simply misses the point. The kinds of critique I have in mind here usually come from perspectives informed by Marxian and Foucaldian ideas. In each case the discourse on privacy is rightly dismissed as a deflection from the real issues at stake. From the Marxian viewpoint, surveillance extends the reach of capitalist social relations, whereas, from the Foucaldian, surveillance places 'individuals' in the grip of ubiquitous power.

Kevin Wilson notes in his study of home networking that the old liberal notion of a 'balance of interests' between the state and the individual simply does not speak to the current situation where big corporations employ massive surveillance techniques. Classically the discourse on privacy states that a balance must be ensured between the right of the individual to be left alone and the duty of the state to obtain necessary information on him. But present conditions, observes Wilson, make a nonsense of this. The modern state, as we have seen, employs an array of surveillance apparatuses to maintain social stability, far beyond what could be considered within a rubric of 'balance'.[43]

At the same time, it is no secret that privacy legislation has not in any case arrived on the statute books due to an altruistic desire of governments to protect their citizens. It is all too often a minimal concession. Ironically, privacy legislation may also be read as a means of making the collection, storage and retrieval of personal data *more* rather than *less* straightforward. In North America, consumer surveillance is in any case frequently exempt, but in all such legislation loopholes and limitations exist. As Wilson says of the USA and Canada, at stake in the privacy debate is not so much the claim to protect the individual from privacy invasions as the establishment of ground rules and limits of acceptable institutional behaviour in the context of rapid changes in the technologies of information collection, storage and transfer'.[44] Surveillance practices continue subtly to encourage people to obey and comply with institutional rules, ironically with the legislative assistance of privacy law.

Public surveillance, once thought of as the domain of the nation state, has in the late twentieth century decisively been joined by consumer surveillance, or as some have it, 'social management'. Even fewer hindrances lie in the path of this latter surveillance than lie in the path of the former. And while modes of privacy critique may still have some limited salience here, several commentators are more concerned about the augmented powers of capital. Kevin Robins and Frank Webster, for instance, complain that this 'gathering in of social knowledge' is part of the establishment of capitalist rationality 'domination across all spheres of society'.[45]

Eleanor Novek and others comment that the peculiar way in which consumers are diminished is by de-skilling. That is, 'when consumers base their purchasing decisions on subsidized information flows [such as direct mail] their ability to identify alternatives is reduced and their normal information sampling behaviour is circumscribed'.[46] It may be objected that this presents the knowledgeability and discernment of consumers in a gratuitously unfavourable light, but Novek's point is as follows. Consumers become increasingly dependent on the reduce stream of information coming from direct mail, with the result that they progressively lose their opportunities for informed consumer choice. 'Social management' is effective in this way, much like its workplace counterpart. And the trading of personal information is viewed, not merely as some intrusion on privacy, but as an erosion of personal autonomy. This last I take to be the real challenge; it will be missed by those hanging on to the discourse on privacy.

That discourse on privacy, as we have seen, arose in a modern context, just as the problems it purports to address arose in a modern context. For those who believe that the diffusion of information technologies and the rise of a databased surveillance society takes us beyond the modern, the issues are seen differently.

A Superpanopticon?

From a postmodern perspective, a focus on the data image shifts the question away from privacy altogether. 'We see databases not as an invasion of privacy', writes Mark Poster, 'but as a multiplication of the individual'.[47] The trouble is that while the electronic self may be 'as socially effective as the one that walks in the street', the processes of creating the data image may constitute new modes of domination.[48]

Poster's claim has to do with the linguistic dimension of the electronic technologies. He sees databases as a 'Superpanopticon'. We have given considerable attention to the 'invisible observation' and 'sequestering' aspects of the panoptic, in which individuals are classified and as it were sorted into different categories and placed under constant inspection. But Poster draws attention to another aspect of the power/knowledge relation. People are not only sorted into categories of creditworthiness, for example in a technical sense; the category also signifies their position in society and may attach meaning to their existence as consumers, workers or citizens. As Poster points out, 'language is not simply a tool for expression; it is also a structure that defines the limits of communication and shapes the subjects who speak'.[49]

To some minds this kind of analysis holds that 'individuals' are in fact a friction, a creation of modern 'discourses' mirages of modernity. Self-identity, for Foucault, is simply the effect of strategies of power, which in the later twentieth century have become 'continuous' and technocratic', unhindered by either divine standards or human action. Some analysts reserve a residual place for capitalist power within this scheme, as in the view that monopoly control of markets makes nonsense of liberal notions of balance and privacy. But Poster's concern is different. In his view, the electronic media alter the rules of the game.

As in the old Panopticon, technologies of power – what Poster now calls 'structures of domination' – are constituted by practices. These practices in turn are organized by discourses. The discourse or 'social text' of the prison served to define the prisoner's experience so that he or she was constantly readjusted to the norm. Today's circuits of communication supersede electronically the old walls, shutters and other architectural facilitation of the inspector's constant gaze, and create the Superpanopticon.

Now we all participate as disciplined consumers and citizens, conforming constantly to the norm by form-filling, producing drivers' licences and credit cards with routine docility. The digital encoding of our personal data imposes a particular 'reading' upon it, for instance one which stresses our supposed consumer preferences, yielding the data-image. Thus we actually participate in the process that multiplies our 'selves'. According to Poster, 'surveillance by means of digitally encoded information constitutes new subjects by the language employed in databases.'[50]

Does privacy dissolve in power, then, as we tack from modern to postmodern analysis? Do the persons we once thought of as being pale palimpsests in the data image actually have no 'reality' at all? And what if the Superpanopticon has emerged in the interlocking databases of government and corporation? Does any critical strategy exist to withstand its power?

Let me address each of these questions in turn, albeit briefly. Firstly, this form of analysis questions sharply the salience of privacy. The rational self of modern individualism may be expected to have privacy problems; these are two aspects of the same, modern, outlook. The rational self was socially constructed; so is privacy. If novel 'selves' are indeed created by electronic surveillance, then the power of this process actually to dominate us in this way seems more interesting than whether some socially-constructed private sphere is threatened.

Secondly, the question of personhood; does no 'real' self exist at all? Leaving aside the question of whether Foucault was concerned about such ontological matters, Poster at least is at pains to stress that 'real' selves still have their being in the world. But he tells us little more than this; perhaps we can no longer know who we are. Jürgen Habermas, for instance, might be thought of as providing some answers here, because he proposes 'communicative action' as the distinguishing trait of humans. But for Poster, Habermas' focus on speech misses the point; electronic languages are intrinsically different. Habermas' ontological and epistemological standpoint gives the theorist a privileged position, says Poster.[51]

Thirdly, there is the question of a critical strategy. As I said earlier, this connects with the chosen mode of analysis. Thus the liberal is content with privacy law because this fits with the rational self and technical solutions. The Weberian focus on bureaucratic structure shows how the unanticipated consequences of action may produce an iron cage, of which surveillance is one aspect. Democratic restrictions could mitigate this. The Marxian, concerned still with the mode of production, maintains a focus on action through which domination and resistance is expressed. The Foucaldian; however, stresses language, not action, as the object of analysis. But it is not yet clear how, having shifted attention away from action, this approval provides any starting point for a critical theory.

Surveillance and Personhood

If we are to develop any kind of critical theory of surveillance that might offer the basis for informed and appropriate responses, some notion of human personhood, along with some understanding of the 'good society', must be involved. Even though it may turn out to be inadequate for a critique of the dimensions of databases indicated by Poster, I wish to hold onto the notion of humans as self-communicating creatures as being crucial to personhood. At this point, let us review some of the arguments that have brought us here. I shall begin by working within the 'modern' discourse of privacy before commenting on what kinds of insights are available from the 'postmodern' position.

Surveillance acquired distinct dimensions in modern societies, which, when viewed negatively, required protection for individuals (or at least for data about them). Privacy emerges as the vehicle for such protection. But surveillance itself has undergone subtle transformations. On the one hand it is electronically enhanced, granting it greater and more pervasive powers within the social fabric. But on the other its role in social control appears to be giving way to the softer social order of consumption, which it nevertheless still services.

The modern issue of surveillance has been countered in a modern fashion, by legislation, which explicitly or implicitly refers to privacy. Privacy, in turn, is understood in modern, liberal terms as balancing individual with societal interests, and those interests are increasingly distilled within consumer capitalism as property interests. The benefits of surveillance are recognized variously as thwarting terrorism, reducing fraud, preventing crime, and enabling participation in elections, granting new opportunities for improved health, as well as in organizations and in the consumer marketplace. And such benefits would hardly be denied, even by those most irritated or most anxious at specific surveillance practices. Thus privacy is considered as one 'value' among others, not dominant, even in Arcadian visions, but perhaps more prominent in the later twentieth century.[52]

Laws relating to personal data tend to be fairly weak, for two reasons. One is that such laws are all too often the product of political expediency and economic threat, and thus are minimal requirements, feebly enforced. They may actually serve to legitimize certain kinds of informational practices, despite lip-service paid to liberal 'individual' values.[53] Another reason, the obverse, is that little attention is paid to the human dignity or self-identity aspects of privacy. Such concerns no doubt seem much to arcane to be considered within the legislative task.

The upshot of this, as we have seen, is that privacy is a matter of self-protection. Those who are aware that data protection and privacy laws exist, and have the resources and motivation to take advantage of them, may do so. Those with entrepreneurial initiative may further take up arms against commercial surveillance by declaring property rights over 'their' personal data. This simply extends the early modern focus on possessive and self-protecting individualism. So although privacy was in the early modern period a privilege of the ruling classes, only later becoming identified with the non-public realm,[54] one could justly argue that we have come full circle once more: privacy is a privilege.

What, however, if we were take as central an emphasis on human personhood and self-identity? A good place to start is the concept of the data-image. Kenneth Laudon, working within a modern framework, offers the notion of data image as a means of drawing attention to the significance of the computerized portrayal of our lives to databanks.[55] What makes us uneasy about the data image, from a 'human dignity' point of view, is well expressed in the following quotation;

> My electronic image in the machine may be more real than I am. It is rounded; it is complete; it is retrievable; it is predictable in statistical terms ... I am in a mess; and I don't know what to do. The machine knows better – in statistical terms. Thus is my reality less real than my image in the store. That fact diminishes me.[56]

Now, why exactly does this 'diminish me? What is going on here?

Return for a moment to where we left Geoffrey Brown's discussion of the control of information. Brown insists that controlling the circulation of personal information is a question of the appropriateness of disclosure within differing contexts.[57] Thus 'access to particular information is systematically related in the appropriate way to the network of social relationships in which that person stands to others by virtue of their places in the role structure'.[58] Breaches of privacy in this view are attacks on the integrity of social identity. The sense of selfhood is diminished and freedom is constrained.

Of course, this approach raise numerous other questions (what if I don't accept some role assigned to me?). But its advantage lies firstly in the emphasis on modern surveillance itself, and not just the consequences of say, inaccurate data, being a potential threat, or at least something less than desirable. And secondly, this kind of approach has much to offer those engaged in the law- and policy-making process. The question of person-hood and social identity also relates back to our previous discussion of how identity is negotiated, which in turn connects with the processes of human communication.

To understand surveillance in relation to social processes of communication opens new doors. To say that we form and maintain self-identity by means of negotiation reminds us of some important factors. Before the advent of modern surveillance systems, communicating the kind of personal data now required by them depended on particular sets of relationships. What might be reported to a doctor, confessed to a priest or admitted to a close friend depended on the nature and quality of relationship. One might say certain things in one context but not in another. Given the commitments of certain professionals and kin to confidentiality, what was spoken to one would not be passed on to another. So personal data, in a world characterised by face-to-face relations, tends to be limited to voluntary disclosure to chosen confidants within relations of trust.

Of course, this could be seen as idealizing traditional situations and disregarding tendencies to gossip, slander and malicious whisper. But even to acknowledge these things is to note that such practices are considered undesirable. The social expectation, and indeed the very possibility of social intercourse, depends on the ongoing exercise of trust and tact. Although Goffman's work may be read as depicting the cynical manipulation of events and people by 'actors' occupying temporary and maybe strategic 'roles', even there an underlying sense of mutual commitments and social collaboration is evident.[59] Today, in the world of abstract systems dependent upon the manipulation of digital symbols, trust is no longer rooted in face-to-face relations.

The situations described here differ in even respect from those of earlier times. Personal data circulates within and between the databases of huge corporations and government departments. The society of strangers is now abstracted into machine systems within which no face-to-face human relations are possible. The data are collected, transmitted, sifted, sorted and shared promiscuously so that voluntary communication, and even consent, is seldom considered. And this is now our taken-for-granted reality. To expect that communicating personal information could be in the nature of voluntary disclosure of select items to specific persons tied to us by the tissues of trust seems simply irrelevant.

But taking such a view of personhood seriously is not entirely anachronism. The idea of controlling personal information already finds expression in many data protection and privacy laws. The British Data Protection Act, for instance, is based on the principles that 'personal data shall be obtained and processed fairly and lawfully, held only for those purposes and only be disclosed to [certain] people ... '. It provides for 'individuals to have access to data held on themselves and, where necessary, have the data corrected or deleted'.[60] So people can, in principle at least, know about data held about them and, if they have the motivation, ensure that they are correct, up-to-date and appropriate.[61] To take a specific case, Boston Public Utilities are now obliged to contact customers before cutting services when defaulters have been discovered through computer matching.

As we have seen, however, the reality is that 'privacy' often remains a privilege. Expressed within data protection law it stands as a necessary minimum requirement, but that hardly touches the deeper problem. Today's surveillance is carried out not only by government but also be large corporations, not only within the nation-state but in networks that transcend humanly created boundaries. The idea of a 'balance of interests' is risible. And very real possibilities exist that the feared totalitarian tendencies of surveillance society are already proliferating, within supposedly democratic polity.

Moreover, this surveillance may further be seen both as an extension of capitalist power and as the burgeoning of new structures of domination which employ digital language as their medium. To say this is not to fall into the trap of imagining that a societal electronic prison is in the making; that was dismissed as postmodern paranoia in chapter Four. Rather, certain aspects of panoptic discipline still manifest themselves in contemporary advanced societies, either to define individual as worthy consumers or to determine who, as deviants, should be subjected to more rigorous panoptic surveillance.

Beyond Privacy

The concept of privacy is inadequate to cover what is at stake in the debate over contemporary surveillance. At worst, the dominant framework for privacy debate – self-possessing, autonomous individualism – leaves us with a world of privilege where self-protection is only available to those who can negotiate it. At best, when understood in relation to a notion of personhood centred on self-communication, and thus resonating more with ideas like human dignity and human freedom, privacy – if that term must be used at all – has a place. In this light, we may see that some surveillance by large impersonal organizations itself is undesirable or at least in need of of strict regulation. The question must always be asked whether this or that surveillance system is permissible at all.

Such questions may be asked, and legal limits may be framed around the movement of information. The key problems would then be perceived in terms of trust and voluntary disclosure, both principles that can be – and in a limited sense have been – translated into law. But far more than this is required if the full consequences of a surveillance society are to be understood and their challenges met. An educative process would have to occur, as well as the mobilization of opinion and action on a number of fronts. The legislative approach is necessary, but far from sufficient.

The inadequacy of privacy is also exposed by changed circumstances. Electronic surveillance in the context of consumer capitalism represents a different social world from that of written documents in government bureaucracies or the Taylorist monitoring of employees in the workplace. In this context our very ability to participate depends upon our possession of certain coded numbers on plastic cards. As Michael Rubin puts it, 'our passport into [American] society is the information we share with others in exchange for recognition as being employable and creditworthy, to obtain medical treatment, and also for the right to pay taxes, and when needed, to obtain governmental assistance'.[62]

Such reliance upon the electronic 'passport' may also be viewed in terms of the data-image that circulates beyond our control and may in real life give us a 'good name' or a 'bad name' that in turn affects our life-chances. The whole system of networked databases serves as a potential mode of domination, disciplining us, however subtly, to adjust to the prevailing norms of consumer citizenship. Either way, reducing the issue to one of 'privacy' simply deflects attention from impugned personhood and a social situation in which electronic languages are permitted to define us and channel our social participation.

Thus the language of surveillance all too often classifies, divides, and excludes, based as it is on Enlightenment epistemologies, now electronically expressed. Some alternative is required that does not simply, and unrealistically, try to dispose of surveillance, but places it in another context. This makes the inclusiveness of a scheme like that of Habermas attractive, because it recalls elements of trust, founded not in some social contract, but in 'covenant',[63] while simultaneously reminding us that without language there cannot be a 'self'.

The important question is, can the idea of personhood relating to self-communication within a community of trust be retained in an era when the distinctive languages of the database are becoming dominant? I believe that the answer is positive, because although the condition of *post*modernity may well be nascent, it is emerging imbricated – overlapping – with modernity. In this view the problem of transcending 'privacy' still confronts us. There is a sense in which the language of the database is still recognisable to modern eyes, and may be challenged in the name of a counterfactual state such as Habermas' 'ideal speech situation'. Simultaneously, however, effort is required on a further front, beyond 'undistorted communication'. To quote Poster, this other theoretical/political problem is to 'account for the way actual language situations contain structures of domination and potentials for emancipating change'.[64] Even here, of course, we cannot evade the question of how humans are defined. Indeed, Poster's position sharpens this challenge.

This of course begs further questions, and thus pushes the debate into the realm not just of personhood, but of the 'good society'. Modern analysis, centred on privacy, ends with a world or privilege. The emerging framework for postmodern surveillance analysis may lead us, at worst, into a world of ubiquitous power. Is any other context available to give a rationale for a critical theory of surveillance? Interestingly enough, the modern and the postmodern analyses refer to dystopian models – *Nineteen Eight-Four* and the Panopticon respectively. These are models of society that warn of what might happen if nothing is done to avert the totalitarian or the maximum security future. But they still beg the question of what sort of society is desirable, as far as surveillance is concerned. It is to this question that we turn next.

11

Against Dystopia, Distance, Division

Now we see but a poor reflection as in a mirror; then we shall see face-to-face. Now I know in part; then I shall know fully, even as I am fully known.

St Paul[1]

Real-Time Dystopia

Does the future lie in Los Angeles? The web of elevated freeways and the pall of carbon-choked smog have in recent years dulled the attraction of that great city by the Pacific. But now another kind of future, equally ambiguous, is discernible there. Today, the neat lawns of LA's Westside sprout 'ominous little signs warning "Armed Response".[2] In Watts, says Mike Davis, one finds a 'panopticon shopping mall surrounded by staked metal fences and a substation of the LA Police Department (LAPD) in a central surveillance tower'. And an ex-police chief crusades for an anti-crime 'giant eye', a geosynchronous law-enforcement satellite. Who needs *Blade Runner* or *Die Hard* when Hollywood itself can evoke images of the future without using film? The freeway web is now overlaid by an electronic web.

In Mike Davis' LA, state-of-the-art electronics and high-tech policing divides the 'fortified cells' of the affluent from the naked social control of the criminalized poor. Private security systems are sold to insulate the rich from the rest. Once the electronic battlefield-style satellite is up and running, social divisions should be even clearer to the LAPD; 'good citizens, off the streets, enclaved in their high-security private consumption spheres; bad citizens, on the streets (and therefore not engaged in legitimate business), caught in the terrible, Jehovan scrutiny of the LAPD's space program'.[3]

Between the time when I was first writing this and the time I came to revise it for publication, areas of the city erupted in riot. This followed the acquittal of a white policeman whom millions had seen beating a black man, on televised amateur video. The precariousness of the situation became far more publicly visible, just as the poignancy of describing it was heightened. Dystopia – the warning-by-trend-analysis that predicts how our worst fears may be realized if nothing is done[4] – may on occasion be overtaken by events.

LA as a real-time dystopia captures neatly one of the themes of this chapter; surveillance analysed in terms of futures to be avoided. Dystopia is the converse of utopia, but they hold an ambiguous relation to each other. Bentham's Panopticon was for him a utopian – ideal – solution to social problems, but the same Panopticon has for Foucault distinctly dystopian undertones. Dystopia describes a situation in terms of trends towards some catastrophe; Orwell's *Nineteen Eighty-Four* provides a prime example.

Despite the rhetoric of community policing, with which cities like LA are awash, in reality the guardians of social order direct from a distance with electronic technologies. And the means of control is classic; divide and rule. Of course, LA's consumers may not exempt themselves from surveillance. Their elite databases and pay-per-cable TV offer opportunities for minute-by-minute monitoring of their lives, over and above credit cards and telemarketing. The difference is that they experience consumption as a realm of freedom, not as a prescribed social order. Here lies the 'bad edge of postmodernity'.[5]

A bleak picture, to be sure. We can make the complacent comment 'it won't happen here', or just hope that when it does, we'll be on the right side of the electronic tracks. Another response is denial; either 'he's got it wrong' or 'it's bound to be exaggerated in LA'. Yet again, fearing there might be some accuracy in Davis' 'fortress LA' – now desperately confirmed by fire and looting – we might turn our energies to discovering and resisting whatever forces brought it about.[6] Within these responses, where does sociology stand? And, in particular, in which direction are we led by the kind of analysis proposed in this book?

Three tasks lie before us. The first is to examine the role of dystopia in surveillance theory. What effects are achieved by framing social analysis in this negative, cautionary mood? The second is to clear some space for an alternative, or at least a complementary, approach by revisiting the Panopticon. This time we would focus on sight and on speech. The third task is to sketch the contours of a new approach to surveillance and to indicate what role it might have in critical social analysis and in political practice.

Dystopia in Surveillance Theory

Much surveillance theory is dystopian. The stark contrasts and helpless fear depicted in *Nineteen Eighty-Four*, *A Handmaid's Tale* or even in the excerpt from Mike Davis' *City of Quartz* may be muted in sociology. But the note of warning, the doom-laden prediction, is often present via the chosen concepts – surveillance capacities, for instance – or the conscious allusions such as those to Big Brother, watching. We have seen how the dystopian yields some strong clues both about surveillance itself and about how it is perceived by its subjects. But at the same time I have tried to show how the unmitigated negativism of the dystopian misleads. Surveillance has two faces.

The time has come to explore these themes a little further. I shall argue not only that dystopias – like *Nineteen Eighty-Four* or the Panopticon – mislead if taken too far within social analysis, but that something was amiss with these dystopias in the first place. One problem is that they are unable to articulate, except by implication, what might be a desirable state of affairs rather than an undesirable one. The other is that they encourage a form of fatalism. Even if we understand dystopia as a warning about what might happen if nothing is done about it, neither *Nineteen Eighty-Four* nor the Panopticon give any clues as to what might be done.

Like it or not, all social theory depends explicitly or implicitly on some social judgement. That is to say, normative notions about persons and about the 'social' inform all sociological explanation.[7] In the case of surveillance, interesting, and indeed fruitful, models originating in the work of George Orwell and Jeremy Bentham have illuminated social theory. As a matter of fact, neither of these authors intended that their work be used in quite this way; their ideas are mediated by others who claim more self-consciously to be social theorists. But they did intend that their work be taken as a criterion of judgement. Orwell's was a warning about incipient political trends; Bentham's potential political panacea.

How have Orwell's and Bantham's ideas been appropriated in social science? On the one hand, James Rule's classic 1970s study of surveillance makes a direct appeal to Orwell. He obtained his four criteria of 'surveillance capacity', so valuable for gauging the growth of surveillance, from an Orwellian picture of a 'total surveillance society'.[8] While his analysis of surveillance is admirably fair, careful and balanced – he eschews apocalyptic conclusions – Rule's basic sociological tool implies a judgement on societies that might more closely come to resemble *Nineteen Eighty-Four*. Other theorists, such as Dandeker, have followed Rule by using the same categories.[9]

Coming at the problem from a slightly different angle, David Flaherty similarly follows this line. 'Surveillance society', made possible by technologies Orwell knew not of, represents the society to be avoided. 'In the waning years of the twentieth century, our technocratic societies can accomplish what George Orwell could only fantasize about. . . Our capacity to create surveillance societies should force us to confront fundamental questions about their desirability . . . '[10] We shudder, says Flaherty, at the thought of living in worlds like *Nineteen Eighty-Four* or Atwood's *The Handmaid's Tale*. This is why we should ask 'at what point does surveillance become unacceptable, whether by private detectives, the police, or welfare and taxation authorities?'[11]

Most theorists pay at least passing attention to the relevance of Orwell to surveillance studies. Some, such as Gary T. Marx writing in the 1980s, explicitly argue for ways in which Orwell also needs to be updated, and analysis based on his images overhauled.[12] Marx maintains that both the massive expansion of surveillance using new technologies and their role within, but also beyond, government means that Orwell's contribution should be rethought. His argument obliges sociology to examine the societal ramifications of surveillance, within supposedly democratic situations.

On the other hand, Bentham's Panopticon is mediated by Michel Foucault, and, *via* his classic history, *Surveiller et Punir*, numerous other theorists of surveillance.[13] It is well-nigh impossible today to find anyone in social theory committed to the Panopticon as an ideal, a social panacea, even though the idea clearly has lost none of its appeal for some contemporary software designed, criminologists, shopping mall architects and police chiefs. Foucault himself, ever reticent to reveal the basis of his 'moral outrage' can hardly be thought an advocate of subordination through uncertainty. For others, the Panopticon patently functions as a postmodern equivalent of Max Weber's equally dystopic 'iron cage' of rationalized society.[14]

To refer to the Panopticon as 'dystopian' does, I know, beg a few questions. Bentham held it up as a utopian solution to social problems, while Foucault simply elaborates the ways in which – by his lights at least – its principles percolate through every layer of social life. His strong implication, however, is that having our daily lives controlled by a prison regime is less than ideal. Even if the Panopticon in Foucault falls short of some criteria of a literary criterion for dystopia, it is hard to deny that some dystopian characteristics are present. The apparent contradiction between utopian and dystopian themes in the Panopticon are opposite sides of the same coin. As Ruth Levitas says, these two are often found close together; 'the hope of what the future could be at best, the fear of what it may be at worst'.[15]

Both models or metaphors – Big Brother and the Panopticon – are used successfully as a means of highlighting what is negative and undesirable about surveillance. Both, interestingly enough, point beyond privacy preoccupations to questions of social control and asymmetries of power, although it must be said that while Orwell is still concerned about a loss of personal dignity, Foucault seems unconcerned about the loss of persons as such. Both models are understood dystopically as 'visions of social control'.[16] And both, significantly, depend upon 'vision' to maintain social control. Although the gaze, the scrutiny of the controlling other, may not literally be present in the electronic counterparts of Orwell's and Bentham's original images, it remains literarily present; the metaphors of seeing and being seen are central, even when the 'eyes' are mere digital impulses.

The dystopic paradigms deriving from Orwell and Bentham are indeed illuminating. They serve the purposes of alerting us to significant social trends or tendencies in the present that have already been discussed imaginatively in the past. They assist our identification of undesirable trends. Although the more dramatic 'thought control' is what we often associate with Orwell, in many ways his vision was far more mundane, and alarmingly contemporary. As Stanley Cohen observes, the control of proles, the mass of the population, depended on nothing more sophisticated than classification, segregation and behaviour modification.[17] Crime control in the later twentieth century, with all the humane talk of decarceration, seems to have some surprising affinities with Orwell; surveillance, anticipation, prevention are its watchwords. One might add that consumer surveillance operates by a smiliar logic as well, though seduction and channelling of choices might here be better terms than 'prevention'.[18]

This kind of exposition ties Orwell even more closely to Bentham, for whom the instrumental channelling of behaviour was paramount. A technique was sought in the Panopticon that would ensure the automatic functioning of the system, so that organizational certainty could be obtained at the price of uncertainty in the people it contained. Though Bentham conceived of his 'moral architecture' as a place for the 'fabrication of virtue', in fact the Panopticon served to redefined virtue itself. This production of virtue is essentially cynical – Bentham unwittingly used 'fabrication' in an ambiguous way. Psychological conditioning of the most deplorable kind here supplants genuine moral responsibility.[19]

There are some differences between Orwell's vision and that of Foucault's Bentham, however. Whereas Orwell's could be viewed as a 'possible but preventable' future, as it is in, say, Rule's hands, Foucault's Panopticon often appears as imminent and inevitable. Whereas the contemporary interpreters of Orwell's dystopia may under certain circumstances galvanize action and resistance – 'Big Brother is watching you' must be the best known anti-surveillance slogan – Foucault's dystopia seems rather to instil paranoia and paralysis. Whereas *Nineteen Eighty-Four* still clings to some shadowy hopes of democracy and decency, *Discipline and Punish* dissolves them in discourses of ubiquitous power.

The differences should not however be exaggerated. Even Orwell's dystopia finally leaves us with almost unrelieved pessimism. True, conflict, struggle, and resistance are present, but in the end only at an elite level. The proles – 85% of the population – are a pretty docile, determinable and one-dimensional lot. Does not even Orwell underestimate their knowledgeability, their capacity for making a difference? As Raymond Willams notes, 'by viewing the struggle as one between only a few people over the heads of an apathetic mass, Orwell created the conditions for defeat and despair'.[20]

But even if Orwell had a more positive message, the problem is that after Foucault it is hard to go back to Orwell. For Foucault has shown how the 'autonomous individuals' or Orwell's elite are indeed the product of post-Enlightenment Western thought. The quest for 'privacy' bound up with that approach is thus equally suspect as a means of counter-surveillance. Even if we grant that Orwell's desire for dignity and decency barked up the right tree, it is not clear how they would be preserved. Foucault's approach, for all its luminary quality, also seems unsatisfactory, because it is unclear exactly what is wrong with the Panopticon or what strategy might be appropriate to question or resist it.

Herein lies the challenge for surveillance theory. I propose that such theory often depends for its criterion of judgement, its normative basis, upon dystopian visions. These have the virtue of directing our attention to the negative, constraining, and unjust aspects of surveillance, and of helping us to identify which kinds of trends are especially dangerous from this point of view. But their disadvantage is that they may thus exaggerate the negative by seeing only one side of surveillance, promote pessimism about whether such negative traits can be countered, and fail to offer any indication as to what the content of an alternative might be.

In the next two sections I shall try to clear conceptual space for considering just such alternatives. Using the Panopticon as the starting point, we consider again its relentless gaze; what is really revealed? Secondly, we turn our attention to what wo do or do not wish to disclose verbally. Beyond this, we also must consider the non-verbal electronic language of databases.

Is Seeing Knowing?

The Panopticon inspector is 'in the know'. What is known is what is seen. But what is seen is also what is disclosed. In the kinds of surveillance that go on outside clearly carceral situations like the prison, much of what is disclosed is what is told. When asked for social insurance numbers or even addresses and telephone numbers, we tell. Verbal and non-verbal communication takes place between data-gatherer and data-subject. But that communication may be involuntary if in fact the data-gatherer obtains the data from a third party, such as an information broker. And once the data-image aquires this sort of life of its own, it seems more appropriate to speak of a data-object than a data-subject. Indeed, the electronic 'gaze' of the Superpanopticon's inspector is fixed on this data-object. What has happened here?

It seems that the categories of knowing, seeing, and saying are conflated and confused. The confusion can be explained, however, by returning to Bentham to discover exactly what was going on in his Panopticon. There, vision of a specific kind is paramount and the ocular is privileged over other kinds of knowing. If we examine that first of all, then we may turn – in the next section – to the issue of 'saying' or disclosing to others in words. The first task involves understanding surveillance from the perspective of the 'inspector', the second, from the perspective of those inspected, or, better, heard.

Recall that Bentham planned his Panopticon as a centrepiece of his aggressively secularist approach to policy.[21] The Panopticon was a weapon wielded in his war against religion. With a social panacea like this prison plan, religion would be rendered redundant. Virtue could be fabricated without reference to religion, the church, theology, or God. Yet paradoxically Bentham's Panopticon retained some religious referents. It was still located in a 'theology', albeit a secular one.[22] The Panopticon inspector is a parody of God; the inspector's vision, a play on omniscience or omniperception. He even used a biblical quotation from the Book of Psalms as an epigram to make this point.

We have argued that Bentham's Panopticon is now viewed as a dystopic vision, following Foucault. That is, the Panopticon is an undesirable, if not avoidable, future. Yet it expresses certain key ideas from the Enlightenment, ideas that have actually become constitutive of modernity. Before trying to see what might be beyond the Panopticon and beyond modernity, perhaps we should look back to see what Bentham overturned in order to construct his secular utopia. Could today's uneasiness with the Panopticon have arisen from Bentham's (mis)reading of his inspirational text? Did he do justice to the source of the essential idea lying behind the Panopticon? How complete was his secular social theology, even as a parody of divine omniscience?

Bentham made much of the unseen observer within the Panopticon; vision was just one-way. Thus the observed became the *object* of vision, echoing the more general subject-object relation characterizing much Enlightenment thought. For the *philosophes*, knowledge was largely constituted in this fashion. Today, this 'objective' knowledge, though increasingly doubted as a source of scientific certainty,[23] still finds a home in computer databases. Electronic surveillance carries this Enlightenment motif into the late twentieth century by its reduction of persons to data-images. The objects of digital 'gaze' can no more look back into the database than Panopticon inmates could see into the rotunda. Discovery of what went on behind the venetian blinds of the inspection tower depended on deliberate, determined, and maybe even devious action on the part of the observed. This is not dissimilar to the effort that so-called data-subjects have to make to get a glimpse at their database files.[24]

Within such a system, the data-image is distanced from the person, and thus also from forms of accountability and responsibility that might be expected in relationships. Though this may be viewed as an advantage insofar as body-language, gender, disability, or ethnicity may diminish as grounds for discrimination, this 'distancing effect' of technology[25] has very negative connotations here.[26] Though perhaps not as dramatic as the ways in which distancing was grotesquely evident in the TV computer games version of the 1991 Gulf War,[27] distancing by electronic surveillance is no less 'objectifying'. This also ties in with the 'maleness' of Enlightenment epistemologies that emphasize the rational at the expense of the emotional, the controlling rather than the caring,[28] and thus give us gender-lopsided data-images. It is undoubtedly the case that electronic surveillance neglects the dimensions of personhood typically associated with femininity.

No such objectifying is found in the psalm quoted by Bentham. One section he used as the epigraph for his secular social theology was 'Thou art about my path, and about my bed; and spiest out all my ways. If I say, peradventure the darkness shall cover me, then shall my night be turned into day'.[29] It should be noted that 'spiest' in seventeenth century English did not have the 'espionage' connotation it now does. Indeed, the psalmist relied on there being some reciprocity of seeing; the seen could see, the known could know.[30]

As well as mutuality there is forgiveness in this psalm; the psalmist appeals to divine amnesia to 'overlook' his sins. In Bentham's books no such thing occurs; his only 'overseeing' is the monitoring, accusatory kind. By the time this is electronically enhanced we get categorical suspicion. Forgiveness, which surely must form the foundational bedrock of any authentically trusting relationships between persons, is largely absent from today's surveillance.[31]

Bentham's *hubris* knew no limits. His inspector was to seek omniperception in the 'all-seeing place'. Comprehensive knowledge was the point of Panoptic architecture. Yet this pretence is perpetuated in electronic systems. Though the data-image is as patently limited as, say, an X-ray image, it tends to be treated as if it gave a full picture. The impression is given that motivation and intention are laid bare; yet only observable behaviour is recorded. However, while it may be 'unreal' to the data-subject, as W. I. Thomas once said in another context, it is real enough in its consquences,[32] Credit-worthiness in a consumer society is actually taken as an index of personal worth and grounds for social inclusion. Reliance on data-images does nothing to mitigate this. Bentham's denial of finitude, seen in his quest for secular omniscience, contrasts starkly with the psalmist's admission 'such knowledge is too wonderful for me'.

Bentham's Panopticon idea also rides roughshod over distinctions properly made between different spheres of social activity. All is harnessed and subordinated to the classificatory impulse that imposes an alien looic of surveillance in all places at all times. As we have seen, surveillance may protect, enable or affirm by ensuring equal treatment before the law, the right to vote, or freedom from danger. But the same surveillance, in a different context, may be oppressive and constraining. If I ask a neighbour to keep an eye on my child, the context makes surveillance enabling. If an arm of the state – say community policing – requires that neighbour to keep an eye on me, the context makes surveillance at least unwelcome and possibly inappropriate.

Bentham did away with such niceties and so does computer matching, consumer clustering, and so on. Ignoring the context-specificity of surveillance may amount to a denial of different spheres of social competence, each with its own integrity and accountability structure. It is a denial of the relational quality of seeing and knowing. When personal data circulates and is recycled in contexts far beyond that purpose for which it was garnered, profound violence is done to the variety and specificity of social relations. Such an insight goes beyond the idea that our incumbency of social roles is what counts. Though relating surveillance to appropriate roles has the virtue of stressing social relations, referring to the relations themselves avoids the implicit individualism of role theory.[33]

Seeing surveillance as a secular parody of divine omniscience puts the Panopticon in a sorry state. It is truly dystopic when viewed as a distortion of divine vision. No wonder the 'Jehovan gaze' of the Los Angeles Police Department's surveillance satellite appears so severe, so menacing. That gaze, when mediated by Bentham and Foucault and magnified by electronics, has everything to do with fear and nothing to do with love. It is precisely love that is lost between the biblical account and Bentham's account, love manifest in reciprocal seeing, protecting, care, and respect for the integrity and accountability of different social spheres. Could this contribute to an alternative normative basis of surveillance theory?

Before attempting to answer that question, we must consider speech as well as sight. Love and trust may be missing in this account of sight – the 'gaze' – but, given the bonding character of language, may we not hope that they will at least be found here? Unfortunately not. At least, not on their own. Power and control may also be discerned in the most intimate of social relations.

Confessing, Controlling, Confidence

The Panopticon, like The Enlightenment, gave priority to vision. But surveillance, despite its literal meaning, also refers metaphorically to verbal communication. What we say is used as evidence. Or rather, under certain circumstances – such as in a police statement – our words will be used to 'see' us in a fresh light, or maybe to trap and constrain us. But confession may also be the route to forgiveness and freedom. As with the visual, the verbal element in surveillance is also context-specific. The paradoxes of surveillance return to haunt us in the realm of communication.

What difference do words rather than sight make to surveillance? In the previous chapter we looked at the ways in which privacy concerns are often expressed in data protection law in terms such as 'control of personal information'. I suggested that in societies characterized by face-to-face relations, personal data is usually limited to voluntary disclosure to chosen confidants within relations of trust. Moreover, I expressed some scepticism about solutions to surveillance issues that reduce the problem to a technical, legal or marketplace level. What is at stake actually relates to self-identity which, though in some ways is 'given', is also established and maintained through verbal communication.[34]

One example of voluntary disclosure in trusting relations is confession to a priest within Catholicism. However, oral confession has also been analysed as a crucial connection between Christianity and social control. Once again, Michel Foucault has played a major role in attempting to explain the modern development of surveillance based upon uttered words; and the explanation is again tied tightly to religious practice, this time in the confessional.

Foucault argues that the traditional Catholic confessional does not so much decline in modern times as fine itself reconstituted and redistributed.[35] Medical, Legal, and scientific discourses on private life which rely on questionnaires, examinations, and surveys help to regulate the individual within administrative and bureaucratic organizations. What began as confession reappears in modern times as answers to census or tax-return questions. The '. . . religious inquiry into the soul overlaps with the secular inquiry into the citizen'.[36] We might add that in electronic times 'inquiry' need not involve the 'citizen' personally at all. Direct checking of databases elicits the involuntary 'confession'.

The only point I wish to consider from Foucault's analysis is the way that for him the confession 'is interwoven with the exercise and presence of power'.[37] The priest represents power; the confessional, control. So, if confession provides the link between religious and secular discourses of power, then Christianity – as in Bentham's Panopticon – is implicated in the development of modern forms of social control. This would seem to disqualify Christianity as a basis of critique. But just such a critique appeared possible after our exposure of Bentham's secular misunderstanding of omniscience.

In Foucault's disciplinary society, power operates not so much through the repression of desire as through classifying, tabulating, and organizing desire. From medieval times the confession allowed for the expression of desire, and for its consideration in terms of a code of appropriate conduct. This emerges in the growth of *self*-control characteristic of modern individualism. A number of questions may be raised about the success of this thesis[38], but for our purposes the most relevant are about the direct Christian connections with social discipline.

Early pastoral care for members of the Christian community did indeed involve total oversight, precisely because total well-being was the goal. Confession was a mutual matter, and this emphasis has been revived from time to time, for instance in the anti-individualistic Methodism of John Wesley.[39] Wesley objected to ways that a commitment to personal, pastoral care had degenerated in the more bureaucratic churches of later centuries.[40] Thus it is the failure at least as much as the success of Christianity that connects which modern disciplinary society.

Furthermore, Foucault blithely ignored the pagan, heroic quest for power as an end in itself, which lies at the root of the same social world.[41]

Foucault cannot both have his cake and eat it. Christian motifs may appear within the surveillance society, but they appear partly as Christian failures, and are fatefully intertwined with motifs of power utterly inimical to Christian teachings. Indeed, the Panopticon inspector, parodying God, would be proud of those latter motifs.

To argue that Christianity cannot wholly be blamed for the emergence of Foucault's disciplinary society is one thing; to suggest that it may make a constructive contribution to its alternative is another. But perhaps in the process of confession, not now to a priest but in a communal context, the outlines of such an alternative may be traced. Mutual confession actually represents the road to total transparency, which of course is anathema to the paranoid. But surely transparency in the context of trust and forgiveness is utterly different from transparency in the thrall of power? It seems very hard to affirm this today. Such transparency is either taken to be self-evidently destructive or, if taken more seriously, is compromised by association with other modern motifs.

Richard Sennett, for instance, excoriates the 'destructive *gemeinschaft*' associated with modern quests for intimacy. People 'opening themselves up to each other' simply impose intolerable burdens on all concerned, he warns.[42] Yet, at the same time, in the 'society of strangers' individuals are involved in a constant quest for affirmation, for self-identity, through communication with others. In Niklas Luhmann's analysis, the mode of communication thus linking people together is 'love'.[43] But it is decidedly a love with limits, resting in the sinking sand of self-centredness.[44] It is not clear that transparency as a virtue can stand up to such critique.

One exception to the rule of scepticism about the use of mutual communication as a normative base for emancipatory theory is Jürgen Habermas. In his 'ideal speech situation', participants find freedom through 'undistorted communication'.[45] For Habermas communicative action is the human distinguishing trait *par excellence*. Here 'the actions of agents involved are co-ordinated not through egocentric calculation of success but through acts of reaching understanding . . . they pursue their individual goals under the condition that they can harmonize their plans of action on the basis of common situation definitions'.[46] This amounts to communication without compulsion. There is much to commend this approach to critical theory, with its clear starting point, its focus on interaction, and its relevance to surveillance as a form of communication.

Several difficulties are also presented by Habermas' approach, however. It is unclear what undistorted communication would be *about*; what is the content of the free choices made by participants?[47] Then, the theme of autonomy remains strong in Habermas as a means of overcoming the technologically-mediated constraints of 'prediction and control'; but it is hard to see how this autonomous freedom is in the end any more than power. More of the same?[48] Habermas also makes metaphorical use of the concept of 'convenant' over against 'contract'. While this wisely connects the reality of human solidarity with the religious, without making that connection tighter it is hard to see how it yields sufficient leverage on the problems presented here.[49] Four, how do we arrive at undistorted communication when electronic media, which as Zygmunt Bauman says 'make sins inevitable and salvation unattainable',[50] already frame our discourse? Such difficulties would have to be faced squarely before 'communicative action' could form the basis for a non-dystopian surveillance theory. It does, however, push us in the right direction.

Foucault connected Catholic confession with the disciplinary society, but his analysis is incomplete. To accept this could open the door for an alternative, maybe even Christian, contribution to the non-carceral society, where oversight involves as much pastoral care as moral supervision. But within involves as much pastoral care as moral supervision. But within existing social theory emancipatory themes relating to communication seem stuck in old discourses of individualism and autonomy. If freedom is power and love self-centred, we are left only with dark dystopian visions of social control. The technologies that distance, the surveillance that divides, will be all there is.

From LA to the Other City

Is the future in LA? Is what faces us a world of electronic technologies that classify us clinically, include and exclude by consumerist criteria, and are backed up by police and welfare departments? As the power of apartheid crumbles in South Africa, will the new 'non-persons', segregated by surveillance systems, be failed consumers?[51] Will something similar occur in the new nation-states of Eastern Europe? Certainly, the Panopticon image captures significant social and technological trends; contemporary surveillance does facilitate moral distance, and it does help to entrench social division and to reinforce the social order of consumerism.

But in terms of other analytical threads woven here, the panoptic is an incomplete paradigm. Surveillance enables as well as constrains, but the Panopticon image implicitly denies this (though not, notably, in Poster's portrayal of the Superpanopticon, where constraint and enabling features still appear).[52] Indeed, the Panopticon, even more than Big Brother, generates only bad news and unremitting dystopia. The Panopticon, with societal surveillance itself, is a product of modernity. So is privacy, its supposed solution. Only the magic of modernity can cope with the idea that we can be emancipated from the negative side of surveillance when its proffered alternative emerges from the same framework.

The other side of modernity does not look inviting either. Foucault's work may not be all we have to go by, but for him postmodernity is ultimately a world of pure power. He eyes the Panopticon unfavourably, but can never tell us exactly why. Moreover, he leaves us feeling uneasy. Individuals may be modern fictions, but where are *persons*? The disciplinary society may have historic links with Christianity, but is not Foucault's version of this story somewhat one-sided?

It is what Foucault omits that is so significant, especially with regard to Christianity. Nowhere in Foucault's work is Bentham's use of Psalm 139 discussed, yet Bentham obtained his metaphor from just that source.[53] But the constrast between the Panopticon and that psalm could not be more pronounced. Bentham's pretended omniscience denies his finitude, collapses all spheres of social interaction into one arena of surveillance, objectifies those upon whom the gaze falls, denies forgiveness and destroys trust by facilitating mutual *malveillance*.[54] When it comes to confession, the disclosure of what is personal, again Foucault can only see power relations at work. No pastoral care, only social control.

Taken together, though, these neglected counterpoints add up to components of an alternative. As modernity falters, it seems clear that such alternatives cannot be grounded in Reason, Science, or whatever. But that does not make them unavailable or illegitimate. Why should social theory not be animated by a hope of peace, rather than of power, of participation, rather than of exclusion, of love, rather than of fear? Desire for a better way of living[55] may thrive better in some historical circumstances than others, but it will take more than a few postmodern pessimists to extinguish it.

Indeed, the need to articulate such desires is expressed with increasing frequency within social theory. They may take the form of a goal, such as Habermas' ideal speech situation, or a call to 'utopian realism' in theorists as ideologically separate as Anthony Giddens and Peter Berger.[56] However, modern utopias are the stepchildren of distinctly *pre*-modern parents, originating in the Western traditions with the biblical prophets. They would both warn of dire outcomes if present unjust and immoral practices were continued *and* promise peace – or *shalom*, all-round well-being based on right relations between God and people, land and people, and people and people – if justice and righteousness were upheld.

One highly important link between Old Testament prophets and modern utopias occurs in St Augustine. He constrasted the *civitas dei* – the City of God – with the *civitas terrena*, the earthly city where self-possessing power and other-denying violence again reign.[57] In this vision, attainable not through struggle but by grace, not through reason but by faith, responsible persons are not reduced to autonomous individuals, and peace – *shal*om – rather than power is the true human condition. The creation provides the initial clues about such *shalom*; the negative distortions of *dominium* – mastery – overlay this, but forgiveness and reconciliation are available in Jesus to correct the distortions and restore the 'peaceable Kingdom'.

Needless to say, predictable but not insignificant objections are raised against this position. The first has to do with Augustine's inappropriate politics; liberation theologians rightly question his elitism, feminists his views on female subordination. However, Augustine can be read in much less elitist ways, as he was, for instance, by early French Christian socialists, who considered he had discorvered a 'social' realm.[58] And the feminist reading – through it correctly exposes unforgivable errors – is also selective. Moreover, it must be observed that while socialist feminism has a similar problem with Karl Marx's ineptitude about gender, it is scarcely sufficient grounds for rejecting the rest of Marx.

Secondly, Augustine hardly fits the 'utopian' category, given his conviction that this world is no more than a 'dark vestibule leading to the great hall of the next'.[59] True enough, and this is why utopianism proper describes so poorly what I argue for here. But at the same time Augustine had no contempt for this world; it was for him the arena of God's purposes. The City of God, the 'other city', provided a present reality which both exposes wrong in, and offers an alternative within, temporal society.[60]

Then it may be objected that Augustine's position requires prior faith, its very epistemology involves *fideism*. To this I say, granted, – as Augustine himself said, 'faith seeks understanding', – but with two qualifications. First, what is the alternative – some position that is empirically demonstrable? This will hardly do in a postempiricist climate! Every authentically critical theory has its baseline; Augustine's was Christian. Then, the implications flowing from this position do not necessarily require Christian commitment. Forms of hope may spring from many sources, but what this one offers does seem relevant to the problems of surveillance. What is yet lacking is an agency capable of making a difference that would turn the hopes to vision.

This is the political problem, to search for agency and the possibility of hope.[61] I have argued that the pessimism and fatalism of dystopian surveillance models deriving from Foucault and from Orwell fail at just these points. In concluding this chapter, let me sketch an alternative, deriving from the 'other city', that takes us beyond dystopia, distance and division.

214   *Counter-Surveillance*

Towards an Alternative

Suveillance should be a major concern of both social analysis and political action because it has become a central feature of contemporary advanced societies. The survey offfered here shows clearly that issues raised by surveillance must no longer be treated in a marginal, piecemeal fashion; no longer, that is, if we wish to avoid a dystopian future. However, while resisting the fulfilment of our worst fears is one thing, attitudes and action would both be better informed if we had more idea of what a desirable future might look like. And while general positive sentiments may appear to counter dystopian pessimism, tackling the political problem of identifying hope and agency requires proposals that come down to the level of specific policies.

Geoffrey Brown rightly concludes that the long-term solution to the problems of surveillance lies in such intangible areas as 'openness, accountability and co-operation'.[62] Implicitly, he too recognizes that remedies typical of modernity are at best strictly limited, and at worst futile. From such practices as openness, accountability, and co-operation could come real alternatives to today's surveillance difficulties. Equally, we may couch the problem, perhaps more sociologically, in terms of *participation*, *personhood* and *purposes*. From 'participation' derive some alternatives to the exclusionary power of much surveillance, from 'personhood' some criteria by which to judge the data-image, and from 'purposes' an antidote to the self-augmenting development of surveillance technologies.

Participation. In its historical origins the growth of surveillance may be traced in part to the expansion of citizenship. That is to say, increasingly full social participation became available to members of nation-states on the basis of established civil, political, economic and social rights. The administration of such rights entailed the use of documentary indentification and the construction of personal dossiers. Whatever constraints this imposes has to be understood in the light of the enablement offered.

However, the language of new technologies, superimposed upon that of bureaucratic organization and the extension of surveillance into the consumer sphere, now threatens some of those rights, so that the equation of constraint and enablement is less easy. The revival of interest in 'citizenship' as a central concept for both social analysis and political practice is to be welcomed in this respect.[63] It both extends and updates earlier pursuits of the just society, with which surveillance was symbiotically intertwined; at the same time in connects to the contemporary quest for full social participation for marginalized and excluded groups.

Surveillance practices seem more and more to reinforce the social order of consumerism, through credit cards, ISDN telephone services, and so on, while simultaneously maintaining existing soical divisions, especially those between consumers and non-consumers or those within the occupational structure and those cut off from it. To seek for a 'balance of interests' between 'individuals' and corporations or 'the state' seems hopelessly inadequate when the starting point is such an asymmetry of power. Strategies to widen or to keep open social participation must of course have a far broader base than merely a focus on surveillance, but such a focus would now be a necessary component of strategy.

As far as public and corporate policy is concerned, the goal of maximum social participation could be sought by means such as regarding computer networks as common carriers, as public utilities. Of course this flies in the face of current deregulation, but it is not necessarily unrealistically utopian to consider this option.[64] Its virtue would be to reduce the power of 'social management' by finding a place for both consumer and non-consumer voices to be heard. Similarly, within what will no doubt continue to be called privacy laws, the emphasis should be shifted away from mere self-protection and towards placing a greater onus on data-gatherers to ensure that data is obtained fairly, in the demonstrably best interests of data-subjects, and used only for those purposes and with as much subject access as possible. Again, this may seem to have a ring of unreality to it, but it only does so because 'privacy' and data protection law is so notoriously cynical and subject-unfriendly.[65]

Personhood. This is the corollary of participation and is closely articulated with it. The specific question that prompts concern here, and that is so central to all contemporary surveillance, is the data-image. We have seen how this artifact crucially affects life-chances and also renders fragile one's very reputation. Both a 'good life' and a 'good name' may be put in jeopardy by it. The data-image objectifies, is based almost entirely on a one-way transmission of information, and is redolent of stereotypical masculine traits, while its categories are clustered around observable behaviour alone. Furthermore, it may turn out to be a means of domination in ways as yet only dimly perceived.

What I mean by this is that our humanness itself, rather than just our life-chances or good name, is increasingly defined in terms of the data-image. Who we are to the ubiquitous machine, the ubiquitous connection, is more significant than who we are to ourselves or to each other. So far from there being a distinctiveness to being human, whether rooted in Habermas' language or in the *imago dei*, humanness may be redefined by surveillance-based powers, to which we are accountable.[66]

These features reflect the quest of efficiency, productivity, accuracy and predictability that are the hallmarks of contemporary surveillance. But no technical reasons exist why other features should not be present as well or instead. Caring and protecting motifs, for instance, would be one area to be explored. And the data-image could also be constructed in such a way as to include intentionality, as well as mere mechanical behaviour, and forgiveness, in that records would be erased when needed no longer. To achieve this, groups of professionals, from systems designers to quality controllers, would have to be involved.

In this vein Alan Dix proposes that 'auditing may be at the heart of a people-friendly company's information policies' and thus that all organizations operating surveillance should employ those who would 'examine information systems for the way they use or misuse personal information'.[67] Such auditors may be able to develop quite new sets of criteria to aid their organizations in this way. However, as Dix wryly observes, 'the main problem with such an information structure is not technical, but that it would conflict with the corporate power structures'.

One specific area in which much attention should be focused is computer matching. As we have seen, this represents a massive and rapidly growing aspect of surveillance, whether in government or in commercial contexts. Yet at the same time it is one about which all too little is known in detail. Its great virtue, as far as those employing it are concerned, is that whole categories of data-subjects may be isolated according to certain criteria. This same 'virtue' however, gives us what Gary T. Marx dubs 'categorical suspicion'.[68] People are targets for consumer advertising campaigns, or suspected of tax evasion or welfare fraud, on the basis of thier involuntary membership of a statistical 'group' that is disclosed, involuntarily, to surveillance operators. As far as computer matching is concerned, a case may be made not only for great vigilance but also, from the criteria applied to participation and personhood alike, for questioning whether some versions of such systems should be permitted at all.

Purpose. Underlying both previous principles – participation and personhood – is the assumption that the purposes of surveillance systems should be the constant subject of sociological scrutiny and political concern. This is so because of the ease with which such purposes may be subverted, obscured or replaced. The story of surveillance in modern societies is studded with references to bureaucratic augmentation and technocratic enlargement, each of which exhibits strong tendencies towards autonomy. That is to say, instrumentality – *dominium*, mastery – predominates.

The alternative here would be to identify, not some fixed and static 'purposes' for appropriate surveillance, but rather some dynamic criteria for gauging their appropriateness. Given the overweening ambition that appears to have attended most surveillance schemes since the Panopticon, a concentration on *limits* would be apt here. Limits to knowledge, the seeking of specificity rather than omniscience, constitute the most obvious of these. But another limit, highly pertinent to an era in which the use of new technologies is serving to blur boundaries between previously discrete domains, would be a sphere-by-sphere check on surveillance operations. What may be ethically or politically unassailable in one social field is often inadmissible in another. This raises queries, again, for computer matching, and also about the extent to which data-subjects may control personal information about them.

These three categories of participation, personhood and purposes are offered as a contribution to finding direction for hope in an analytical field dominated by dystopia. They comport well with Augustine's 'other city' but may fit equally with other commitments. They are intended as means by which the normative content of surveillance theory may be weighed, and by which new theory may be devised. And they can be added to, particularly as we come to understand better the peculiar consequences of electronic languages on life-chances and on the constitution of 'individuals'.

Beyond theory, such categories could find a role within political practice at both the policy and the movement/mobilization levels discussed in the previous chapter. Change agencies are still available, Orwellian pessimism or Foucaldian fatalism notwithstanding. Consumers and citizens show they are far more knowledgable and competent than certain deterministic theories allow. Some activists and responsible advocates do make a difference to the climate of opinion.[69] And symbolic victories such as that against the excesses of the Lotus Household Marketplace do much to spur further questioning and redirecting surveillance practices. From individual actors to collective strategies, green shoots are visible.

12

Beyond Postmodern Paranoia

Postmodern Paranoids

Modernity established surveillance as a central social institution. Today, the expansion of surveillance using electronic technologies, to settle with the articulation of surveillance with consumerism and its ever-stretching global reach, poses big questions for surveillance and modernity. As far as surveillance is concerned, at least, a good case can be made that modernity is either entering a new phase or, possibly, is being superseded. Surveillance studies throw fuel on the fire of postmodern debate, and rightly so.

However, this requires that the ways we think about surveillance also undergo revision. At present, surveillance theory is dominated by models and metaphors deriving from the modern era. The discourse of Big Brother demonstrates this most clearly; Orwell's prescience was limited to state power and primitive technology, and left a legacy of pessimism. Globalization and the subtle sophistication of information technology were not anticipated by him. Even in the case of the Panopticon, whose relevance to postmodern analysis is currently being explored to advantage, at best fear and at worst paranoia is engendered. Such paranoia is also evident, of course, outside academy, by those whose have replaced the .38 with the camcorder, and who put their trust in high-tech home security systems.

But paranoia patently will not do as a response to contemporary surveillance. Without doubt, the expansion of electronic surveillance represents one aspect of a major challenge to social participation and to human personhood. But paranoia is a pathological response. It is blind to the subtleties of surveillance which, as I have shown, enables and empowers as well as constrains and limits action. And paranoia produces political paralysis. Either a form of fatalism takes over, or else energies are spent protecting privacy as a sphere of privilege.

Not that such pessimism and paranoia is inexplicable. For one thing, by its very nature electronic surveillance is only hazily visible. The unknown is frequently feared. For another, the withdrawal into the private, individual, consumer domain makes any potential external threat appear magnified. Thirdly, the contemporary climate of decline is conducive to dystopia;[1] economic recession, ecological catastrophe, famine and incurable disease, all on a global scale, leave little room for hope.

So we have a complex problem. The sites of surveillance have been enlarged to include the new and vast terrain of consumerism, which simultaneously may be viewed as a source of social order in itself. The medium of surveillance has shifted decisively from paper files and direct observation to computer files that filter data through a grid of electronic language and are networked by telecommunications. The theories attempting to explain surveillance trends are rooted in metaphors generated by modernity, and are often misleadingly one-dimensional. Their practical logic leads either to technical tinkering with legal fixes or to resigned political passivity.

Despite the laudable effort to reconsider surveillance in late-modern or postmodern terms, few theorists seem able to escape the insidious sway of pessimism and paranoia. The message of this book, however, is that the paranoid posture is inappropriate. Surveillance is paradoxical and ambiguous, exhibiting more than one face. The Panopticon in particular, orginating in Cartesian obsessions with the 'gaze', inevitably deflects attention from the dual character of surveillance, which, to oversimplify, spells control *and* care, proscription *and* protection. Let me try to summarize the main themes of this study that take us beyond postmodern paranoia.

Surveillance Society Today

Rather late in the day, sociology started to recognise surveillance as a central dimension of modernity, an institution in its own right, not reducible to capitalism, the nation-state or even bureaucracy.[2] As such, surveillance shows more than one face. The prominent paradox is that surveillance simultaneously represents both a means of social control and a means of ensuring that citizens' rights are respected. For example, the state that keeps tabs on the population can be influenced by that population by means of those tabs. Despite this paradox, the fact remains that the kinds of models used to try to understand surveillance focus on the darker, negative side of social control.

No sooner had sociology got a clear fix on surveillance, however, than the focus became fuzzy again. Events seem to be overtaking surveillance analysis in at least two important respects. First, in the later twentieth century surveillance adopted a new medium, electronic technologies. Suddenly the talk is of a 'new surveillance', qualitatively different from that which existed before.[3] Some such pronouncements are little more than high-tech hype, inflated imagery derived from technological determinism. But, that said, several changes do seem to follow in the train of new technologies.

In terms of pervasiveness and intensity, for example, surveillance is certainly amplified by electronics. This holds both for systems deliberately established to monitor and check and for those which, despite being originally set up with different aims in view, also promote closer surveillance. We have seen how this is the case both in government administration and within the capitalistic workplace. Surveillance, which became part of everyday life with the coming of modernity, now penetrates even more deeply into those routines. And we participate with it, routinely, often unconsciously, as the self-disciplined bearers of our own surveillance.

Far-reaching consequences follow. New categories of social relationship emerge, structured by the data-image. This data-image reconstitutes 'selves' by piecing together bits of data drawn from diverse sources. These days, instead of surveillance being contained within discrete spheres, new technologies permit a blurring of boundaries. Computer networks transgress conventional conduits of personal information. Creating myriads of new channels that defy definition. Computer matching in particular makes visible this effect, which, in conjunction with statistical analysis, isolates groups and identifies potential deviants with ease.

Secondly, surveillance moved into a new site, consumption. Again, this situates surveillance within broader social transformations – in this case, the growth of consumer capitalism – but nonetheless, surveillance itself must be rethought in its consumer phase. Paradoxically – again! – the consumer society exercises social control *via* individual freedom, even though the marketplace is under heavy surveillance. TV ads in particular help to structure the social order of consumption.[4] In both instances the process is also globalized.

Two things should be noted here. Surveillance carefully sifts consumers, clustering them in crude categories to be taught specific skills and educated according to their economic station. This is hardly a coercive form of surveillance, though; judging by the evidence from marketing companies, it is one that does contribute to the consumerist order and people cheerfully comply. On the other hand, such surveillance at the same time classifies together those whose market position disqualifies them from participation in the consumerist cornucopia. This same group are much more likely to experience surveillance of a more carceral kind, not only from corporations but also from welfare and policing departments. Let me stress that I am not elevating consumerism to the plane of a desirable social order, but rather commenting on the lot of those cut off from it. Consumer surveillance reproduces and reinforces such divisions.

In short, contemporary surveillance exists in an expanding range of settings, within each of which surveillance capacities are augmented and to which new technologies increasingly contribute. New categories of social relationship are emerging, based on the data-image, which more and more has consequences for life-chances, personal reputations and maybe even our ontological status as humans. While the soft social control of surveillance may be scarcely perceptible, and for many is relatively innocuous, it also serves to perpetuate social division, particularly those on the axis of consumption.

The idea of a surveillance society may usefully draw attention to the far-reaching ramifications of this central dimension of modernity. To examine 'surveillance society' is to examine social relations today in terms of surveillance, as one might in terms of capitalism, patriarchy and so on. Equally, it can mislead, either through association with other technology-driven notions like the 'information society'[5] or through neglect of the 'two faces' of surveillance. It is worth being clear about these potential pitfalls. They relate to the two major contexts within which, I have insisted, the sociology of surveillance should be located; the historical and the normative.

As to the first, one crucial conclusion of our analysis is this; while computer and telecommunications technologies do contribute to alterations in the nature of contemporary surveillance, to focus on the allegedly new and neglect the long-term historical context is profoundly mistaken. Just as modern societies were from the outset 'information societies'[6] so they are by definition 'surveillance societies'. Continuity as well as discontinuity may be discerned within surveillance practices and processes. Some of the latter may be traceable to electronic influence. But even if we grant that electronics does bias communication in new ways, this still must be seen in a broader context than surveillance only.[7] Technological determinism wrapped in the language of 'computers controlling you' simply will not do.

Turning to the second context, normativity, we focus on the failure to theorize both faces of surveillance, which is visible in the models adopted for its critique. The paradox may be acknowledged – people find social benefit in surveillance – but the emphasis is firmly negative; surveillance is control, constraint, the probing eye, unfreedom. In other words, the prominent models of Big Brother and the Panopticon are dystopic, concerning – in sociological treatments – fearful futures. Not only so, but when used today, the need to update these models is implied. An article entitled 'Big Brother 1994', for instance, refers to an analysis of connections between consumer and government surveillance,[8] while Poster's 'Superpanopticon' clearly suggests a surveillance situation resembling but transcending Bentham's prison architecture. My contention is that they need not only updating but rethinking.

Thus the context within which surveillance should be rethought is not only the historical – which yields strong clues as to why the new technologies are shaped in a particular way – but also the theoretical and critical. As I have suggested, surveillance theory has benefited tremendously from sociological insight, but in terms of producing a normative theory difficulties still remain. Regrettably, some of the most telling insights come from theory that emphasises the negative and that ultimately offers no buffer against paranoia.

As an alternative to this, I propose that the social analysis of surveillance be harnessed to a consideration of elements of the 'good society' as opposed merely to those of the 'bad'. The question then becomes, what 'good society'? Not a utopia as such, but a state of affairs that has utopian aspects. I have indicated that Habermas' situation of 'undistorted communication' has much to offer in this respect. Its focus on language and communication fit it well for the analysis of surveillance – which may be viewed as a communicative process – and also highlights questions of self or personhood and of social participation. This position on its own is however inadequate. Further work that examines the consequences of electronic framing of discourse is also required.

My personal position, which became evident both from my critique of Foucault's failure to understand Psalm 139 and from the shortcomings of Habermasian theory – less than a full commitment to the 'covenant' metaphor, and an inability to encompass the subtleties of 'database discourse' – involves a return to Augustine's 'other city' for guidance. Social participation is there based on human solidarity which is literally 'given', and not on effort, let alone on market-position. Likewise personhood is understood not as the self-possessing individualism attacked by Augustine – and which flourishes within privacy discourse today – but as the *imago dei*, which again accents solidarity, dignity and responsibility.

It is imperative that some clear conception of elements of a 'good society' be articulated with the analysis of surveillance, so that constructively critical theory can be made available. My understanding of the present situations convinces me that notions akin to *participation, personhood* and *purposes* would serve well. Preoccupation with pessimistic prognoses or with privacy could be sidestepped and genuine progress made towards appropriate responses. But their virtue would not merely be analytical, as if that activity ever took place in a moral and political vacuum. The concepts of participation, personhood and purpose would also serve to reorient policy and practice in the surveillance realm.

For the Future

To eschew fatalism or paranoia is one thing. To face the future with realism and hope is another. I have tried to sketch a vision that catches some elements of hope, and to couple that to the realism of sociological analysis. But even this is of little use without the identification of some agency or agencies, capable of transforming present situations into something different and desirable. Surveillance, as explored in this book, is neither overwhelmingly negative in its effects nor incorrigibly evil in its character. But it is undergoing certain rapid changes at present, so that it is hard to get a handle on what exactly is happening.

The first agency then, would actually be responsible social analysis. In understanding better the meaning of electronic languages and of the relation between consumption, social order, and surveillance, common obstacles to appropriate political action would be removed. The more this could be considered within the educative processes of contemporary society, the better. Our worst fears of surveillance will be realized much more easily in contexts where such complacent assumptions reign as that computerized efficiency equals progress or that privacy laws protect citizens. Thus educative initiatives should be welcomed. In the USA, for instance, university and college computer science accreditation requires the inclusion of 'social and ethical implications of computing'.[9] In Britain, the Open University's 'Introduction to Information Technology' includes similar questions.

Such public awareness of surveillance issues could further be raised through professional groups and organizations, especially those directly concerned with computing, information management, and so on. Recall the importance of 'mobilization' responses mentioned in Chapter Eight, and the dramatic results of the computer networking of the Computer Professionals for Social Responsibility group in blocking development of the Lotus Household Marketplace software in 1991. Their attempts to argue for limits to consumer surveillance expansion fits in exactly with my criteria of participation, personhood and purposes. Resisting the growth of electronic surveillance *per se* would be a futile gesture. Attempting to channel it in ethically and politically appropriate directions is sociologically much more *à propos*.

More broadly, other kinds of movements may also contribute to the containment of surveillance. If we are right to think of 'surveillance as a site of struggle in its own right',[10] then there is every reason to expect various kinds of groups and movements to contest this territory, no doubt in the name of privacy. Consumer groups and organizations represent one important sector which, as we have seen, has already flexed its muscles. In Britain banking practices and consumer blacklisting have come in for criticism, and in the USA more *ad hoc* groups have mobilized to resist unwanted direct marketing.

Of course, creating policies and laws equal to the realities of today's surveillance society is another task for which agencies exist. Without relaxing my indictment of privacy laws for being cynical, sieve-like and subject-unfriendly, it may still be said that such laws are a necessary minimum. Weak law is better than none at all. Precedents for some protection are set that way, and the foundation for improvements laid. In a situation where surveillance becomes increasingly global, it is interesting that legal limits similarly start to have international implications. The European Convention on Data Protection, for instance, may well have beneficial effects on citizens well beyond Europe, as well as within it. As Europe requires trading partners to comply with the convention, the USA and Canada may well be obliged to extend legislation to the currently untouched field of consumer surveillance.

Needless to say, the political problem involves not only identifying agencies that might spur transformative activity, but also searching for appropriate ways of doing so. It is clear, for instance, that some kinds of regulation of surveillance practices could wind up with as much invasive bureaucratic machinery as the practices they intend to reduce. It is equally clear that if surveillance is not to be viewed in a paranoid fashion, then space must be made not only for viewing it as a 'necessary evil' but as a 'greater good'. The case of caller ID telephone services is a case in point. Technical means are available for maintaining such services for women or minority groups in danger while denying them to direct marketers. The question of which purposes would be served is critical here.

Which brings us back to the main point. Surveillance is a central institutional area of contemporary societies, and as such calls for forms of social analysis and political action that include but also transcend the local and the piecemeal. Without doubt legal, technical and even educational remedies to the problems raised by surveillance are inadequate, just as analytical approaches tied to modern paradigms are also inadequate.

Contemporary surveillance must be understood in the light of changed circumstances, especially the growing centrality of consumption and the adoption of information technologies.

Imaginative analysis, informed by constructively critical theory based on notions of participation, personhood, and purpose, would not only go a long way towards relieving us of the pessimism and paranoia bequeathed to us by the dominant models, but would create space for genuine alternatives. We may not see them clearly yet, but they are not too much to hope for.

Notes

Where full publication details of books referred to are not given, they can be found in the Select Bibliography.

CHAPTER 1   BODY, SOUL AND CREDIT CARD

1   Quoted in David Rubin 'Realism in the Social Sciences', in Lisa Appiginesi and Hilary Lawson, *Dismantling Truth*, London, Weidenfeld and Nicholson, 1989, p. 58.

2   The concept of the surveillance society was first used by Gary T. Marx to refer to a situation in which 'with computer technology, one of the final barriers to total control is crumbling' ('The Surveillance Society: the threat of 1984-style techniques' in *The Futurist*, June 1985, pp. 21–6). It was taken up later by others, such as David Flaherty in his *Protecting Privacy in Surveillance Societies*.

3   James B. Rule's *Private Lives, Public Surveillance* won the C. Wright Mills award of the SSSP in 1974 as the best social science work dealing with current social issues.

4   Anthony Giddens, *The Nation-State and Violence*.

5   For example, Sandra Lee Bartky 'Foucault, femininity and the modernization of patriarchal power' in Irene Diamond and Lee Quinby (eds) *Feminism and Foucault: Reflections on Resistance*, Boston, Northeastern University Press, 1988.

6   Michel Foucault, *Discipline and Punish; the Birth of the Prison*. (The Panopticon is discussed in Chapter Four of this book.)

7   I use the term 'surveillance society' to suggest, not that the widespread adoption of information technologies has given rise to a totally new situation, but that it has amplified and accelerated certain tendencies and processes. I do

imply that surveillance is an increasingly significant dimension of contemporary social life, and one that should be examined sociologically and politically.

8 It is used as such by Christopher Dandeker in *Surveillance, Power and Modernity*, for example.
9 Alvin Toffler, *The Third Wave*, London, Pan, 1980.
10 Karl Marx, *Capital*, Harmondsworth, Penguin, 1976, vol 1, p. 435.
11 I spell this out at more length in 'New technology and the limits of Luddism', *Science as Culture*, 7 (1989), pp. 122–34.
12 Gary T. Marx, *Undercover: Police Surveillance in America*.
13 By January 1993 the task force had not yet been approved. It was recommended formally in *Privacy and Computer Matching*, a report for the Standing Committee on the Legislative Assemby, Toronto, IPC, 1991.
14 Cited in Simon Davies, *Big Brother: Australia's Growing Web of Surveillance*.
15 See for example Michael Rubin, *Private Rights, Public Wrongs*, and David Flaherty, *Protecting Privacy in Surveillance Societies*.
16 John Shattuck, 'Computer matching is a serious threat to individual rights', *Communications of the ACM*, June 1984, pp. 538–451.
17 David Burnham, *The Rise of the Computer State*.
18 Kevin Wilson, *Technologies of Control: The New Interactive Media for the Home*.
19 Jacques Ellul, *The Technological Society*.
20 Anthony Giddens, *Social Theory and Modern Sociology*, Cambridge, UK, Polity Press, 1985.
21 Anthony Giddens, *The Nation-State and Violence*, p. 303.
22 James B. Rule, *Private Lives, Public Surveillance*.
23 Christopher Dandeker, *Surveillance, Power and Modernity*.
24 Zygmunt Bauman, *Modernity and the Holocaust*, Cambridge, UK, Polity Press, 1989, pp. 101–2.
25 Quoted in Duncan Campbell and Steve Connor, *On the Record*.
26 The first meetings of Privacy International were held in Sydney, Australia, but the organization is linked to Computer Professionals for Social Responsibility in Washington DC. See *The International Privacy Bulletin*, Kensington, Australia, University of New South Wales, vol 1, October 1992.
27 Quoted in Gary T. Marx, *Undercover*, p. 54.
28 Geoffrey Brown, *The Information Game: Ethical Issues in a Microchip World*, p. 4.
29 The work of Geoffrey Brown is at least a partial exception. His analysis certainly is technologically informed, and his social-political instincts lead him in a similar direction to that taken later in this book.
30 David Flaherty, *Protecting Privacy in Two-Way Electronic Services*; *Privacy in Colonial New England*; and *Privacy and Government Databanks: An International Perspective*, White Plains NY, Knowledge Industry, 1979.
31 See for example Elizabeth Pleck *Domestic Tyranny: The Making of Social Policy against Family Violence from Colonial Times to the Present*, New York, Oxford University Press, 1987.

32   Caller ID is examined in Chapter Eight of this book.

33   Speech to US Telephone Association, Washington DC, 13 September 1989; quoted in Simon Davies, *Big Brother*.

34   See Gary T. Marx 'Privacy and the home; the king doesn't have to enter your cottage to invade your privacy', *Impact Assessment Bulletin*, 7 (1) pp. 31–59.

35   See for example Carol Pateman, 'Feminist Critiques of the Public/Private Dichotomy' in S. I. Benn and G. A. Gaus (eds), *Public and Private in Social Life*, Bechenham, Croom-Helm, 1983.

36   See for example Christopher Bryant 'The dialogical model of applied sociology' in C. Bryant and D Jary (eds) *Giddens' Theory of Structuration; A Critical Appreciation*, London and New York, Routledge, 1991.

37   See Barry Smart, *Modern Conditions*, Postmodern Controversies.

38   Jean-François Lyotard, *The Postmodern Condition*.

39   Daniel Bell, *The Coming of Postindustrial Society*.

40   Mark Poster, *The Mode of Information*.

41   Ibid., pp. 97–8.

42   Kenneth Laudon refers to this as a 'data-image' in *The Dossier Society: Value Choices in the Design of National Information Systems*. It is a recurring theme of later chapters in this book.

43   See Robert S. Fortner, 'Physics and metaphysics in an information age', *Communication* (9), 1986, pp. 151–72.

44   See further David Lyon, 'Bentham's Panopticon; from moral architecture to electronic surveillance', *Queen's Quarterly* 98:3, 1991; also 'Whither Shall I flee? Surveillance, omniscience and normativity in the Panopticon' forthcoming in *Christian Scholars' Review*, 1994.

45   The primary implication of globalization for responses to surveillance is that increasing communication, and the co-ordination of governmental and trade agreements, mean that data protection policies are also increasingly compatible. See for example Colin Bennett, *Regulating Privacy: Data-Protection and Public Policy in Europe and the United States*, where he discusses the 'convergene' of policy-making in this sphere.

46   See Anthony Giddens, *Social Theory and Modern Sociology*, Cambridge UK, Polity Press, 1987, pp. 30–1.

CHAPTER 2   SURVEILLANCE IN MODERN SOCIETY

1   V. H. Galbraith, *Domesday Book: Its Place in Administrative History*, Oxford, Oxford University Press, 1974, p. 172.

2   V. H. Galbraith, *op. cit.*, p. 182.

3   Quoted in R. W. Finn, *An Introduction to the Domesday Book*, London, Longmans, 1963, p. 7.

4   V. H. Galbraith, *op. cit.*, p. 166.

5   R. W. Finn, *op. cit.*, p. 3.

6   Harold Adams Innis, *The Bias of Communication*.

7 See also James Carey, *Culture and Communication*, pp. 142ff.
8 The concept of 'surveillance capacity' appears in James B. Rule, *Private Lives, Public Surveillance*, and is discussed later in this book.
9 Christopher Dandeker, *Surveillance, Power and Modernity*, p. 217.
10 See Sidney Pollard, *The Genesis of Modern Management*.
11 Christopher Dandeker, *op. cit.*, p. 10.
12 I have just such a different standpoint in mind, which is worked out in Chapters Eleven and Twelve of this book. Surveillance need not be viewed solely in the myopic and negative light of power in the 'disciplinary society'. If one accepts the implicitly critical tone of such a view and is explicit about alternatives to it, why should not some other category – such as 'peace' rather than 'power' – act as the normative guide for social theory?
13 Alexis de Tocqueville, *Democracy in America*, Glasgow, Collins 1968.
14 David Lyon, *The Information Society: Issues and Illusions*. See also Jacques Brieur, Andrew Clement, Richard Sizer and Diane Whitehouse (eds), *The Information Society; Evolving Landscapes*, New York and Heidelberg, Springer-Verlag, and Toronto, Captus Press Inc.
15 Anthony Giddens, *The Nation-State and Violence*.
16 William McNeill, *The Pursuit of Powr: Technology, Armed Force and Society since AD 1000*, pp. 125–43.
17 Martin Shaw, *War, State and Society*, London, Macmillan, 1984, p. 5.
18 This view of the dimensions of modernity is discussed in several of Giddens' books, notably *The Nation-State and Violence* and *The Consequences of Modernity*. One problem with it, however, is that the cultural dimension is ambiguously placed or absent altogether. Culture appears as a 'fifth dimension' in his *Social Theory and Modern Sociology*, Cambridge UK, Polity Press, 1987, pp. 28–9. While I think it could be misleading to limit the institutional dimensions of modernity to four – where, for instance, would modern patriarchy fit in? – this certainly makes for a neat and suggestive scheme within Giddens' work.
19 Christopher Dandeker, *Surveillance, Power and Modernity*.
20 Christopher Dandeker, *op. cit.*, p. 223.
21 Arthur Marwick, *Total War and Social Change*, London, Macmillan, 1988.
22 H. O. Dovey, 'Why National Registration had to go', *Public Administration*, 64, 1986 (winter), pp. 459–62.
23 Quoted in David Beetham, *Max Weber and the Theory of Modern Politics*, Cambridge, Polity Press, p. 81.
24 Anthony Giddens, *Social Theory and Modern Sociology*, Cambridge UK, Polity, 1987, p. 156.
25 The term comes from Kenneth Laudon, *The Dossier Society*.
26 Quoted in J. E. Hodgett, 'The Civil Service when Kingston was capital of Canada', *Historic Kingston*, 5, 1956.
27 Stanley Cohen, *Visions of Social Control*, p. 210.
28 T. H. Marshall, *Citizenship and Social Class*.
29 T. H. Marshall, *op. cit.*, p. 11. Some of the most significant contributions to the

debate over this thesis come in Anthony Giddens, *The Nation-State and Violence*, pp. 201ff., and in David Held, 'Citizenship and Autonomy' in David Held and John Thompson (eds), *Social Theory of Modern Societies*, Cambridge and New York, Cambridge University Press, 1989, and Bryan Turner, 'Towards a Theory of Citizenship', *Sociology*, 24 (2), 1990, pp. 189–217.

30   Nicholas Abercrombie et al., *Sovereign Individuals of Capitalism*. This is also discussed in David Lyon, 'Citizenship and Surveillance' Communication and Information Technologies Working Paper no. 23, Queen's University, Kingston, Ontario, 1991.

31   David Beetham, *Bureaucracy*, Milton Keynes, Open University Press/ Minneapolis, University of Minnesota Press, 1987, p. 16.

32   E. P. Thompson, 'Time, work-discipline and industrial capitalism', *Past and Present*, 38, 1967.

33   Anthony Giddens, *Social Theory and Modern Sociology*, Cambridge UK, Polity Press, 1987, p. 152.

34   Anthony Giddens, *The Nation-State and Violence*, pp. 191ff.

35   See Christopher Dandeker, *Surveillance, Power and Modernity*, p. 35.

36   Anthony Giddens, *The Nation-State and Violence*, pp. 201ff.

37   Further comments on similar lines are in David Held 'Citizenship and Autonomy' in Held (ed) *Political Theory and the Modern State*, Cambridge UK, Polity Press, 1989.

38   Jürgen Habermas, *Legitimation Crisis*, London, Heinemann, 1976, pp. 20–4.

39   See for example Scott Lash and John Urry, *Disorganized Capitalism*, and David Harvey, *The Condition of Postmodernity*.

40   See for example Desmond Ball and Jeffrey Richelson, *The Ties That Bind*, Boston, Unwin Hyman; and Jeffrey Michelson, *The US Intelligence Community*, Cambridge MA, Ballinger, 1989.

41   Governments in North America are increasingly under pressure from the European Community to abide by its Convention on Data Protection as a condition of continuing trade.

42   Privacy International, founded in 1992, is discussed later in this book.

43   Dandeker comments on different kinds of rule in relation to different kinds of surveillance in *Surveillance, Power and Modernity*, pp. 46ff.

CHAPTER 3   NEW SURVEILLANCE TECHNIQUES

1   The term 'papermongers' is used by Charles Tilley in *The Formation of Nation-States in Europe*.

2   A. N. Maiden, 'Watching Big Brother', *Time*, 11 February 1991, pp. 40, 46.

3   Duncan Campbell and State Connor, *On the Record*, p. 15.

4   David Flaherty, *Protecting Privacy in Surveillance Societies*, p. 3.

5   Simon Davies, *Big Brother*, p. iv.

6   James B. Rule, *Private Lives, Public Surveillance*, p. 13.

7   Mark Poster, *The Mode of Information*, p. 98.

8   The image comes from Anthony Giddens, *The Consequences of Modernity*, p. 139.

9   *The Independent*, London UK, 12 January 1990.

10 David Burnham's *The Rise of the Computer State*, for instance, is sub-titled 'a chilling account of the computer's threat to society'. In this particular case, however, Burnham's is a 'soft' determinism. See David Lyon, 'The New Surveillance: Electronic Technologies and the Maximum Security Society', *Crime, Law and Social Change*, 1992, 17:2.

11 David Held, 'Power and Legitimacy in Contemporary Britain' in G McLennan et al., (eds), *State and Society in Contemporary Britain*, Cambridge UK, Polity Press, 1984, p. 356.

12 See among others Steven Yearley, *Science, Technology and Social Change*, and Donald McKenzie and Judy Wajcman (eds), *The Social Shaping of Technology*, Milton Keynes, Open University Press, 1985.

13 My own critical and normative perspectives on technology have been honed through reading work such as that of Jacques Ellul (eg *The Technological Bluff*, Grand Rapids, Eerdmans, 1990); Langdon Winner, *The Whale and the Reactor*, Chicago, University of Chicago Press, 1986; Egbert Schurmann, *Technology and the Future*, Toronto, Wedge, 1980; and Stephen Monsma *et al*, *Responsible Technology*, Grand Rapids, Eerdmans, 1986.

14 This is ably discussed in James Carey, *Communication as Culture; Essays on Media and Society*, pp. 142ff.

15 See William Melody, 'Some Characteristics of Knowledge in an Information Society', Canada House Lecture no 31, London UK.

16 Anthony Giddens, *The Nation-State and Violence*, chapter 7.

17 This was touched on in Chapter One and we shall return to it later.

18 The categories which follow are suggested by Geoffrey Brown, *The Information Game*.

19 Lotus' Household Marketplace was mentioned in Chapter One and reappears later.

20 Duncan Campbell and Steve Connor, *On the Record*.

21 James Leith, *The Financial Times*, London, 17 July 1985.

22 Roger Clarke, 'Information Technology and Dataveillance', *Communications of the ACM*, 31 (5), p. 499.

23 Shown on *We Know where you Live*, Coronet/Nova Films, 1991.

24 Roger Clarke, *op. cit.*, p. 500.

25 Roger Clarke, *op. cit.*, p. 501.

26 See David Lyon, 'British Identity Cards: the unpalatable logic of European membership?', *The Political Quarterly*, 62, (3), 1991, pp. 377–85.

27 Roger Clarke 'Just another piece of plastic for your wallet: the Australia Card scheme', *Prometheus* 5 (1), 1987, pp. 29–45

28 Gary T. Marx, *Undercover*.

29 Gary T. Marx and Nancy Reichman, 'Routinizing the discovery of secrets: computers as informants', *American Behavioral Scientist*, 27 (4), 1984, p. 430.

30   *Time*, 26 July 1976, cited in 'We know where you Live'. (note 23 above).
31   John Shattuck, 'Computer Matching is a serious threat to individual rights', Communications of the ACM, 27 (6), 1984, pp. 538–41.
32   John Shattuck, *op. cit.*
33   James Rule, *Private Lives, Public Surveillance*, pp. 37–40.
34   The concept of surveillance capacities has been picked up by Christopher Dandeker in his *Surveillance, Power and Modernity*, and by others.
35   R. Baldwin and R. Kinsey, *Police Power and Politics*, London, Quartet, 1982.
36   For Norberto Bobbio this is a danger for democracy. Such 'invisible power', as he calls it, is at variance with the 'ideal of democracy as the apotheosis of visible power'. *The Future of Democracy*, p. 97.
37   James Rule *et al.*, 'Documentary identification and mass surveillance in the United States', *Social Problems*, 31 (2), 1983, p. 232.
38   Gary T. Marx, *Undercover*, p. 208.
39   G. Goodwin and L. Humphreys, 'Freeze-dried stigma: cybernetics and social control', *Humanity and Society*, (6), November 1982.
40   Stanley Cohen, *Visions of Social Control*.
41   Gary T. Marx. *Undercover*.
42   Kevin Robins and Frank Webster, 'Cybernetic Capitalism; information, technology, everyday life' in Janet Wasko and Vincent Mosco (eds), *The Political Economy of Information*, Madison, University of Wisconsin Press, 1988, p. 71.
43   See James B. Rule, 'For Whose Eyes Only?', *The New York Times*, 4 March 1990; and David Lyon, 'British Identity Cards: the unpalatable logic of European membership?', *The Political Quarterly*, 62 (3), 1991, pp. 377–85.
44   This book does not itself pretend to offer an exhaustive empirical account of contemporary surveillance; it rather highlights a cluster of important questions raised by surveillance as a *problematique*. But empirical research is being produced in a number of contexts. Workplace surveillance, for instance, is analysed in a series of important studies by James B. Rule and his associates (see bibliography), while the most recent findings on consumer surveillance appear in Oscar Gandy's *The Panoptic Sort*.

CHAPTER 4   FROM BIG BROTHER TO THE ELECTRONIC PANOPTICON

1   James Martin and Adrian Norman, *The Computerized Society*, Harmondsworth, Penguin/New York, Random House, 1973.
2   Theodore Lowi, 'The political impact of information technology', *IEEE Transactions on Communications*, 23 (10), 1975 reproduced in Tom Forester (ed.) *The Microelectronics Revolution*, Oxford, Blackwell/Cambridge USA, MIT Press, 1980 p. 466.
3   A case in point is Oscar Gandy's *The Panoptic Sort*.
4   "Do you begin to see, then, what kind of world we are creating? It is the exact opposite of the stupid, hedonistic utopias that the old reformers imagined . . .

a world which will not grow less but more merciless as it refines itself".
George Orwell, *Nineteen Eighty-Four*, Harmondsworth, Penguin, 1954.

5 George Orwell, *op. cit.*

6 See Gary T. Marx, 'Fraudulent identification and biography'

7 US Government denials regarding national databases are documented, for instance in David Flaherty's *Protecting Privacy in Surveillance Societies.*

8 Gary Marx makes much of this connection between computer surveillance and detectability. See Chapter Three of this book.

9 I am indebted to Bob Fortner for this point. See R. S. Fortner, 'Physics and metaphysics in an information age', *Communication*, (9), p. 166.

10 Stanley Cohen, *Visions of Social Control*, pp. 142. 202.

11 George Orwell, *Nineteen Eighty-Four*, Harmondsworth, Penguin, 1954, p. 60.

12 I do not think that this term implies a conservative view of people in poverty and disadvantage, or that it suggests a necessarily static social grouping. It seems to me that the 'underclass' is a concept which captures the reality of life for those cut off from the means of consumption within present-day capitalist societies. See for example Kirk Mann, *The Making of the English Underclass?*, Milton Keynes/Pennsylvania, Open University Press, 1991.

13 This view of consumerism as social control is put most elegantly in the work of Zygmunt Bauman, especially in his *Freedom.*

14 Gary T. Marx discusses other aspects of social control as 'engineering' in his forthcoming paper 'The engineering of social control: the search for the silver bullet', J. Hogan (ed), *Crime and Inequality*, Chicago, University of Chicago Press.

15 Gary T. Marx, *Undercover*, p. 231. The theme is also explored in Andrew Scull, *Decarceration.*

16 Gary T. Marx, *Undercover*, p. 232.

17 Among such criticism of Foucault, Michael Ignatieff's *A Just Measure of Pain* stands out.

18 Mark Poster discusses this in *The Mode of Information* and *Critical Theory and Poststructuralism.*

19 Jeremy Bentham, *Collected Works*, ed John Bowring, London, 1843.

20 Gertrude Himmelfarb, 'The Haunted House of Jeremy Bentham', *Victorian Minds*, New York, Knopf, 1968, p. 32.

21 Jeremy Bentham, *op. cit.*, p. 39.

22 Quoted in David Lyon, 'Bentham's Panopticon', *Queen's Quarterly*, 1991, 98 (3).

23 Bentham's immodest ambitions for the Panopticon were connected with its role in the contemporary prison reform movement in England. On his hopes of personal gain from involvement in the administration of the Panopticon, see David Lyon, 'Bentham's Panopticon' (above). The 'clockwork image' metaphor derives from Donald MacKay, *The Clockwork Image*, Leicester UK, Intervarsity Press, 1974.

24 Jeremy Bentham, *op. cit.*, p. 40.

25 This is discussed in Zygmunt Bauman, *Modernity and Ambivalence.*

26 Jeremy Bentham, *op. cit.*, p. 40.
27 I am using the term 'panoptic' to refer only to the principles embodied in the Panopticon.
28 Jeremy Bentham, *op. cit.*, p. 64.
29 Jeremy Bentham, *op. cit.*, p. 64.
30 Michel Foucault, *Discipline and Punish*, p. 201.
31 Michel Foucault, *Discipline and Punish*, p. 201.
32 Michel Foucault, *Discipline and Punish*, p. 204.
33 Michel Foucault, *Discipline and Punish*, p. 221.
34 Anthony Giddens, *The Nation-State and Violence*, p. 183.
35 Michel Foucault, *Discipline and Punish*, p. 228.
36 The Panopticon may also be seen in relation to other kinds of technique, particularly perhaps that using biotechnology. But the surveillance power even of biotechnology depends upon microelectronics.
37 Anthony Giddens, *The Nation-State and Violence*, pp. 14–15, pp. 175ff.
38 Stanley Cohen, *Visions of Social Control*, p. 222.
39 Gary T. Marx, *Undercover*, p. 220.
40 Diana Gordon, 'The Electronic Panopticon: a case-study of the development of the National Criminal Records System', *Politics and Society*, (15), 1986, pp. 483–511. See also on Canada David Flaherty *Protecting Privacy, The Surveillance Society*, 1989 and on Britain, Duncan Campbell and Steve Connor, *On the Record*.
41 Diana Gordon, *op. cit.*, p. 487.
42 Diana Gordon, *op. cit.*, p. 487.
43 See Nancy Reichman, 'Computer matching: towards computerized systems of regulation', *Law and Policy*, October 1987, pp. 387–415: Canadian Information and Privacy Commissioner, *Privacy and Computer Matching*, Toronto/Ontario, Information and Privacy Commissioner, 1991.
44 Oscar Gandy, 'The surveillance society: information technology and bureaucratic social control', *The Journal of Communication*, 39 (3), 1989. See also R. G. Meadow, *New Communications Technologies in Politics*, Washington DC, Washington Program of the Annenberg School of Communications, 1985, and M. J. Weiss, *The Clustering of America*, New York, Harper and Row, 1989.
45 Shoshana Zuboff, *In the Age of the Smart Machine*.
46 Shoshana Zuboff, *op. cit.*, pp. 315–17
47 James B. Rule and Paul Attewell, 'What do Computers do?', *Social Problems*, 36 (3), pp. 225–40.
48 Shoshana Zuboff, *op. cit.*, p. 326.
49 Shoshana Zuboff, *op. cit.*, p. 323.
50 Frank Webster and Kevin Robins, 'Plan and Control: towards a cultural history of the information society', *Theory and Society*, 1989, 18.
51 See Vincent Mosco, *The Pay-Per Society*.
52 See for example Oscar Gandy, 'Information Privacy and the Crisis of Control' in Mark Raboy and Peter Bruck (eds), *Communication: For and Against Democracy*, Montreal/New York, Black Rose Books, 1989; and and Eleanor

Novek, Nikhil Sinha and Oscar Gandy, 'The Value of your Name', *Media, Culture and Society*, (12), 1990, pp. 525–43.

53 Kevin Robins and Frank Webster, 'Cybernetic Capitalism: information, technology and everyday life', in Vincent Mosco and Jane Wasko, *The Political Economy of Information*, Madison, University of Wisonsin Press, 1988, p. 72.

54 Mark Poster, *Critical Theory and Poststructuralism*, p. 122.

55 Mark Poster, *The Mode of Information*, p. 97.

56 Mark Poster, *Critical Theory and Poststructuralism*, p. 123.

57 Kevin Robins and Frank Webster, *op. cit.*, p. 62.

58 Shoshana Zuboff, *In the Age of the Smart Machine*, pp. 415–22.

59 See for example Gary Stix, 'Call and Tell', *Scientific American*, April 1991, pp. 152–3.

60 See the discussion in Christopher Dankeker, *Surveillance, Power and Modernity*, p. 27.

61 Anthony Giddens, *The Nation-State and Violence*, p. 185.

62 This is discussed in Chapter Three of this book, and in Harold Adams Innis, *The Bias of Communication*, Toronto, University of Toronto Press, 1951. The stretching of relationships in time and space is referred to variously as 'time-space compression' (by David Harvey, *The Condition of Postmodernity*) and 'time-space distantiation' (by Anthony Giddens in a number of his works, eg *The Constitution of Society*, Cambridge UK, Polity Press, 1984, especially Chapter 5).

63 For further historical reflection on this process see Edward Shils, 'Privacy and Power' in his *Center and Periphery*, and Gary T. Marx, 'Privacy and the home; the King doesn't have to enter your cottage to invade your privacy', *Impact Assessment Bulletin*, 7 (1), 1989, pp. 31–59.

64 Again, see Zygmunt Bauman, *Intimations of Postmodernity*, for a lucid exposition of this theme.

65 See Michael Featherstone 'Lifestyle and Consumer Culture', *Theory, Culture and Society*, (4), 1987, pp. 55–70.

66 Clifford Shearing and Philip Stenning, 'From the Panopticon to Disneyworld: the Development of Discipline', in A. Doob and E. L. Greenspan (eds), *Perspectives in Criminal Law*, Toronto, Canada Law Books, 1985, p. 336.

67 Clifford Shearing and Philip Stenning, *op. cit.*, pp. 339–40.

68 Clifford Shearing and Philip Stenning, *op. cit.*, p. 347. See also S. Mugford and P. O'Malley, 'Heroin Policy and Deficit Models', *Crime, Law and Social Change* 15 (1), 1991, pp. 19–36.

69 As well and embeddedness, other features noted by Shearing and Stenning remain significant for the analysis of consumer surveillance; it is preventative, co-operative, non-coercive, consensual, non-carceral, instrumental, and effective.

70 Jean-Paul Lyotard, *The Postmodern Condition*.

71 See Max Weber, 'Science as a Vocation' in Hans Gerth and C. Wright Mills, *From Max Weber*, Glencoe, Free Press, 1946.

72 Michel Foucault, *Discipline and Punish*, p. 308.

73   Foucault himself seems to hint at this when he says that 'resistance to the Panopticon will have to be analysed in tactical and strategic terms, positing that each offensive from the one side serves as leverage for a counter-offensive from the other'. From Colin Gordon, (ed.), *Power Knowledge*, Brighton, Sussex, Harvester Press, 1980, p. 163.

74   Nicholas Abercrombie et al., *Sovereign Individuals of Capitalism*, p. 179. See also Edward Shils, 'Privacy and Power', in his *Center and Periphery*.

75   Anthony Giddens, *The Nation-State and Violence*, p. 11

76   Anothny Giddens, *The Constitution of Society*, Cambridge UK, Polity Press, 1984, p. 374.

77   See Bob Jessop 'Capitalism, nation-states and surveillance' in David Held and John B. Thompson (eds) *Social Theory of Modern Societies; Anthony Giddens and his critics*, Cambridge and New York, Cambridge University Press, 1989.

78   At this point it is worth attending to the sensible critique made by Richard Kilminster that Giddens' individual actors are somewhat rationalistic creatures and that Giddens underestimates the extent to which such actors are already embedded in interdependent relationships with others. This is important for surveillance studies. See Richard Kilminster, 'Structuration theory as world-view', in Christopher G. A., Bryant and David Jary (eds), *Giddens' Theory of Structuration: A Critical Appreciation*, London and New York, Routledge, 1991.

79   See Martin Jay, 'In the Empire of the Gaze: Foucault and the denigration of vision in twentieth century thought', in Lisa Appigenesi (ed), *Postmodernism: ICA Documents*, London, Free Association Books, 1989.

80   See Harry Strub, 'The theory of panoptic control', The *Journal of the History of the Behavioural Sciences*, (25), 1989, pp. 40–59, and James Crimmons, 'Bentham on Religion: Atheism and the Secular Society', *Journal of the History of Ideas*, (47), 1986, pp. 95–110.

81   This is argued further in David Lyon, 'Bentham's Panopticon: From moral architecture to electronic surveillance', *Queen's Quarterly*, 62 (3), 1991, p. 98.

82   See Mary Dietz, 'Context is all: Feminism and theories of citizenship' in Chantal Mouffe (ed), *The Dimensions of Radical Democracy*, London and New York, Verso, 1992.

CHAPTER 5   THE SURVEILLANCE STATE: KEEPING TABS ON YOU

1   *Montreal Gazette*, 17 September 1990, p. A9; Canadian Privacy Commissioner, *Annual Report 1989–90*, Ottawa, Ministry of Supply and Services, 1990, p. 4.

2   Detailed studies of how this occurs appear for instance in Kenneth Laudon, *The Dossier Society*, and in the work of Rob Kling.

3   Computer matching is also known as data matching, record linkage and so on.

4 James B. Rule, Douglas MacAdam, Linda Stearns, David Uglow, 'Documentary identification and mass surveillance in the United States', *Social Problems*, 31 (2), 1983, p. 230.

5 Kenneth Laudon, *The Dossier Society*.

6 Mark Poster, *The Mode of Information*, p. 95.

7 Mark Poster, *Critical Theory and Poststructuralism*, p. 69.

8 Mark Poster, *The Mode of Information*, p. 96.

9 This perspective on the state is consonant with some of Anthony Giddens' work, especially *The Nation-State and Violence*, but also tries to take account of the critique of Giddens, for example Bob Jessop, 'Capitalism, Nation-states and Violence' in David Held and John B. Thompson (eds) *Social Theory of Modern Societies*, Cambridge UK and New York, Cambridge University Press, 1989, and David Jary, 'Society as "time-traveller"', in Christopher Bryant and David Jary (eds), *Giddens' Structuration Theory; a Critical Appreciation*, London and New York. Routledge, 1991.

10 Quoted in Statistics Sweden, *Statistics and Privacy*, report from a conference in Stockholm, 24–6 June, 1987, p. 11.

11 Jan Freese, 'The future of data protection', *Proceedings of a Seminar on Openness and Protection of Privacy in the Information Society*, Voorburg, Netherlands, Embassy of Sweden and Netherlands Central Bureau of Statistics, p. 108; quoted in David Flaherty, *Protecting Privacy*, p. 96.

12 Gert Persson, 'Computerized personal registers and the protection of privacy, *Current Sweden*, 344, February 1986, pp. 1–10, quoted in Flaherty, *Protecting Privacy*, p. 98.

13 'Sweden axes "Orwellian" research project', *Times Higher Educational Supplement*, 697, 14 March 1986, p. 8.

14 See Anne Ackeroyd 'Ethnography, personal data, and computers' in R. S. Burgess (ed) *Conducting Qualitative Research*, JAI Press Inc., 1988.

15 'Anger over axed research', *Times Higher Educational Supplement*, 701, 11 April 1986, p. 10.

16 Frederic Jameson, *Postmodernism; the Cultural Logic of Late Capitalism*, Durham NC, Duke University Press, 1991, p. 38.

17 Rober Cadenhead, 'High Tech prevented muzzling of Soviets', *The Whig-Standard*, Kingston, Ontario, 22 August 1991, pp. 1, 7.

18 On this see among others Gary T. Marx 'The iron fist and the velvet glove; totalitarian potentials within domestic structures,' in J. F. Short (ed) *The Social Fabric*, 1986.

19 Michael R. Rubin, *Private Rights, Public Wrongs*.

20 Georg Simmel, *Sociology*, Glencoe, Ill., Free Press, 1950.

21 Weber's key concept was 'rationalization', applied above all to economic organization. This theme reappears – though without much acknowledgement of Weber – in Ellul's work.

22 *Wall Street Journal*, 5 April 1985, p. 19.

23 Michael R. Rubin, *Private Rights, Public Wrongs*, p. 38.

24 Cited in Roger Clarke, 'The resistible rise of the national personal data system', *Software Law Journal*, (5), pp. 29–59.

25 James B. Rule, *Private Lives, Public Surveillance*, pp. 21–3.

26 US Congress Senate Committee on Governmental Affairs, hearing 6 June 1984. *Computer Matching; Taxpayer Records*, Washington DC, Government Printing Office. Cited in Oscar Gandy 'The surveillance society; information technology and bureaucratic social control', Journal of Communications 39 (3), 1989, p. 69.

27 Philip Elmer-Dewett, 'Peddling Big Brother', *Time*, 24 June 1991, p. 62.

28 This is the thrust of Anthony Gidden's comments in *Modernity and Self-Identity*, p. 151. An example of an electronic surveillance system *increasing* the liberty of certain groups would be alarms installed in cities (as in Leicester, UK) to reduce racist attacks in housing areas with a high density of visible minorities.

29 Christopher Dandeker, *Surveillance, Power and Modernity*, p. 194.

30 Such anonymity is also seen in the 'technical control' of workers in large modern corporations. See Richard Edwards, *Contested Terrain*, New York, Basic Books, 1979, pp. 112ff., and Chapter Seven of this book.

31 Mark Poster, 'Databases as Discourses' paper presented at the Strategic Research Workshop on *New Technology, Surveillance, and Social Control*, Queen's University, Kingston, Ontario, May 1993.

32 James B. Rule *et al.*, 'Documentary identification and mass surveillance', *Social Problems*, 31 (2), p. 232.

33 See Joseph Weizenbaum, *Computer Power and Human Reason*, San Francisco, WH Freeman, 1976/Harmondsworth, Penguin, 1986.

34 Quoted in Duncan Campbell and Steve Connor, *On the Record*, p. 89.

35 The British National Consumer Council, quoted in Michael O'Higgins 'An operational strategy in lieu of a policy strategy', in D. C. Pitt and B. C. Smith, *The Computer Revolution in Public Administration*, Brighton, Harvester Press, 1984.

36 Ontario Ministry of Health, *Health Number Registration*, Toronto, n.d.

37 *Idem.*

38 'Why the new OHIP card is so essential', *Toronto Star*, 3 November 1990, p. D4

39 Similar criteria may be applied to other forms of record-linkage, such as those done for credit-worthiness. At a given moment, checking may apparently reveal someone to be a very bad credit risk, when in fact the poor predictive value of the test failed to isolate the factor that would demonstrate otherwise.

40 Jean-Yves Nau, 'The law that's blind to progress', *Guardian Weekly*, 5 May 1991, p. 16.

41 Ontario Ministry of Health, *Health Number Registration*, Toronto, n.d., p. 7

42 See for example Mark Mills, 'Memory cards; a new concept in personal computing', *Byte*, January 1984, p. 164.

43 *Globe and Mail* (Toronto), 13 May 1989, p. A3.

44 *Globe and Mail* (Toronto), 26 February 1990, p. A7.

CHAPTER 6   THE SURVEILLANCE STATE: FROM TABS TO TAGS

1   For details, see Chapter Three of this book.
2   See for example Robert Lilly and Richard Ball, 'A brief history of house arrest and electronic monitoring', *Northern Kentucky Law Review*, 17 (3), pp. 343–74.
3   From Control Data in Minneapolis, Minnesota.
4   See for example Stanley Cohen, *Visions of Social Control*, pp. 220–5, and Richard Ball *et al* (eds) *House Arrest and Correctional Policy*, London and Beverly Hills, Sage, 1988.
5   See Mike Davies, *City of Quartz*, especially the chapter 'Fortress L. A.'.
6   From time to time a War Measures Act is passed, as in Canada in 1970, or a National Guard is called in to deal with rioting, as in California in 1992.
7   The Senate Judiciary Subcommittee on Constitutional Rights, *Surveillance Technology*, Washington DC, Office of Technology Assessment, 1976.
8   In 1990 a British farmer with fields 'set aside' because of European over-production told me that the farming press had warned that satellite surveillance would check that farmers were not in fact using fields they had claimed were set aside. By 1992 this was a reality. See 'Spies in the sky zero in on farm cheats', *The European*, 23–6 July 1992, p. 1.
9   Roger Clarke, 'Information technology and dataveillance', *Communications of the ACM*, 31 (5), 1988, p. 500, and Chapter Three of this book.
10   See Kenneth Laudon, *The Dossier Society*, and Diana Gordon 'The electronic Panopticon: a case study of the development of the National Criminal Records system', *Politics and Society*, (15), 1986, pp. 483–509.
11   'Protests at computer ID cards', *The Guardian*, London and Manchester, 1 March 1986.
12   'Germans computerize identity cards', *New Scientist*, 20 February 1986.
13   John Gardiner-Garden, *The Australia Card*, Education and Welfare Group, Department of the Parliamentary Library, Canberra, ACT, 1987. Roger Clarke, 'Just another piece of plastic for your wallet; the "Australia Card" scheme', *Prometheus* 5 (1), pp. 29–45.
14   'ID card's fatal clause', *Transnational Telecommunications and Data Report*, January 1988. See also Roger Clarke, 'The resistable rise of the national personal data system', *Software Law Journal*, (5), February 1992, pp. 29–52.
15   David Lyon, 'British Identity Cards; the unpalatable logic of European membership?', *The Political Quarterly*, 62 (3), pp. 377–85.
16   Ralph Howell MP, quoted in Lyon *op. cit.*, p. 380.
17   Roger Clarke, 'Information technology and dataveillance', *Communications of the ACM*, 31 (5), 1988.
18   See Roger Clarke, 'The resistable rise of the national personal data system', *Software Law Journal*, (5), February 1992, p. 30.
19   See, for example, the comments about the Canadian Social Insurance Number as a *de facto* ID reference, in Canadian Human Rights Commission, *Report of*

the *Privacy Commissioner on the Use of the Social Insurance Number*, Ottawa, 1981.

20 *Identity Cards and the Threat to Civil Liberties*, Civil Liberty Briefing No 12, London, Liberty, 1988.

21 Steve Connor, 'The invisible border guard', *New Scientist*, 5 January 1984.

22 Farley Mowat, *My Discovery of America*, Toronto, MacLelland and Stewart, 1985.

23 *Statistics and Privacy*, a report from a conference in Stockholm, Statistics Sweden, June 1987, p. 11.

24 See James Rule *et al.*, 'Documentary identification and mas surveillance in the United States', *Social Problems* 31 (2), 1983, pp. 228ff. Doubts about the reliability of computer-stored data continue to be raised, as they have been ever since Project Match, the notoriously error-studded computer matching experiments of the US Department of Health, Education and Walfare. In 1977, Project Match obtained raw hits suggesting that 33,000 individuals were in paid employment and simultaneously obtaining benefits. Most were invalid, and of the 7,100 remaining cases, only 638 were deemed strong enough to be investigated; this resulted in just 55 prosecutions and 35 minor convictions, amounting to less than $10,000 in fines. See source in note 25 below.

25 US Congress, Office of Technology Assessment, *Federal Government Information Technology; Electronic Record Systems and Individual Privacy*, Washington DC, OTA, 1986, p. 41.

26 Gary T. Marx and Nancy Reichman, 'Routinizing the discovery of secrets; computers as informants', *American Behavioural Scientist*, (27) 4, p. 424.

27 See Simon Davies, *Big Brother*, p. 65–6, and David Flaherty, *Protecting Privacy in Surveillance Societies*, pp. 344ff.

28 Gary T. Marx and Nancy Reichman, 'Routinizing the discovery of secrets; computers as informants', *American Behavioural Scientist*, 27 (4), 1984, p. 429.

29 Canadian Information and Privacy Commissioner, *Privacy and Computer Matching*, Toronto, IPC, 1991, p. 3.

30 See Daniel B. Radner 'Inter-agency data matching projects for research purposes', *Social Security Bulletin*, July 1988, pp. 22, 56–7; Priscilla M. Regan, 'Privacy, government information and technology', *Public Administration Review*, Nov-Dec 1986, pp. 629–34; Kenneth J. Langan, 'Computer matching programs; a threat to privacy', *Journal of Law and Social Problems*, 1979, 15 (2) pp. 143–80; Nancy Reichman, 'Computer matching; towards computerized systems of reglation', *Law and Policy*, October 1987, pp. 387–415.

31 George Papaulou, *Privacy Laws and Business*, Dec 1989, p. 8.

32 Nancy Reichman, Computer matching; towards computerized systems of regulation', *Law and Policy*, October 1987, p. 407.

33 Canadian Privacy Commissioner, *Annual Report*, Ottawa, Ministry of Supply and Services, 1988, p. 6.

34 *Ibid*, p. 4.

35 Nancy Reichman, 'Computer matching; towards computerized systems of regulation', *Law and Policy*, October 1987, pp. 387–415.

36 John Shattuck, 'Computer matching is a serious threat to individual rights', *Communications of the ACM*, June 1984, pp. 538–41.

37 Gary T. Marx, *Undercover*, p. 219.

38 US Congress, Office of Technology Assessment, *Federal Government Information Technology; Electronic Records Systems and Individual Privacy*, Washington DC, OTA, 1986, p. 39.

39 A further problem is that some governments do not even know the extent of matching in their own jurisdictions. Surveys are currently being carried out in Britain and in Ontario to determine how widespread this practice is.

40 Diana Gordon, 'The Electronic Panopticon', *Politics and Society*, 15, 1987, p. 483.

41 Kenneth Laudon, *The Dossier Society*, Chapters 5 and 6.

42 Duncan Campbell and Steve Connor, On the Record, p. 226.

43 Jim Boothroyd, 'Help from on high', *Police Review* (UK), May 19, 1989, pp. 110–13.

44 See Stephen Ackroyd *et al.*, *New Technology and Practical Police Work; A Case of Arrested Development?* Milton Keynes, Open University Press, 1991.

45 S. Manwaring-Wright, *The Policing Revolution; Police Technology, Democracy, and Liberty in Britain*, Brighton, Harvester, 1983.

46 The waning of private police in early modern times was not irreversible, and private policing is increasing again in the 1990s. See Clifford Shearing (ed), *Private Policing*, Newbury Park CA, Sage, 1987.

47 Christopher Dandeker, *Surveillance, Power and Modernity*, P. 127.

48 See Michael Fooner, *Interpol*.

49 R. Baldwin and R. Kinsey, *Police Power and Politics*, London, Quartet, 1982; Ackroyd *et al.*, *New Technology an Practical Police Work; a Case of Arrested Development?*. Milton Keynes, Open University Press, 1991.

50 Gary T. Marx, *Undercover*, pp. 219–19.

51 Barry Leighton, 'Visions of community policing; rhetoric and reality in Canada', *Canadian Journal of Criminology*, 33 (3/4), 1991, pp. 493, 495.

52 Some doubt exists about the quality of police information, particularly in the realm of data-analysis. See for example Pierre Tremblay and Claude Rochon, 'D'une police efficace à une police informée; lignes directrices d'un programme global de traitement de l'information', *Canadian Journal of Criminology*, 33 (3/4), 1991.

53 See Christopher Dandeker, *Surveillance, Power and Modernity*, p. 132, and J. L. Lambert, *Police Powers and Accountability*, Brighton UK, Croom-Helm, 1986. The problem of 'certainty' being sought in data of dubious authority is touched on by James B. Rule, 'Documentary identification and mass surveillance', *Social Problems*, 31 (2), 1983.

54 Duncan Campbell and Steve Connor, *On the Record*, p. 227.

55 See for example Kenneth Laudon, *The Dossier Society*.

56 See for example Mike Nellis, 'Keeping tags on the underclass', *Social Work*

Today, May 25 1989, pp. 18–19.

57 Ronald Corbett and Gary T. Marx, 'Critique; No soul in the new machine; Technofallacies in the electronic monitoring movement', *Justice Quarterly*, 8 (3) 1991, pp. 399–414.

58 Steven Spitzer, 'The rationalization of crime control in capitalist society', in Andrew Scull and Stanley Cohen (eds), *Social Control and the State*, New York, Basil Blackwell Inc, 1986. Stanley Cohen is probably the best-known proponent of the view that social control systems are bifurcating in this exclusionary/inclusionary manner.

59 Quoted in Dandeker, *Surveillance, Power and Modernity*, p. 104.

60 Peter Wright, *Spycatcher; the Candid Biography of a Senior Intelligence Officer*, Toronto, Stoddart, 1989.

61 Jeffrey T. Richelson, *America's Secret Eyes in Space; The Keyhole Spy Satellite Program*, New York, Harper Business, 1990.

62 Jeffrey T. Richelson and Desmond Ball, *The Ties that Bind*, 1985

63 Richard Norton-Taylor, 'Blinded by the light of technology', *Guardian*, Manchester and London, 6 June 1990.

64 See *The Globe and Mail*, Toronto, June 1992.

65 See Richard Norton-Taylor, *op. cit.*

66 *The Computer and Political Control*, Campaign against the Model West Germany, Bochum, 1979.

67 Alan Borovoy, *When Freedoms Collide; the Case for our Civil Liberties*, pp. 67ff.

68 *The Independent*, London, 18 July 1991, p. 7.

69 G. J. Mulgan, *Communication and Control*, p. 133.

70 See Anthony Giddens' use of Linblom and Dahl in *The Nation-State and Violence*, pp. 198ff.

71 'Video Vigilantes', *Newsweek*, 22 July 1991, pp. 42–7.

72 Bryan Turner, among others, has begun useful work in this direction. See his 'Outline of a Theory of Citizenship', *Sociology*, 24 (2), May 1990, pp. 189–217, reprinted in the stimulating collection edited by Chantal Mouffe (ed.), *The Dimensions of Radical Democracy*, London and New York, Verso, 1992.

CHAPTER 7   THE TRANSPARENT WORKER

1 Robin Murray, 'Life after Henry (Ford)', *Marxism Today*, October 1988, p. 11.

2 This is discussed briefly in David Lyon, *The Information Society*, Chapters 3 and 4, and more fully in Scott Lash and John Urry, *Disorganized Capitalism*.

3 In this connection I refer the reader to the work of James Rule and of Barry Wilkinson, discussed later in this chapter.

4 See Scott Lash and John Urry, *Disorganized Capitalism*.

5 Asa Briggs, *Victorian Cities*, Harmondsworth, Penguin, 1968.

6 Sidney Pollard uses illustration in his *The Genesis of Modern Management*.

7 Of course, Karl Marx and his disciples have been pretty sceptical of the benefit

to workers; but it was on this basis that the means of industrial democracy developed in the twentieth century was built. That the benefits of capitalist and worker are unequal does not mean that the workers' benefits are unreal. See Anthony Giddens, *The Nation State and Violence*, p. 191.

8 Karl Marx, *Capital*, vol 1, p. 436. Compare Donald McKenzie, 'Marx and the machine', *Technology and Culture*, 25, 1984, pp. 473–502.

9 Harry Braverman, *Labour and Monopoly Capital*, New York, Monthly Review Press, 1974.

10 Max Weber, *Economy and Society*, Berkeley, University of California Press, 1978. The 'visible hand' idea is from M. Unseem, *The Inner Circle*, London and New York, Oxford University Press, 1984.

11 Christopher Dandeker, *Surveillance, Power* and *Modernity*, p. 10.

12 Michel Foucault, *Power/Knowledge*, p. 161.

13 Christopher Dandeker, *op. cit.* Dandeker's evidence for capitalist reliance upon military methods is not entirely compelling, but there is at least an 'elective affinity' worth exploring. In Chapter Eight of this book, on commercial surveillance, some further connections are made.

14 David Dickson, *Alternative Technology*, London, Fontana, 1989, p. 73.

15 Joanna Yates, *Control through Communication*.

16 Robin Murray, 'Life after Henry (Ford) (1988), *Marxism Today*, October 1988, p. 8.

17 See Christopher Dandeker, *Surveillance, Power and Modernity*, p. 182.

18 Harry Braverman, *Labour and Monopoly Capital*, New York, Monthly Review Press, 1974.

19 Richard Edwards, *Contested Terrain*, London, Heinemann, 1979.

20 See Stephen Wood (ed), *The Degradation of Work? Skill, Deskilling*, and the Labour Process, London, Hutchinson, 1983.

21 David Noble, *America by Design; Science, Technology, and the Rise of Corporate Capitalism*, Oxford and New York, Oxford University Press, 1977.

22 Jane Barker and Hazel Downing, 'Word Processing and the transformation of patriarchal relations of control in the office', *Capital and Class*, 10, 1980, pp. 64–99, referring to Braverman, *Labour and Monopoly Capital*, p. 347.

23 See for example S. S. Clegg, 'Radical revisions; power, discipline and organizations', *Organization Studies*, (10), 1988, pp. 97–116.

24 See Frank Webster and Kevin Robins, *Information Technology, a Luddite Analysis*, Norwood NJ, Ablex, 1986.

25 See for example Masao Nemoto, *Total Quality Control for Management; Strategies and Techniques from Toyota and Toyoda Gosei*, Englewood Cliffs NJ, Prentice-Hall, 1987.

26 See Chapter Eight of this book.

27 See for example L. Fuller and V. Smith, 'Consumers' reports: management by customers in a changing economy', *Work, Employment and Society*, (5), 1991, pp. 1–16.

28 The matter of journal citations may have other disciplinary effects not mentioned here. See David A. Nock, 'Star Wars: aspects of the social

construction of citations in Anglo-Canadian sociology', *Canadian Review of Sociology and Anthropology*, 29 (3), 1992, pp. 346–61.

29   Jim Steinhart, '"Handcuffs" can tie up customers', *The Globe and Mail*, Toronto, 12 February 1992, p. B4. On SABRE see for example Charles Wiseman, *Strategic Information Systems*, p. 18.

30   The intellectual parent of this group is Daniel Bell, in *The Coming of Postindustrial Society*.

31   For instance, Claus Offe, *The End of Organized Capitalism*, Cambridge, UK, Polity Press, 1987, and Scott Lash and John Urry, *Disorganized Capitalism*,

32   Christopher Dandeker, *Surveillance, Power and Modernity*, pp. 153–6.

33   Quoted in Geoff Bickerton and Jane Stinson, 'Working in 1984', *Rights and Freedoms*, Ottawa, January/February 1984, p. 9.

34   Michael Miller, 'Productivity Spies', *The Wall Street Journal*, June 3 1985, pp. 1, 15.

35   'One million jobs subject to security, group says', *The Independent*, London, January 29 1990.

36   'New group aims to fight employers' blacklisting' — *The Independent*, London, June 9, 1989. In countries such as Canada, Sweden and Australia no-one can lose their job without evidence against them being heard, or without the right to fair appeal.

37   'Computer terrorism coming to Britain' – *The Independent*, London, November 28, 1991.

38   'Fingerprinting: the high-tech key to office security' – *The Independent*, London, October 3, 1988. See also comments in Gary T. Marx and Sanford Sheriden, 'Monitoring on the job', *Technology Review* November-December 1986, pp. 66–7.

39   Reported on *Tomorrow's World*, BBC TV, November 29, 1990.

40   *The Globe and Mail*. Toronto, September 12, 1990, p. B4.

41   Gary T. Marx, 'The case of the omniscient organization', *Harvard Business Review*, March-April 1990, pp. 4–12.

42   Gary T. Marx and Sanford Sheriden, 'Monitoring on the job', *Technology Review*, November-December 1986, p. 63–72.

43   Shoshana Zuboff, *In the Age of the Smart Machine*.

44   In an interesting study of resistance on the part of both managers and potential workers to "telecommuting", Constance Perin argues that the "panopticon discourse" predominates, so that "appearance" in physical, face-to-face settings is more significant than an alternative "performance" discourse. What she does not explore, however, is the extent to which metaphorical visibility *via* information technology might intervene in such situations to blur the distinction. See Constance Perin, 'The moral fabric of the office; Panopticon discourse and schedule flexibilities', *Research in the Sociology of Organizations*, (8), 1991, pp. 241–68.

45   L. Jackson, 'Office automation provides opportunity to examine what workers actually do', *Industrial Engineering*, 16 (1), 1984, pp. 90–3, quoted in Andrew Clement 'Office automation and the technical control of information workers'

in Vincent Mosco and Janet Wasko (eds), *The Political Economy of Information*, Madison WI, University of Wisconsin Press, 1988.

46 James B. Rule and Peter Brantley, 'Surveillance in the workplace; a new meaning to "personal computing"' (unpublished).

47 James B. Rule and Paul Attewell, 'What do computers do?', *Social Problems*, 36 (3), 1989, p. 237.

48 Ibid., pp. 237–8.

49 David Knights and Andrew Sturdey, 'New technology and the self-disciplined worker in the insurance industry', in Ian Varcoe, Maureen McNeil and Steven Yearley (eds), *Deciphering Science and Technology*, London UK, MacMillan, 1990.

50 James B. Rule and Peter Brantley, *op. cit.*, p. 21.

51 James B. Rule and Peter Brantley, *op. cit.*, p. 25–6.

52 The study is reported in Graham Sewell and Barry Wilkinson, 'Someone to watch over me; Surveillance; Discipline and the Just-in-Time Labour Process', *Sociology*, 26:2, 1992, pp. 271–89.

53 Shoshana Zuboff, *In the Age of the Smart Machine*, pp. 346, 350.

54 James B. Rule and Peter Brantley, *op. cit.*, p. 23.

55 David Knights and Andrew Sturdey, *op. cit.*, p. 129. The present author also found similar evidence in a small-scale unpublished study of computerization in a local government education welfare office in Bradford, West Yorkshire.

56 See also the discussion of alternatives in Andrew Clement, 'Office automation and the technical control of information workers', in V. Mosco and J. Wasko (eds), *The Political Economy of Information*.

CHAPTER 8 THE TARGETED CONSUMER

1 Unsolicited mail from advertisers has increased throughout this century, but the term 'junk mail' did not appear until the advent of the computer-generated address list.

2 This theme started life in the work of Theodor Adorno (see, for example, *The Culture Industry*, London and Boston, Routledge, 1992), reappears in the – sometimes hysterical – speculations of Jean Baudrillard (see, for example, *The Ecstasy of Communication*, New York, Semiotext(e), 1987, and *For a Critique of the Political Economy of the Sign*, St Louis, Telos Press, 1981), but is expounded briefly and best by Zygmunt Bauman in *Freedom*, Chapter 3, and in *Intimations of Postmodernity*.

3 Paul Fisher, 'Piecing together the facts', *The Guardian*, Manchester and London, 2 November 1989, and Duncam Campbell and Steve Connor, *On the Record*, pp. 56–7.

4 Anne Field and Robert Neff, 'Big Brother Inc may be closer than you thought', *Business Week*, 9 February 1987, pp. 84–6.

5 See Jeffrey Rothfeder *et al.*, 'Is nothing private?', *Business Week*, 4 September 1989, p. 37.

6   Vincent Mosco, *The Pay-Per Society*, pp. 37–8.

7   Michel Foucault, *Power/Knowledge*.

8   Vincent Mosco, *op. cit.*, p. 38.

9   Kevin Robins and Frank Webster, 'Cybernetic capitalism; information, technology, everyday life', in Vincent Mosco and Janet Wasko (eds), *The Political Economy of Information*, Madison, University of Wisconsin Press, p. 65.

10 Frank Webster and Kevin Robins, 'Plan and Control; towards a cultural history of the information society', *Theory and Society* (18), 1989, p. 334. This is also discussed from a different viewpoint in Christopher Dandeker, *Surveillance, Power and Modernity*, pp. 63, 175.

11 Manuel Castells, *The Informational City*; Scott Lash and John Urry, *Disorganized Capitalism*, Cambridge UK, Polity Press, 1988.

12 Kevin Robins and Frank Webster, 'Cybernetic capitalism; information, technology, everyday life' in Vincent Mosco and Janet Wasko (eds) *The Political Economy of Information*, Madison, University of Wisconsin Press, p. 70.

13 See Jeffrey Rothfeder et al., 'Is nothing private?', *Business Week*, 4 September, 1989, p. 37.

14 It would also perhaps be approved by those wishing to extend the influence of those "consuming" state services; see for example Peter Saunders 'The sociology of consumption: a new research agenda' in Per Otnes (ed), *The Sociology of Consumption*, Oslo, Solum Forlag A/G, 1988. But contrast Zygmunt Bauman, *Freedom*, pp. 84ff.

15 'We know where you live', Coronet/Nova Films, 1991.

16 John Moore, 'They want you to be a junk mail junkie', *The Independent*, London, 16 October 1990, p. 25.

17 'Not giving credit where it's due', *Information Week*, 19 August 1991, p. 36.

18 See for example Herbert Schiller, *Who Knows? Information in the Age of the Fortune 500*, Norwood NJ, Ablex, 1981.

19 The innovative legislation of the Ontario government in its 1987 Freedom of Information and Protection of Privacy Act may pave the way for future developments in policy that assume the same definition of information for both access and limitations on access.

20 Gary Stix, 'Call and Tell', *The Scientific American*, April 1991, p. 152.

21 *Ibid.*, p. 153.

22 Computer Professionals for Social Responsibility discovered this when checking how consumers could delete their names from the database. See Langdon Winner, 'A victory for computer populism', *Technology Review*, May-June 1991, p. 66.

23 David Flaherty, *Protecting Privacy in Surveillance Societies*, p. 1.

24 *The Times*, London, 4 April 1987.

25 *The Times*, London, 13 January 1990.

26 Tom Forester (ed), *Computers in the Human Context*, Oxford and New York, Basil Blackwell, 1989, p. 220.

27 David Flaherty, *Protecting Privacy in Two-Way Electronic Services*; Kevin Wilson, *Technologies of Control*.

28 Kevin Wilson, *op. cit.*, p. 9.

29 Kevin Wilson, *op. cit.*, p. 97.

30 The strengthened European Community is putting pressure upon North American trading partners to abide by common data protection legislation, which may eventually end the anomaly whereby European laws cover public and private spheres but North American only governmental. See Management Board of Cabinet, *Information Bulletin*, 2 (3), Toronto, 1991.

31 See David Collingridge, *The Control of Technology*, Milton Keynes, Open University Press, 1982.

32 Charles Wiseman, *Strategic Information Systems*, Homewood IL, Irwin, 1988, p. 25.

33 'Privacy inquiry to assess new technology', *The Australian*, 21 October 1991. 'Prank callers warmed – your number's up', *The Australian*, 16 December 1991.

34 Mary Gooderham, 'Caller ID system termed threat', *Globe and Mail*, Toronto, 9 April 1991, p. A7.

35 Oscar Gandy, 'Caller ID: a two-edged sword', in Dan Wedemayer and Mark Lofstrum (eds) *Pacific Telecommunication: Weaving the Technological and Social Fabric*, Hawaii, Pacific Telecommunications Council, 1990.

36 See Gary Stix, 'Call and Tell', *Scientific American*, April 1991, pp. 152–3: James E. Katz, 'Caller ID, Privacy and Social Processes', *Telecommunications Policy*, October 1990, pp. 372–410.

37 Some implications of this are discussed in Peter Shields and Rohan Samarajiva, 'Emergent institutions of the "intelligent network": towards a theoretical understanding', *Media, Culture and Society*, (14), 1992, pp. 397–419.

38 The Canadian Radio and Television Commission, for instance, ordered during 1992 that Bell Canada abandon its charges for blocking disclosure of callers' numbers *via* Caller ID. *Globe and Mail*, Toronto, 5 May, 1992, p. B5.

39 See Peter Shields and Rohan Samarajiva, *op. cit.*: James Katz, 'Public concern over privacy: the phone is the focus', *Telecommunications Policy*, 14 (4), 1991, pp. 373–411: Gary T. Marx, 'Hang up on Caller ID', *The Washington Post*, 20 January 1990, p. A17.

40 The discussion of smart cards began in Chapter Five, in the context of health-care.

41 *Vancouver Sun*, 20 December 1989, p. D1.

42 *The Globe and Mail*, Toronto, 5 March 1991, p. C2.

43 This linking of market-data and government departments already occurs in some contexts. See for example R. C. Baker, Roger Dickinson, and Stanley Hollander, 'Big Brother 1994: marketing data and the IRS', *Journal of Public Policy and Marketing*, 5, pp. 227–42.

44 Christopher Dandeker, in *Surveillance, Power and Modernity*, pp. 175–6, notes the ways that consumer surveillance has benefited from lessons learned in military contexts.

45 This is discussed in David Lyon, *The Information Society*.
46 William Melody, *Some Characteristics of Knowledge in an Information Society*, p. 7.
47 William Melody, *op. cit.*, p. 9.
48 Jeffrey Steinberg, 'Putting your business on the map', *MacUser*, March 1991, p. 159.
49 Charles Wiseman, *Strategic Information Systems*.
50 Vincent Mosco, The *Pay-Per Society*, p. 38.
51 See Chapter Three. The notion of surveillance capacity derives from James B. Rule, *Private Lives, Public Surveillance*.
52 Rob Kling, 'Value-conflicts and social choice in electronic funds transfer system developments', *Communications of the ACM*, 21 (8), 1978.
53 Inaccurate files are fairly commonplace. American credit bureaux admit that, with nine million credit reports requested annually by customers, three million consumers request reverification or updating of records. See 'Not giving credit where credit is due', *Information Week*, 19 August 1991, p. 36.
54 Zygmunt Bauman makes this point eloquently in *Freedom*.
55 This idea originates in the work of Jean Baudrillard, *De la Séduction*, Paris, Editions Galilée, but is helpfully discussed in many places, including Zygmunt Bauman, *Freedom*, Mark Poster, *The Mode of Information*, and Clifford Shearing and Philip Stenning, 'From the Panopticon to Disneyworld: the development of discipline' in E. Doob and E. L. Greenspan (eds), *Perspectives in Criminal Law*, Aurora: Canada Law Books Inc, 1985.
56 See for example a report on the Canadian Direct Marketing Association in *Marketing Magazine* (Canada), 26 October 1992.
57 Such a re-calibration of surveillance theory would of course have to bear in mind the role of TV advertising, on which Jean Baudrillard has produced some important insights. Mark Poster's preliminary treatment of this, in Chapter Two of *The Mode of Information*, and in particular of the ways that advertisements constitute people as consumers, is most helpful.
58 Zygmunt Bauman, *Intimations of Postmodernity*, p. 225.

CHAPTER 9   CHALLENGING SURVEILLANCE

1 Jacques Ellul, *Perspectives on our Age*, Toronto, CBC, 1981, p. 71.
2 Ronald Inglehart, *Culture Shift in Advanced Industrial Society*: Alberto Melucci, *Nomads of the Present*.
3 See for example, Christopher Bryant, 'Sociology without philosophy? The case of Giddens' structuration theory', *Sociological Theory*, 10, 1992.
4 See for example Numbers 1–4, 1 Samuel 8.
5 David Flaherty, *Privacy in Colonial New England*, p. 15.
6 David Flaherty, *op. cit.*, p. 18.
7 See Nicholas Abercrombie et al., *Sovereign Individuals of Capitalism*, and David Lyon, *Citizenship and Surveillance in an Information Society*.

8   The phrase, remember, is from Gary T. Marx, *Undercover*, p. 219.
9   Gary T. Marx, *Undercover*, p. 208.
10 See also David Lyon, 'The new surveillance? Electronic technologies and the maximum security society', *Crime, Law and Social Change*, 17 (2), 1992.
11 Harold Adams Innis, *The Bias of Communication*.
12 Noted in James Beniger's *The Control Revolution*, in a fairly uncritical fashion: and by Kevin Robins and Frank Webster, much more critically, in 'Plan and control: Towards a cultural history of the information society', *Theory and Society*, 18, 1989, pp. 323–351.
13 This phrase is Foucault's. See Chapter Four.
14 Shoshana Zuboff, *In the Age of the Smart Machine*, and Diana Gordon, 'The Electronic Panopticon', *Politics and Society*, 15, 1986.
15 Mark Poster, *Critical Theory and Poststructuralism*,
16 Mark Poster, *op. cit.*, p. *123*.
17 *Ibid.*
18 Mark Poster, *op. cit.*, p. 111.
19 By using the term "empirical study" I do not for a moment intend to suggest that a wedge can be driven between this and, say, "critical theory". On the contrary, theory is ever underdetermined by so-called facts, and those facts are invariably theory-laden. All I mean by "empirical" is "supported by observable evidence", that is, the kinds of descriptive activity undertaken in Chapters Five to Eight.
20 James B. Rule *et al.*, 'Documenary identification and mass surveillance', *Social Problems*, 31 (2), 1983.
21 Jacques Ellul, *Perspectives on our Age*, p. 56.
22 See for example Anthony Giddens, *The Consequences of Modernity*.
23 This side is spelled out in popular form in Mark Dery, 'Terrorvision', *Mondo 2000*, 1992, pp. 46–9.
24 See David Lyon, *Information Technology and Community Development*, London UK, Community Development Foundation, 1990.
25 David Flaherty, *Protecting Privacy in Surveillance Societies*, p. 94.
26 David Flaherty, *op. cit.*, pp. 23, 97, 167, 244, 307.
27 For a comparative survey of how data protection and privacy legislation has evolved in the UK, USA, Sweden, and Germany, see Colin Bennett, *Regulating Privacy*.
28 This view coincides to some extent with that of Geoffrey Brown in *The Information Game*.
29 Paul Sieghart (ed) *Microchips with Everything*, London, Comedia, p. 102.
30 Norman Lindop, *Report of the Committee on Data Protection*, Cmnd 7341, London, 1978, HMSO.
31 In the USA data protection is left to citizens and the courts; the UK relies on registration, Germany on an Ombudsman, Sweden on a licensing system, and Canada on a Privacy Commission.
32 Paul Sieghart (ed), *op. cit.*, p. 106.
33 During the BBC documentary film '*The Intelligent Island*', screened in May

1990 and also on Singapore Broadcasting Corporation, 5 August 1990. See 'BBC calls Singapore the Intelligent Island', *Straits Times*, 6 August 1990.

34   Philip Elmer-Dewitt, 'Peddling Big Brother', *Time*, 24 June 1991, p. 62.

35   David Flaherty, *Protecting Privacy in Surveillance Societies*, p. 321.

36   David Flaherty, *op. cit.*, pp. 405–6.

37   Duncan Campbell and Steve Connor, *On the Record*.

38   Geoffrey Brown, *The Information Game*, p. 138.

39   See David Lyon, 'Surveillance Societies, Privacy and Social Control: Trends and Counter-Trends', *Artificial Intelligence and Society*, 1992.

40   David Lyon, 'British identity cards: the unpalatable logic of European membership', *Political Quarterly*, 62 (3), 1991.

41   Roger Clarke, 'Just another piece of plastic for your wallet', *Prometheus*, 5 (1), 1987, pp. 25–45.

42   Peter Graham, 'The Australia card', *The Australian Quarterly*, Autumn 1986, pp. 4–14.

43   See 'ID card's fatal clause', *Transnational Data and Communications Report*, January 1988, p. 26.

44   Langdon Winner, 'A victory for consumer populism', *Technology Review*, May/June 1991, p. 66.

45   Anthony Giddens, *The Nation-State and Violence*, p. 314: *Modernity and Self-Identity*. p. 207.

46   Alain Touraine, *Social Research*, 52, (4), 1989, p. 763.

47   See Zygmunt Bauman, *Freedom*, p. 95.

48   Alberto Melucci, *Nomads of the Present*, and 'Symbolic Challenge of Contemporary Movements', *Social Research*, 52 (4), 1989.

49   Alberto Melucci, 'Symbolic Challenge of Contemporary Movements', *Social Research*, 52 (4), 1989, p. 805.

50   Alberto Melucci, *op. cit.*, pp. 813–14.

51   See for example National Consumer Council, *Taking Liberties*, London, NCC, 1988.

52   Since 1991, an annual conference has been mounted by a coalition of mainly North American computer networking groups, under the title 'Computers, Freedom and Privacy'.

CHAPTER 10   PRIVACY, POWER, PERSONS

1   See on this Eleanor Novak, Nikhil Sinha and Oscar Gandy, 'The value of your name', *Media, Culture and Society*, (12), 1990, pp. 525–543.

2   See Norman Stockman, 'Barrington Moore's "Privacy"', *Theory, Culture and Society*, (6), 1989, p. 142.

3   Neil Vidmar and David Flaherty, 'Concern for personal privacy in an electronic age', *Journal of Communication*, (35), 1986, pp. 91–103.

4   Communication Canada, *Privacy Revealed*, Ottawa, 1993. See also Barbara Wickens, 'Preserving individual privacy', *Maclean's*, 26 April 1993, pp. 20–1.

5 James E. Katz and Annette R. Tassons, 'Public opinion trends: privacy and information technology', *Public Opinion Quarterly*, (54), 1990, pp. 125–43.

6 Richard Lacayo, 'Nowhere to hide', *Time*, 11 November 1991, pp. 34–40.

7 Louis Harris and Associates Inc. *The Equifax Report on Consumers in the Information Age*, Atlanta Ga., Equifax Inc., 1990.

8 Oscar Gandy, 'The anticipatory responses: Avoiding the destructive gales of popular resistance', paper from the 19th Annual Telecommunications Policy Research Conference, Solomon's Island, Md., 1991.

9 It is in fact doubly paradoxical, given the conspicuousness attending symbolic consumption!

10 Georges Duby, Foreword to Paul Veyne (ed), *A History of Private Life*.

11 Hannah Arendt, *The Human Condition*, pp. 29–30.

12 Yvonne Thébert, 'Private life and domestic architecture in Roman Africa', in Paul Veyne, *A History of Private Life*.

13 Alvin Gouldner, *The Dialectic of Ideology and Technology*, p. 99.

14 Alvin Gouldner, *op. cit.*, p. 103.

15 Anthony Giddens, *Modernity and Self-Identity*, p. 152.

16 Alvin Gouldner, *op. cit.*, p. 104.

17 Jürgen Habermas, *The Theory of Communicative Action*.

18 The work of the early Scottish political economist James Stewart makes this clear; capitalism depends upon the confinement of the majority of the population and a curtailing of their private spaces. See the comments in John Milbank, *Theology and Social Theory: Beyond Secular Reason*, p. 36.

19 Edward Shils, 'Privacy and Power', in *Center and Periphery*.

20 Nicholas Abercrombie et al., *Sovereign Individuals of Capitalism*, p. 151.

21 See Zygmunt Bauman, *Freedom*. However, to speak of privacy as a social relation could be read as the reductionism of secular reason. As I shall argue, privacy in some aspects may be related to human dignity, which, though social, is also "given" in a transcendental sense.

22 Robert Fortner, 'Physics and metaphysics in an information age', *Communication*, (9), pp. 151–72.

23 Several social theorists have examined this question, including Norbert Elias in *The Civilising Process: The History of Manners*, Oxford and New York, Blackwell, 1978, and Anthony Giddens, *Modernity and Self-Identity*.

24 Erving Goffman, *The Presentation of Self in Everyday Life*.

25 Christopher Bryant, 'Privacy, Privatisation and Self-Determination', in John Young (ed), *Privacy*, London, Wiley, 1978.

26 J. S. Mill, *On Liberty*, quoted in Steven Lukes, *Individualism*, New York, Harper and Row, 1973, p. 63.

27 Christopher Bryant, *op. cit.*, p. 76.

28 Hannah Arendt, *The Human Condition*, p. 338.

29 Quoted in Steven Lukes, *Individualism*, New York, Harper and Row, 1973, p. 66.

30 Nicholas Abercrombie et al., *Sovereign Individuals of Capitalism*, pp. 81–3.

31 Alan Westin, *Privacy and Freedom*, New York, Athenaeum, 1967.

32   The point is well made by Geoffrey Brown, *The Information Game*, p. 68.
33   Geoffey Brown, *op. cit.*, p. 69.
34   Norman Lindop, *Report of the Committee on Data Privacy*, Cmnd 7341, London, 1978, HMSO.
35   Sisela Bok, *Secrets*.
36   Geoffrey Brown, *op. cit.*, p. 74.
37   As depicted in the production '*We know where you live*', Coronet/Nova Films, 1991.
38   James B. Rule, 'My Mailbox is mine', *The Wall Street Journal*, 15 August 1990, p. A8.
39   Alan F. Westin, 'How the American public views consumer privacy issues in the early 1990s – and why', House Committee on Government Operations, Washington DC, 10 April 1991. See also Oscar Gandy, 'The anticipatory response: avoiding the destructive gales of popular resistance', paper given at the 19th Annual Telecommunications Policy Research Conference, Solomons Island, MD, 30 September 1991.
40   A similar situation obtains with Caller ID, in which telephone companies charge subscribers for having the Caller ID facility blocked.
41   See Gary T. Marx, 'For Sale: personal information about you', *Washington Post*, 11 December 1989, p. A15.
42   A Swedish view is that 'names and personal data are not commercial assets to be bandied around without the express permission of their subjects'. Quoted in Eleanor Novek, Nikhil Sinha and Oscar Gandy, 'The value of your name', *Media, Culture and Society*, 1990, 12, p. 540.
43   Kevin Wilson, *Technologies of Control*, pp. 49ff.
44   Kevin Wilson, *op. cit.*, p. 52.
45   Kevin Robins and Frank Webster, 'Information as capital: a critique of Daniel Bell', in J. Slack and F. Feges (eds), *The Ideology of the Information Age*, Norwood NJ, Ablex, 1987, pp. 95–117.
46   Eleanor Novek, Nikhil Sinha and Oscar Gandy, 'The value of your name ', *Media, Culture and Society*, 1990, 12, p. 536.
47   Mark Poster, *The Mode of Information*, pp. 97–8.
48   Mark Poster, *Critical Theory and Poststructuralism*, p. 123.
49   Mark Poster, *Critical Theory and Poststructuralism*, p. 128.
50   Mark Poster, *The Mode of Information*, p. 94.
51   Mark Poster, *Critical Theory and Poststructuralism*, p. 131.
52   Richard F. Hixson, *Privacy in a Public Society*, p. 25.
53   Kevin Wilson, *Technologies of Control*, p. 52.
54   Richard Sennett, *The Fall of Public Man*, Cambridge UK and New York, Cambridge University Press, Chapter 5.
55   Kenneth Laudon, *The Dossier Society*.
56   Stafford Beer, in *Computing Weekly*, 21 August 169, quoted in Geoffrey Brown, *The Information Game*, p. 75.
57   Tom Kitwood discusses this in relation to social research; what social analysts can know is limited to what respondents are willing to reveal to people

personally unknown to them. See *Disclosures to a Stranger*, London, Routledge, 1978.

58 Geoffrey Brown, *The Information Game*, p. 77.

59 Anthony Giddens, *Social Theory and Modern Sociology*, Cambridge UK, Polity Press, 1987, p. 113.

60 The Data Protection Registrar, *Data Protection Act, 1984: Introduction to the Act*, Wilmslow UK, Office of Data Protection Registrar, 1989, p. 10.

61 Unfortunately, this does highlight the minimalist approach of privacy legislation; it tends to affirm rights of *self*-protection, and is also enacted not in regard to ideals of personhood and dignity, but to expedience.

62 Michael Rubin, 'Guilty until proven innocent', *Information Management Review*, 2:1, 1986, p. 65.

63 Jürgen Habermas, *The Philosophical Discourse of Modernity*, pp. 303–6.

64 Mark Poster, *The Mode of Information*, p. 80.

CHAPTER 11 AGAINST DYSTOPIA, DISTANCE, DIVISION

1 1 Corinthians, 13:13.

2 Mike Davis, *City of Quartz*, p. 223.

3 Mike Davis, *op. cit.*, p. 253. See also the treatment of Los Angeles in Edward J. Soja *Postmodern Geographies*, London and New York, Verso, 1989.

4 Dystopia frequently takes fictional form, of course. But even there, novels such as *Nineteen Eighty-Four* are essentially fictive extrapolations from existing trends.

5 Mike Davis, *op. cit.*, p. 224.

6 In an interview, Michel Foucault once suggested that the political task involves criticizing 'the working of institutions which appear to be both neutral and independent . . . so that one can fight them', Paul Rabinow (ed.), *The Foucault Reader*, New York, Pantheon, p. 6. Exactly how one 'fights' such institutions or their related 'disciplinary technologies' remains unclear in Foucault's work.

7 This postempiricist position is widely, though far from universally, accepted today. See for example Christopher Bryant, 'Sociology without philosophy: the case of Giddens' structuration theory', *Sociological Theory* (forthcoming). My own statement of the case may be found in 'Valuing in Social Theory: Postempiricism and Christian Responses', *Christian Scholars' Review*, 12 (4), 1983, pp. 324–8.

8 James B. Rule, *Private Lives, Public Surveillance*, Chapter 1.

9 Christopher Dandeker, *Surveillance, Power and Modernity*.

10 David Flaherty, *Protecting Privacy in Surveillance Societies*, p. 6.

11 David Flaherty, *op. cit.*, p. 12.

12 Gary T. Marx, The iron first in the velvet glove: Totalitarian potentials within democratic structures', in J. F. Short (ed), *The Social Fabric*, Beverly Hills CA, Sage Publications, 1986.

13 I use the original French title of Foucault's book to recall its direct relevance to our theme. The Panopticon has of course been used by people committed merely to the metaphor, or to forms of cultural Marxism (such as Webster and Robins) as well as by those who follow more closely Foucault's own 'textual' analysis (such as Shoshana Zuboff or Mark Poster).

14 Diana Gordon, for instance, sees government databases incarcerating us all in such a neo-Weberian fashion. See her 'The Electronic Panopticon: a case-study of the National Criminal Records System', *Politics and Society*, (15), pp. 483–511.

15 Ruth Levitas, *The Concept of Utopia*, London and New York, Philip Allan, 1990, p. 139.

16 See Stanley Cohen, *Visions of Social Control*.

17 Stanely Cohen, ibid., pp. 142ff.

18 In the case of consumption, however, we consumers have become more completely the bearers of our own surveillance, and are less affected by the original Panopticon criterion that we comply because we know we are watched. In fact, self-discipline has largely taken over. The Panopticon *per se* has done its work.

19 On the psychology of the Panopticon see Harry Strub, 'The theory of panoptical control: Bentham's Panopticon and Orwell's *Nineteen Eighty-Four*', *Journal of the History of the Behavioural Sciences*, 25, pp. 40–59.

20 Raymond Williams, *Orwell*, Fontana Modern Masters series, Glasgow, Fontana, 1971, p. 79.

21 In David Lyon, 'Whither shall I flee? Surveillance, omniscience and normativity in the Panopticon' forthcoming, *Christian Scholar's Review*, 1994.

22 The location of social theory in secular theology is discussed in John Milbank, *Theology and Social Theory*, Oxford and New York, Basil Blackwell, 1990.

23 The collapse of 'foundationalism' in science is one of the hallmarks of postmodern epistemology. See for example Hilary Lawson and Lisa Apiganesi, *Dismantling Truth: Reality in a Post-Modern World*, London, Weidenfeld and Nicolson, 1989.

24 Though enshrined as a 'right' within data protection laws, actually seeing the record is frequently frustrated by the insistence that we identify exactly which file is required (known best to the systems operator, of course) and by the demand for payment.

25 See Jacques Ellul, *The Technological Society*. The theme of technological distancing is brought out poignantly in Zygmunt Bauman's *Modernity and the Holocaust*, and Bauman in turn leans on the work of the Jewish philosopher Emmanuel Levinas.

26 See Judith Perrolle, *Computers and Social Change*. Perrolle's claims about the persistent distancing effect of computer technology occurs in the context of computer interfaces, but the same argument can be made in this context. She utilizes Habermas' notion of the 'ideal speech situation', which is further explored in this chapter.

27 Stephen Brockman, 'Total Entertainment', *Queen's Quarterly*, 98 (3), 1992, pp. 748–57.

28 See for example Evelyn Fox-Keller, *Reflections on Gender and Science.*
29 Psalm 139.
30 In Psalms 34:5 and 123:2 the psalmist has eyes.
31 The common practice of maintaining files 'just in case' usually works to the disadvantage of the data-subject.
32 W. I. Thomas, 'If a situation is defined as real, it is real in its consequences'. From *The Unadjusted Girl*, Boston, Little, Brown and Co, 1923, p. 41.
33 This comment about role is a gentle critique of Geoffrey Brown, *The Information Game.* The problem with the concept of role is its association with the 'individual-and-society' models of social relations that are at least implicitly individualistic and thus deny the ontological communality of human being.
34 Robert Fortner, 'Privacy is not enough: Personhood and high technology', *The Conrad Grebel Review*, 1989, 7 (2), pp. 159–77.
35 Michel Foucault, *A History of Sexuality*, London, Allen Lane, 1979, p. 59.
36 Nicholas Abercombie et al., *Sovereign Individuals of Capitalism*, p. 57.
37 Mike Hepworth and Bryan Turner, *Confession: Studies in Deviance and Religion*, p. 97.
38 See for example comments in Hepworth and Turner, *op. cit.*
39 See Nicholas Abercrombie et al., *Sovereign Individuals of Capitalism*, p. 59.
40 John Milbank, *Theology and Social Theory: Beyond Secular Reason*, p. 292.
41 *Op. cit.*, chapter 10.
42 Richard Sennett, 'Destructive Gemeinschaft' in Norman Birnhaum, *Beyond the Crisis*, London and New York, Oxford University Press, 1977.
43 Niklas Luhmann, *Love as Passion: the Codification of Intimacy*, Cambridge MA, MIT Press, 1986.
44 Compare Zygmunt Bauman, *Modernity and Ambivalence*, p. 203.
45 Jürgen Habermas, *A Theory of Communicative Action*, Cambridge UK, Polity Press, vol. 2 1987.
46 Jürgen Habermas, *The Theory of Communicative Action*, Boston, Beacon Press, 1984, vol. 1, p. 286.
47 See Anthony Giddens, *Modernity and Self-Identity*, p. 213.
48 John Milbank, *Theology and Social Theory*, pp. 274–5.
49 See on the notion of 'covenant', Sander Griffioen, 'The metaphor of the covenant in Habermas', *Faith and Philosophy*, 8, (4), pp. 524–40. I am grateful to the author for this observation.
50 Zygmunt Bauman, *Modernity and Ambivalence*, p. 276. This notion of our communication being framed by electronic discourse brings us back to Mark Poster's question of how far Habermas's critical theory is useful for discussing 'database discourses'.
51 See the somewhat apocalyptic comments on South African 'non-persons' and surveillance, in Malcolm Warner and Michael Stone, *The Databank Society*, London, Allen and Unwin, p. 77. Compare the more recent analysis of Jonathan Crush, 'Power and Surveillance on the South African Gold Mines', *Journal of South African Studies* 18 (4) 1992 pp. 825–844.

52 Such constraint and enabling may not simply be understood in 'modern' terms of the conscious subject, however. Mark Poster's admirable effort to conjoin critical theory with poststructuralism helps him maintain a healthy distance from the excesses of each.

53 Foucault was given the opportunity to comment on the 'eye of God' in an interview, but spoke only of related matters. See *Power/Knowledge*, p. 157.

54 *Op. cit.*, p. 158.

55 This is Ruth Levitas's analytical definition of utopia; see *The Concept of Utopia*, London and New York, Philip Allan, 1990, p. 198.

56 Anthony Giddens issues such a call of utopian realism in *The Consequences of Modernity*, while Berger's occurs in *Pyramids of Sacrifice*, New York, Basic Books, 1975.

57 St Augustine's contemporary relevance is discussed for instance in John Milbank, *Theology and Social Theory*, and Leslie Newbigin, *Foolishness to the Greeks*, London, SPCK, 1986.

58 John Milbank, *op. cit.*, p. 408.

59 M. Eliav-Feldon, quoted in Krishnan Kumar, *Utopianism*, Milton Keynes, Open University Press/Minneapolis, University of Minnesota Press, 1991, p. 35.

60 The consummation of the City of God would be the 'new heaven and earth', but this does not exclude a utopianism that transcends social realities without itself being metaphysically transcendental, except in inspiration. See Krishan Kumar, *Utopianism*, Milton Keynes, Open University Press/Minneapolis, University of Minnesota Press, 1991, p. 36.

61 Ruth Levitas, *The Concept of Utopia*, p. 200.

62 Geoffrey Brown, *The Information Game*, pp. 142–4.

63 For example, Chantal Mouffe (ed.), *The Dimension of Radical Democracy*. For a somewhat different perspective, see Adam Seligman's helpful discussion in *The Idea of Civil Society*, which is in the T. H. Marshall 'citizenship' lineage, but also comments on the need for 'alternative sources of information' (p 203), a plea that could be extended to the realm of electronic media.

64 It is proposed, for instance, by Kevin Wilson, *Technologies of Control*, p. 157.

65 The British Data Protection Act of 1984 illustrates this perfectly. The UK wished to trade with other European countries and thus had to show its compliance with the Council of Europe's Data Protection Convention. All loopholes, many of which affect subject access, were exploited by the UK. See Geoffrey Brown, *The Information Game*, p. 138.

66 This comment about the 'defining' capacity of new surveillance technologies builds upon the argument made earlier in David Lyon, *The Information Society*, pp. 16–17, 132.

67 Alan Dix, 'Information processing, context and privacy', *Computer-Human Interaction*, INTERACT '90, North-Holland, Elsevier Science Publishers, 1990.

68 In the USA, one could cite Marc Rotenberg of Computer Professionals for Social Respobsibility; in Canada, the advocacy of the previous Federal Privacy

Commissioner, John Grace,; in Britain, the effective investigative journalism of Duncan Campbell; or in Australia, the energetic Simon Davies, who played a central role in the formation of Privacy International.

CHAPTER 12 BEYOND POSTMODERN PARANOIA

1 On this see Ruth Levitas, *The Concept of Utopia*, London and New York, Phillip Allan, 1988, p. 195.
2 The Weberian perspective of a theorist such as Christopher Dandeker would locate surveillance socially as a bureaucratic phenomenon; see *Surveillance, Power and Modernity*. But those who follow Foucault – including Anthony Giddens, on this point – would treat surveillance as a modern institution *sui generis*. See Anthony Giddens, *The Consequences of Modernity*.
3 Gary T. Marx, *Undercover*, Chapter 10.
4 See Mark Poster, *Jean Baudrillard*, and *The Mode of Information*, Chapter 2.
5 David Flaherty, for instance, sees 'surveillance societies' as 'one component of being information societies' (*Protecting Privacy in Surveillance Societies*, p. 1). But although he is an historian, with a keen sense of the *longue durée*, one feels that these concepts really refer to the 'computer age'.
6 The point is made by Anthony Giddens in *The Nation-State and Violence* and discussed further in David Lyon, *The Information Society*.
7 Jean Baudrillard's work on signs, consumerism, and electronic media, for instance, is only indirectly about surveillance, but should be theorized alongside that concerning surveillance. See various discussions in Jean Baudrillard, *From Marxism to Postmodernism and Beyond* (ed. Douglas Kellner, Cambridge UK, Polity Press, 1989), and Mark Poster, *The Mode of Information*.
8 R. C. Baker, Roger Dickinson, and Stanley Hollander, 'Big Brother 1984: marketing data and the IRS', *Journal of Public Policy and Marketing*, (5), 1988, pp. 227–42.
9 See, for example, materials from the Research Center on Computing and Society at Southern Connecticut State University.
10 Anthony Giddens, *The Consequences of Modernity*, p. 160.

Select Bibliography

Abercrombie, Nicholas et al. *Sovereign Individuals of Capitalism*. London and Boston: Routledge, 1986.

Ackeroyd, Anne, Ethnography, personal data and computers. In R.G. Burgess (ed.), *Conducting Qualitative Research*, JAI Press Inc, 1988.

Arendt, Hannah, *The Human Condition*. New York: Anchor Books, 1959.

Baker, B.R.C., Dickinson, Roger and Hollander, Stanley, Big Brother 1994: Marketing Data and the IRS. *Journal of Public Policy and Marketing*, 5, 227–42, 1988.

Barker, Jane and Downing, Hazel, Word Processing and the Transformation of Patriarchal Relations of Control in the Office. *Capital and Class*, 1980.

Bauman, Zygmunt, *Freedom*. Minneapolis: University of Minnesota Press, 1988.

Bauman, Zygmunt, *Modernity and Ambivalence*. Cambridge, UK: Polity Press, 1991.

Bauman, Zygmunt, *Intimations of Postmodernity*. Boston and London: Routledge, 1992.

Bell, Daniel, *The Coming of Postindustrial Society*. London: Peregrine, 1974.

Beniger, James, *The Control Revolution: The Technological and Economic Origins of the Information Society*. Cambridge MA: Harvard University Press, 1986.

Bennett, Colin, *Regulating Privacy: Data Protection and Public Policy in Europe and the United States*. Ithaca: Cornell University Press, 1992.

Bentham, Jeremy *Jeremy Bentham: Collected Works*, edited by J. Bowring. London. 1843.

Bobbio, Norberto *The Future of Democracy*. Cambridge, UK: Polity Press, 1987.

Bok, Sisela *Secrets: on the Ethics of Concealment and Revelation*. New York: Vintage Books, 1983.

Borovoy, Alan *When Freedoms Collide: The Case for our Civil Liberties*. Toronto: Lester and Orpeen Dennys. 1988.

Brown, Geoffrey *The Information Game: Ethical Issues in a Microchip World*.

London and New York: Humanities Press, 1990.

Bryant, Christopher, Privacy, Privatization and Self-Determination. In J. Young (ed.), *Privacy*, London: Wiley, 1978.

Burnham, David *The Rise of the Computer State*. New York: Vintage, 1983.

Campbell, Duncan and Connor, Steve *On the Record: Surveillance, Computers and Privacy*. London: Michael Joseph, 1986.

Carey, James *Communication as Culture: Eassays on Media and Society*. Boston MA and London: Unwin-Hyman, 1989.

Castells, Manuel *The Informational City: Information Technology, Economic Restructuring and the Urban-Regional Process*. New York: Basil Blackwell, 1989.

Clarke, Roger, The resistable rise of the national personal data system. *Software Law Journal*, 5, 29–59, 1992.

Clarke, Roger, Information Technology and Dataveillance. *Communications of the ACM*. 31(5), 499, 1988.

Clarke, Roger, Just another piece of plastic for your wallet: the Australia Card scheme. *Prometheus*, 5(1), 29–45, 1987.

Clegg, S.S., Radical Revisions: Power, Discipline and Organization. *Organization Studies*, 10, 97–116, 1988.

Clement, Andrew, Office Automation and the Technical Control of Information Workers. In V. Mosco and J. Wasko (eds.), *The Political Economy of Information*, Madison WI: University of Wisconsin Press, 1988.

Cohen, Stanley *Visions of Social Control*. Cambridge, UK: Polity Press, 1985.

Corbett, Ronald and Marx, Gary T., Critique: No soul in the new machine: Technofallacies in the electronic monitoring movement. *Justice Quarterly*, 8(3), 399–414, 1991.

Crimmons, James, Bentham on Religion: Atheism and the Secular Society. *Journal of the History of Ideas*, 47, 95–110, 1986.

Dandeker, Christopher *Surveillance Power and Modernity*. Cambridge, UK: Polity Press, 1990.

Data Protection Registrar *Data Protection Act 1984: Introduction to the Act*. Wilmslow, UK: Office of Data Protection Registrar, 1989.

Davies, Simon *Big Brother: Australia's growing web of surveillance*. Sydney: Simon and Schuster, 1992.

Davis, Mike *City of Quartz*. London: Verso, 1988.

Ellul, Jacques *The Technological Society*. New York: Vintage Books, 1964.

Ellul, Jacques *Perspectives on our age*. Toronto: CBC, 1981.

Flaherty, David *Privacy in Colonial New England*. Charlottesville: University Press of Virginia, 1972.

Flaherty, David *Protecting Privacy in Two-Way Electronic Services*. White Plains, NY: Knowledge Industry Services, 1985.

Flaherty, David *Protecting Privacy in Surveillance Societies*. Chapel Hill, NC: University of North Carolina Press. 1989.

Fooner, Michael *Interpol: Issues in World Crime and International Criminal Justice*. New York: Plenum Press, 1989.

Fortner, Robert, Physics and Metaphysics in an Information Age: Privacy, Identity, Dignity. *Communication*, 9, 151–72, 1986.

Fortner, Robert, Privacy is not enough: Personhood and High Technology. *The Conrad Grebel Review*, 7(2), 159–77, 1989.

Foucault, Michel *Discipline and Punish: The Birth of the Prison.* New York: Vintage, 1977.

Foucault, Michel, In C. Gordon (ed.), *Power/Knowledge*, Brighton UK: Harvester/ New York: Pantheon, 1980.

Fox-Keller, Evelyn *Reflections on Gender and Science.* New Haven, CT and London, UK: Yale University Press, 1985.

Freese, Jan *The future of data protection.* Proceedings of Seminar on Openness and Protection of Privacy in the Information Society, Voorburg NL: Embassy of Sweden and Netherlands Central Bureau of Statistics, 1987.

Fuller, L., and Smith, V., Consumers' Reports: Management by Customers in a Changing Economy. *Work Employment and Society*, 5, 1–16. 1991.

Gandy, Oscar, The Surveillance Society: Information Technology and Bureaucratic Social Control. *Journal of Communication*, 39(3), 69, 1989.

Gandy, Oscar, Information Privacy and the Crisis of Control. In M. Raboy and P. Bruck (eds.), *Communication: For and Against Democracy*, Montreal and New York: Black Rose Books, 1989.

Gandy, Oscar, Caller ID: A Two-Edged Sword. In. D. Wedemeyer and M. Lofstrum (eds.) *Pacific Telecommunication: Weaving the Technological and Social Fabric.* Hawaii: Pacific Telecommunications Council, 1990.

Gandy, Oscar *The Panoptic Sort: Towards a Political Economy of Information.* Boulder, CO: Westview Press, 1993.

Giddens, Anthony *The Nation-State and Violence.* Cambridge UK: Polity Press, 1985.

Giddens, Anthony *The Consequences of Modernity.* Cambridge, UK: Polity Press, 1990.

Giddens, Anthony *Modernity and Self-Identity.* Cambridge, UK: Polity Press/ Stanford, CA: Stanford University Press, 1991.

Goffman, Erving *The Presentation of Self in Everyday Life.* New York: Anchor, 1959.

Goodwin, G. and Humphreys, L., Freeze-dried stigma: cybernetics and social control. *Humanity and Society*, 6, November, 1982.

Gordon, Diana, The Electronic Panopticon: a Case-Study of the Development of the National Criminal Records System. *Politics and Society*, 15, 483–511. 1987.

Gouldner, Alvin *The Dialectic of Ideology and Technology.* New York: Seabury Press, 1976.

Graham, Peter, The Australia Card: A Burden rather than Relief? *The Australia Quarterly*, Autumn, 4–14, 1986.

Habermas, Jürgen *The Theory of Communicative Action.* Cambridge, UK: Polity Press, 1986.

Habermas, Jürgen *The Philosophical Discourse of Modernity.* Cambridge, UK:

Polity Press/Cambridge MA: MIT Press, 1987.

Harvey, David *The Condition of Postmodernity.* Oxford and New York: Basic Blackwell, 1989.

Hepworth, Mike and Turner, Bryan *Confession: Studies in Deviance and Religion.* London: Routledge and Kegan Paul, 1982.

Hixson, Richard F. *Privacy in a Public Society.* Oxford and New York: Oxford University Press, 1987.

Ignatieff, Michael *A Just Measure of Pain: The Penitentiary in the Industrial Revolution.* New York: Pantheon, 1978.

Inglehart, Ronald *Culture Shift in Advanced Industrial Society.* Princeton, NJ: Princeton University Press, 1990.

Innis, Harold Adams *The Bias of Communication.* Toronto: University of Toronto Press, 1951.

Jay, Martin, In the Empire of the Gaze: Foucault and the Denigration of Vision in Twentieth Century Thought. In L. Appigenesi (ed.), *Postmodernism: ICA Documents.* London: Free Association Books, 1989.

Jessop, Bob, Capitalism, nation-states and surveillance. In D. Held and J.B. Thompson (eds.), *Social Theory of Modern Societies: Anthony Giddens and his critics,* Cambridge and New York: Cambridge University Press, 1989.

Katz, James E., Caller ID. Privacy and Social Processes. *Telecommunications Policy,* October, 372–410, 1990.

Katz, James, Public Concern over Privacy: The Phone is the Focus. *Telecommunications Policy,* 14(4), 373–411.

Katz, James E. and Tassone, Annette R., Public Opinion Trends: Privacy and Information Technology. *Public Opinion Quarterly,* 54, 125–43, 1990.

Knights, David and Sturdey, Andrew, New Technology and the Self-Disciplined Worker in the Insurance Industry. In. I. Varcoe, M. McNeil and S. Yearley (eds.), *Deciphering Science and Technology,* London UK: MacMillan, 1990.

Lacayo, Richard, Nowhere to hide. *Time,* November 11 1991, 34–40.

Langan, Kenneth J., Computer Matching Programs: a Threat to Privacy. *Journal of Law and Social Problems,* 15(2), 143–80, 1979.

Lash, Scott and Urry, John *The End of Organized Capitalism.* Cambridge, UK: Polity Press, 1987.

Laudon, Kenneth *The Dossier Society: Value Choices in the Design of National Information Systems.* New York: Columbia University Press, 1986.

Liberty, *Identity Cards and the Threat to Civil Liberties.* Civil Liberty Briefing No 12. London: Liberty, 1988.

Lilly, Robert and Ball, Richard, A Brief History of House Arrest and Electronic Monitoring. *Northern Kentucky Law Review,* 17(3), 343–4, 1987.

Lilly, Robert and Himan, Joan *The Electronic Monitoring of Offenders* (Second Series). Leicester: De Montfort University Law Monographs, 1991.

Louis Harris and Associates Inc. *The Equifax Report on Consumers in the Information Age.* Atlanta, GA: Equifax, 1990.

Lyon, David *The Information Society: Issues and Illusions.* Cambridge, UK: Polity Press, 1988.

Lyon, David, New Technology and the Limits of Luddism. *Science as Culture*, 7, 122–34. 1989.

Lyon, David *Citizenship and Surveillance in an Information Age*. Kingston: Queen's University, Studies in Communication and Information Technologies, Working Paper No. 23, 1991.

Lyon, David, British Identity Cards: the Unpalatable Logic of European Membership? *The Political Quarterly*, 62(3), 377–85, 1991.

Lyon, David, The New Surveillance? Electronic Technologies and the Maximum Security Society. *Crime, Law and Social Change*, 17, 1992.

Lyon, David, Surveillance Societies, Privacy and Social Control: Trends and Counter-Trends. *Artificial Intelligence and Society*, 1992.

Lyon, David, Whither Shall I Flee? Surveillance, Omniscience and Normativity in the Panopticon. *Christian Scholars' Review*, vol. 33, 1994.

Lyon, David, Bentham's Panopticon: From Moral Architecture to Electronic Surveillance. *Queen's Quarterly*, 98, 1991.

Lyotard, Jean-François *The Postmodern Condition*. Manchester: University of Manchester Press/Minneapolis: University of Minnesota Press, 1984.

MacKenzie, Donald and Wajcman, Judy (eds.), *The Social Shaping of Technology*. Milton Keynes: Open University Press, 1985.

Manning, Peter, Technological Dramas and the Police: Statement and Counter-Statement in Organizational Analysis. *Criminology*, 30(3), 327–46, 1991.

Marshall, T. H. *Citizenship and Social Class*. London and New York: Cambridge University Press, 1950.

Marx, Gary T., The surveillance society: the threat of 1984-style techniques. *The Futurist*, June, 21–26, 1985.

Marx, Gary T., The Iron Fist in the Velvet Glove: Totalitarian Potentials Within Democratic Structures. In J.F. Short (ed)., *The Social Fabric*, Beverly Hills CA: Sage Publications, 1986.

Marx, Gary T., *Undercover: Police Surveillance in America*. Berkeley: University of California Press, 1988.

Marx, Gary T., The Case of the Omniscient Organization. *Harvard Business Review*, March-April, 4–12, 1990.

Marx, Gary T., 'Fraudulent Identification and Biography', in D. Altheide et al., *New Directions in the Study of Law and Social Control*. New York: Plenum Press, 1990.

Marx, Gary, T. forthcoming: The Engineering of Social Control: The Search for the Silver Bullet. In J. Hogan (ed.), *Crime and Inequality*, Chicago: University of Chicago Press.

Marx, Gary T. and Reichman, Nancy, Routinizing the Discovery of Secrets: Computers as Informants. *American Behavioral Scientist*, 27(4), 430, 1984.

Marx, Gary T. and Sherizen, Sanford, Monitoring on the job. *Technology Review*, Nov-Dec, 1986.

McNeil, William *The Pursuit of Power: Technology, Armed Force and Society since A.D. 1000*. Chicago: University of Chicago Press, 1982.

Melody, William *Some Characteristics of Knowledge in an Information Society*.

London: Canada House Lectures No. 31, 1986.

Melucci, Alberto *Nomads of the Present*. London: Hutchinson Radius, 1989.

Milbank, John *Theology and Social Theory: Beyond Secular Reason*. Oxford and New York: Basil Blackwell, 1990.

Mosco, Vincent *The Pay-Per Society: Computers and Communications in the Information Age*. Toronto: Garamond, 1989.

Mouffe, Chantal (ed.) *The Dimensions of Radical Democracy*, Lown & New York, Veso, 1992.

Mulgan, G.J. *Communication and Control*. New York and London: The Guilford Press, 1991.

Nellis, Mike, The electronic monitoring of offenders in England and Wales. *British Journal of Criminology*, 31(2), 165–85, 1991.

Novek, Eleanor, Sinha, Nikhil and Gandy, Oscar, The Value of Your Name. *Media, Culture and Society*, 12, 525–43, 1990.

Orwell, George *Nineteen Eighty-Four*. Harmondsworth: Penguin, 1954.

Pateman, Carol, Feminist Critiques of the Public/Private Dichotomy. In S.I. Benn and G.A. Gaus (eds.) *Public and Private in Social Life*, Beckenham: Croom-Helm, 1983.

Perin, Constance, The moral fabric of the office: Panopticon discourse and schedule flexibilities. *Research in the Sociology of Organization*, 8, 241–68, 1991.

Perrolle, Judith *Computers and Social Change: Information, Property and Power*. Wadsworth, 1987.

Pollard, Sidney *The Genesis of Modern Management*. London: Arnold, 1965.

Poster, Mark *Critical Theory and Poststructuralism: In Search of a Context*. Ithaca, NY: Cornell University Press, 1989.

Poster, Mark *The Mode of Information*. Cambridge, UK: Polity Press, 1990.

Poster, Mark (ed.) *Jean Baudrillard: Selected Writings*. Cambridge, UK: Polity Press, 1988.

Radner, Daniel B., Inter-Agency Data Matching Projects for Research Purposes. *Social Security Bulletin*, July, 1988.

Regan, Priscilla M., Privacy, Government Information and Technology. *Public Administration Review*, Nov-Dec, 1986.

Reichman, Nancy, Computer Matching: Towards Computerized Systems of Regulation. *Law and Policy*, October, 387–415, 1987.

Report of the Committee on Data Privacy, Chair: Sir Norman Lindop, Cmnd. 7341. London: HMSO.

Richelson, Jeffrey T. and Ball, Desmond *The Ties that Bind: Intelligence Cooperation between the UKUSA Countries – the UK, USA, Canada, Australia and New Zealand*. Boston, London, Sydney: Allen and Unwin, 1985.

Richelson, Jeffrey T. *The US Intelligence Community*, Cambridge, MA: Ballinger, 1989.

Robins, Kevin and Webster, Frank, Plan and Control: Towards a Cultural History of the Information Society. *Theory and Society*, 18, 323–51, 1989.

Robins, Kevin and Webster, Frank, Cybernetic Capitalism: Information, Technology, Everyday Life. In V. Mosco and J. Wasko (eds.), *The Political Economy of*

Information, Madison: University of Wisconsin Press, 1988.

Robins, Kevin and Webster, Frank, Information as capital: a critique of Daniel Bell. In J. Slack and F. Feges (eds.), *The Ideology of the Information Age*, Norwood, NJ: Ablex, 1987.

Rothfeder, Jeffrey, *Privacy for Sale*. New York: Simon and Schuster, 1992.

Rubin, Michael *Private Rights, Public Wrongs*. Norwood, NJ: Ablex, 1988.

Russel, K. and Lilly, R. *The Electronic Monitoring of Offenders*. Leicester, UK: Leicester Polytechnic Law School, 1989.

Rule, James *Private Lives, Public Surveillance*. London: Allen-Lane, 1973.

Rule, James and Attewell, Paul, What Do Computers Do? *Social Problems*, 36(3), 1989.

Rule, James et al., Documentary Identification and Mass Surveillance. *Social Problems*, 31(2), 1983.

Scull, Andrew *Decarceration: Community Treatment and the Deviant – A Radical View*. Englewood Cliffs, NJ: Prentice-Hall, 1977.

Seligman, Adam *The Idea of Civil Society*. New York: The Free Press, 1992.

Sewell, Graham and Wilkinson, Barry, Someone to Watch Over Me: Surveillance, Discipline and the Just-in-Time Labour Process. *Sociology*, 26(2), 271–89, 1992.

Shattuck, John, Computer Matching is a Serious Threat to Individual Rights. *Communications of the ACM*, 27(6), 548–41, 1984.

Shearing, Clifford and Stenning, Philip, From the Panopticon to Disneyworld The Development of Discipline. In E. Doob and E.L. Greenspan (eds.), *Perspectives in Criminal Law*, Aurora: Canada Law Books, 1985.

Shields, Peter and Samarajiva, Rohan, Emergent institutions of the 'intelligent network': Towards a theoretical understanding. *Media, Culture and Society*, 14, 397–419, 1992.

Shils, Edward, Privacy and Power. In *Center and Periphery: Essays in Macrosociology*. Chicago: University of Chicago Press, 1975.

Sieghart, Paul (ed.) *Microchips with Everything*. London: Comedia, 1983.

Smart, Barry *Modern Conditions, Postmodern Controversies*. London and New York: Routledge, 1992.

Spitzer, Steven, The Rationalization of Crime control in Capitalist Society. In A. Scull and S. Cohen (eds.) *Social Control and the State, 1986*.

Standing Committee on the Legislative Assembly 1991: *Privacy and Computer Matching*. Toronto: IPC.

Strub, Harry, The Theory of Panoptical Control: Bentham's Panopticon and Orwell's *Nineteen Eighty-Four*. *The Journal of the History of the Behavioural Sciences*, 25, 40–59, 1989.

Thompson, E.P., Time, work-discipline and industrial capitalism. *Past and Present*, 38, 1967.

Tilley, Charles *The Formation of Nation-State in Europe*. Princeton, NJ: Princeton University Press, 1975.

Turner, Bryan, Towards a Theory of Citizenship. *Sociology*, 24(2), 189–217, 1990. Reprinted in Mouffe, Chantal, 1992: *The Dimensions of Radical Democracy*.

US Congress, Office of Technology Assessment *Federal Government Information Technology: Electronic Records Systems and Individual Privacy* Washington, DC: OTA, 1986.

Veyne, Paul (ed.) *A History of Private Life*. Cambridge, MA and London, UK: Harvard University Press, 1987.

Vidmar, Neil and Flaherty, David, Concern for Personal Privacy in an Electronic Age. *Journal of Communication*, 35, 91–103. 1986.

Webster, Frank and Robins, Kevin *Information Technology: A Luddite Analysis*. Norwood, NJ: Ablex, 1986.

Weiss, M.J. *The Clustering of America*. New York: Harper and Row, 1988.

Wilson, Kevin *Technologies of Control: The New Interactive Media for the Home*. Madison, WI: University of Wisconsin Press, 1988.

Winner, Langdon, A Victory for Computer Populism. *Technology Review*, May/June, 1991.

Wiseman, Charles *Strategic Information Systems*. Homewood, IL:Irwin, 1988.

Wood, Stephen (ed.) *The Degradation of Work? Skill, Deskilling and the Labour Process*. London: Hutchinson, 1983.

Yates, Joanna *Control through Communication*. Baltimore and London: John Hopkins University Press, 1989.

Yearley, Steven *Science, Technology and Social Change*. New York and London: Unwin-Hyman, 1989.

Zuboff, Shoshana *In the Age of the Smart Machine*. New York: Basic Books, 1988.

Index

LIBRARY
ST. LOUIS COMMUNITY COLLEGE
AT FLORISSANT VALLEY